An OPUS book

A History of Western Philosopy: 6

# ENGLISH-LANGUAGE PHILOSOPHY
## 1750 to 1945

## OPUS General Editors

Walter Bodmer
Christopher Butler
Robert Evans
John Skorupski

OPUS books provide concise, original, and authoritative introductions to a wide range of subjects in the humanities and sciences. They are written by experts for the general reader as well as for students.

## A History of Western Philosophy

This series of OPUS books offers a comprehensive and up-to-date survey of the history of philosophical ideas from earliest times. Its aim is not only to set those ideas in their immediate cultural context, but also to focus on their value and relevance to twentieth-century thinking.

*Classical Thought\**
Terence Irwin

*Medieval Philosophy*
David Luscombe

*Renaissance Philosophy\**
Brian P. Copenhaver and
Charles B. Schmitt

*The Rationalists\**
John Cottingham

*The Empiricists\**
R. S. Woolhouse

*Continental Philosophy since 1750\**
Robert C. Solomon

*English Language Philosophy since 1945*
Barry Stroud

\*Already published

A History of Western Philosophy: 6

# English-Language Philosophy 1750 to 1945

JOHN SKORUPSKI

Oxford   New York

OXFORD UNIVERSITY PRESS

1993

Oxford University Press, Walton Street, Oxford OX2 6DP

Oxford New York Toronto
Delhi Bombay Calcutta Madras Karachi
Kuala Lumpur Singapore Hong Kong Tokyo
Nairobi Dar es Salaam Cape Town
Melbourne Auckland Madrid

and associated companies in
Berlin Ibadan

Oxford is a trade mark of Oxford University Press

British Library Cataloguing in Publication Data
Data available

Library of Congress Cataloging in Publication Data
Skorupski, John. 1946–
English–language philosophy, 1750 to 1945 / John Skorupski.
p. cm.—(A History of Western philosophy : 6) 'An OPUS book'—Ser. t.p.
Includes bibliographical references.
1. Philosophy, Modern—18th century. 2. Philosophy, Modern—19th century.
3. Philosophy, Modern—20th century. I. Title. II. Series.
190—dc20 B803.S54 1993 92–27017
ISBN 0–19–219211–6
ISBN 0–19–289192–8 (Pbk.)

1 3 5 7 9 10 8 6 4 2

Typeset by Graphicraft Typesetters Ltd., Hong Kong
Printed in Great Britain by
Biddles Ltd.
Guildford and King's Lynn

*For*
*Katie and Julia*

# Preface

This is a philosopher's, not a historian's, history. When past thinkers are magicked into contemporaries, the feeling for philosophy's slow rhythms and brief flourishes is lost—I have tried to avoid that. But I have been more opinionated than a historian of ideas would care to be, and much more selective. I tell the story from a present philosophical vantage point, without forswearing hindsight.

I have chosen themes which stand out in retrospect, and gone into some detail in discussing the philosophers who developed them. The result is not encyclopaedic. To add mere lists of names does not help, so I have not done so—even though the list of philosophers who consequently receive no, or next to no, mention in the following pages alarms me. Not even the philosophers discussed are always discussed comprehensively; for example, Peirce's logic and speculative cosmology, and Russell's social and political views, are not treated here. The omission I most regret is of Moore's important views on scepticism, which are germane to my main theme, and a part of his contemporary reputation. They had to be omitted for lack of space. My choices are, I believe, fairly uncontroversial, but they are certainly choices—other stories could have been told.

The main theme in the story I tell is a debate between naturalism, the Enlightenment philosophy which sees human beings wholly as a part of nature, and rejections of naturalism which followed Kant's influential criticism of it. The possibility of intelligible experience, the existence of a priori knowledge, were its crux. Broader cultural claims, about religion and ethics and political life, were staked on it. The stakes were placed because some form of post-Kantian idealism seemed to very many people in the nineteenth century to be the only way of saving reason, faith and freedom. So this became the critical contest in that century's philosophy.

Chapters 4 and 5 deal with the analytic philosophy of this

century. It is in the English language that the analytic tradition has been dominant, and so it belongs most naturally in this volume. In dealing with it, however, I have of course been led to consider philosophers who have been of great importance for it but who wrote in German—or in one case, in French.

Analytic philosophy turns on two sorts of effort to end the nineteenth-century contest between naturalism and idealism. The first appears in Chapter 4, where I call it 'conceptual realism'. This had been a diversionary action in the nineteenth century, unfolding not in the English world or in Protestant Germany, but in Catholic Central Europe, the cockpit of resistence to both naturalism and the 'Critical' philosophy of Kant. Independently, it was propounded with magnificent clarity and insight by the German philosopher-mathematician, Gottlob Frege, and then, rather differently and independently again, in the brief period of conceptual realism in Cambridge before the Great War.

From a Kantian standpoint such realism must seem 'pre-Critical'. But the second phase of analytic philosophy saw an attempt to end the contests of nineteenth-century metaphysics which could, rather, be called 'post-Critical'—it was Wittgenstein's and Carnap's attempt at a dissolution of metaphysics (Chapters 5 and 6). Post-Critical analytic philosophy, which belongs to the tradition of the Critical even while it seeks to dissolve it, is widely influential in contemporary culture—yet among English-language philosophers it is, if anything, in decline. But it may yet have history on its side.

The question underlying ethics and political philosophy in the nineteenth century has not lost its force either—how to respond to the rise of commerce and science and the decline of religion; what place to find in such a society for the life of the spirit. Even in relation to this great question, philosophy continued to proceed with some considerable autonomy; but many of its connections with other cultural, scientific, and religious currents were bound up with it. The sharp distinctions between empirical, conceptual, and normative, much insisted on by philosophers in the first half of this century, appeared to sever the connections and abandon the question. There is truth in that appearance, yet it is also misleading; I have tried to bring this out to some extent, though I have only been able to do so by the way.

I thank Oxford University Press for their patience in putting up with many delays which have interrupted the writing of this book. Andy Hamilton's comments on Chapters 3–6 have been invaluable, as have Bob Hale's on Frege in Chapter 4, Chris Hookway's on Peirce in Chapter 3, and John Kenyon's on the whole thing.

# Contents

# Abbreviations

All references are by volume (where relevant) and page number.

B　　The Works of Jeremy Bentham, ed. John Bowring (Edinburgh, 1843).

Bf　　Jeremy Bentham, A Fragment on Government, ed. J. H. Burns and H. L. A. Hart (London, 1988).

Bi　　Jeremy Bentham, An Introduction to the Principles of Morals and Legislation, ed. J. H. Burns and H. L. A. Hart (London, 1970).

BRa　F. H. Bradley, Appearance and Reality, 2nd edn. (London, 1902).

BRe　F. H. Bradley, Ethical Studies, 2nd edn. (Oxford, 1927).

BRk　F.H. Bradley, 'On our Knowledge of Immediate Experience', Mind, 18 (1909), 40–64.

BRp　F. H. Bradley, 'A Personal Explanation', International Journal of Ethics, 5 (1894–5), 383–4.

Bs　　Jeremy Bentham's Economic Writings, ed. Werner Stark, i–iii (London, 1952–4).

C　　The Collected Works of Samuel Taylor Coleridge, general editor: Kathleen Coburn (London and Princeton, NJ, 1969– ). Works cited in this edition as multiple volumes are cited by the number of the work and the number of the volume. Thus C 7i = work 7, vol. i.

Ca　　Rudolf Carnap, The Logical Structure of the World, trans. Rolf A. George (London, 1967).

Cg　　Collected Letters of Samuel Taylor Coleridge, ed. E. L. Griggs (Oxford, 1956).

Cl　　Rudolf Carnap, The Logical Syntax of Language, trans. Amethe Smeaton (London, 1937).

Db　　Dictionary of Philosophy and Psychology, ed. J. M. Baldwin (London and New York, 1901–5).

Fb　　Gottlob Frege, Conceptual Notation and Related Articles, trans. and ed. Terrell Ward Bynum (Oxford, 1972).

Fbl　 Gottlob Frege, The Basic Laws of Arithmetic, trans. and ed. Montgomery Furth (Berkeley, Calif. and Los Angeles, 1964).

Ff　　Gottlob Frege, The Foundations of Arithmetic, trans. J. L. Austin (Oxford, 1974).

Fp　　Gottlob Frege, Posthumous Writings, ed. Hans Hermes, Friedrich

Kambartel, Friedrich Kaulbach, trans. Peter Long and Roger White (Oxford, 1979).

Ft    *Translations from the Philosophical Writings of Gottlob Frege*, ed. Peter Geach and Max Black (Oxford, 1960).

G    *Works of Thomas Hill Green*, ed. R. L. Nettleship (London, 1885–8).

Gp    T. H. Green, *Prolegomena to Ethics*, 5th edn. (Oxford, 1906).

Je    William James, *Essays in Radical Empiricism* (*The Works of William James*), eds. Fredson Bowers and Ignas K. Skrupskelis (Cambridge, Mass. and London, 1976).

Jm    J. Kenna, 'Ten Unpublished Letters from James to Bradley', *Mind*, 75 (July 1966), 309–31.

Jp    William James, *Pragmatism and the Meaning of Truth* (London, 1978).

Jpe    William James, *A Pluralistic Universe* (London, 1909).

Jpr    William James, *The Principles of Psychology* (London, 1890).

M    *Collected Works of John Stuart Mill*, general editor: John M. Robson (London and Toronto, 1963).

Ma    Ernst Mach, *The Analysis of Sensations* (New York, 1959).

Me    Ernst Mach, 'The Economical Nature of Physical Inquiry', in *Popular Scientific Lectures*, trans. T. J. McCormack, 4th edn. (Chicago, 1910).

Mn    G. E. Moore, 'The Nature of Judgement', *Mind*, 8 (1899), 176–93.

Mp    G. E. Moore, *Principia Ethica* (Cambridge, 1989).

Ms    Ernst Mach, *The Science of Mechanics* (Chicago, 1960).

N    Otto Neurath, *Empiricism and Sociology*, ed. Marie Neurath and Robert S. Cohen (Dordrecht, 1973).

Ns    Otto Neurath, 'Sociology and Physicalism', in A. J. Ayer, ed., *Logical Positivism* (New York, 1959).

P    *The Collected Papers of Charles Sanders Peirce*, i–vi, ed. Charles Hartshorne and Paul Weiss (Cambridge, Mass., 1931–5); vii–viii, ed. Arthur W. Burks (Cambridge, Mass., 1958).

R    *The Works of Thomas Reid, D.D., with Selections from his Unpublished Letters, Preface, Notes and Supplementary Dissertations, by Sir William Hamilton, Bart.*, 6th edn. (Edinburgh and London, 1863).

Ra    Bertrand Russell, *Autobiography* (London, 1978).

Ri    Bertrand Russell, *Introduction to Mathematical Philosophy* (London, 1919).

Rl    Bertrand Russell, *A Critical Exposition of the Philosophy of Leibniz* (Cambridge, 1900).

Rlk     Bertrand Russell, *Logic and Knowledge*, ed. Robert C. Marsh (London, 1956).

Rm      Bertrand Russell, *My Philosophical development* (London, 1959).

Rp      Bertrand Russell, *The Principles of Mathematics* (London, 1992).

Rpp     Bertrand Russell, *The Problems of Philosophy* (London, 1962).

Rw      Bertrand Russell and Alfred North Whitehead, *Principia Mathematica* (Cambridge, 1952).

Sc      Paul Arthur Schilpp, ed., *The Philosophy of Rudolf Carnap* (La Salle, Ill., 1963).

Sg      Moritz Schlick, *General Theory of Knowledge*, trans. Albert E. Blumberg (La Salle, Ill., 1985).

Sm      Paul Arthur Schilpp, ed., *The Philosophy of G. E. Moore* (Evanston and Chicago, 1942).

Sp      Moritz Schlick, *Philosophical Papers* (2 vols., Dordrecht, 1979).

Sr      Paul Arthur Schilpp, ed., *The Philosophy of Bertrand Russell* (Evanston and Chicago, 1946).

Wc      Ludwig Wittgenstein, *Culture and Value*, ed. G. H. von Wright, trans. Peter Winch (Oxford, 1980).

Wv      Ludwig Wittgenstein, *Wittgenstein and the Vienna Circle: Conversations Recorded by Friedrich Waismann*, ed. Brian McGuinness, trans. Joachim Schulte and Brian McGuinness (Oxford, 1979).

# Between Hume and Mill: Reid, Bentham, Coleridge

David Hume (1711–76) stands eminent among the shapers of modern thought. He and Kant (1724–1804) were the supremely great philosophers of the enlightenment—yet both sowed seeds from which the romantic reaction to enlightenment would grow.

In his lifetime, Hume was an intensely controversial figure. The underminer, as it seemed, of both faith and reason, he was fiercely opposed but could not be ignored. Yet for two-thirds of the 19th century his influence lapsed. It was only in its final third that interest in Hume revived. Ernst Mach, the Viennese physicist and philosopher, saw in Hume a forefather, and with this estimate the philosophers of the Vienna Circle later agreed. In Britain, at about the same time as Mach, there was a re-markable surge of interest in the romantic philosophy of Ger-many: Hume now entered the canon as the last great empiricist in Britain, the pivotal figure who had interrupted Kant's 'dogmatic slumber' by taking empiricism to its limit. Hume's revival is a phenomenon of the *fin de siècle* and comes directly or indirectly from Continental influence.

Over the first third of the century, German philosophy worked its way through a sharp reaction against Enlightenment thought (the reaction whose delayed impact in Britain we have just noted). At the deepest level, it was a reaction against *natur-alism*—the metaphysical groundnote of enlightenment thought, and also, one may say, the equilibrium point of British philo-sophy, at least since Locke and Newton. Naturalism conceives human beings as wholly a part of nature: the proper object of a natural science of man. It will be a conception of utmost importance throughout this study.

Kant saw a fundamental link in Hume's thought between his

naturalism and his rigorously sceptical analysis of reason. The latter, Kant argued, followed inexorably from the former, and it was Hume's great merit to have made the link unprecedentedly clear: if naturalism is true, knowledge is impossible (and so, in particular, naturalism cannot be known to be true). Kant reversed this implication: since knowledge *is* possible, naturalism must be false; that was the starting-point of his Critical Philosophy. It is no exaggeration to say that only by contrast to the alternative Kant developed—his 'transcendental idealism'—does naturalism itself come fully into focus as a philosophical doctrine. This has a reverse side. If transcendental idealism, and the even more ambitious idealist philosophies which attempted to supersede it, can be shown to be meaningless—as twentieth-century lines of thought which we shall later encounter have held that they are—then naturalism will also fade out of focus. A doctrine whose denial lacks meaning will itself lack meaning.

But this is to anticipate. At that time there was no question but that the doctrine had meaning. When Kant contraposed the entailment he detected in Hume—from the premise that human beings are wholly a part of nature to a radically sceptical conclusion—he forced naturalism out of the background of inexplicit ideas which shape a period of thought, and made it a debatable philosophical thesis. It remained at the heart of nineteenth-century philosophical debate. Kant opened the door to nineteenth-century idealism, and it rushed unceremoniously past him, agreeing with him that mind was not a part of nature, but pressing on boldly to the even more liberating doctrine that nature itself was an externalization, or self-objectification, of Mind. These ideas developed in German philosophy from Kant to Hegel.

Hume's role as a catalyst in the evolution of German idealism impressed philosophers in Britain at the end of the century. In contrast, in its first third, British philosophy traversed a period in which Hume was eclipsed just because of his scepticism. It was seen not as Kant saw it, as implicit in the very 'Attempt to introduce the experimental Method of Reasoning into Moral Subjects'—which Hume had announced in the frontispiece of his *Treatise of Human Nature*. It showed, rather, some defect in the assumptions Hume had brought to the attempt—so Reid and his associates thought. Or it stemmed from Hume's literary pretensions—an irrelevant blemish on the soberly scientific aspect of his thought. This was the view of Bentham and the philosophers associated with him.

Thomas Reid (1710–96) and Jeremy Bentham (1748–1832) are two of the great names in the interregnum in British philosophy between Hume and Mill; Samuel Taylor Coleridge (1772–1834) is the third. Reid provided the earliest home-grown critique of Hume; Bentham developed the associationist and utilitarian strain which he found in Hume and other writers of the eighteenth century, such as David Hartley. The opposition between their two schools concerned the proper form and content of a natural science of man, not the conditions of its possibility. It was Coleridge who laboured to open up the minds of Britons to the Critical Philosophy, and its extraordinary German aftermath.

They all exercised great influence, penetrating far beyond philosophy into the general culture of Britain and America. But the influence of Reid and other philosophers of the school of 'Scottish common sense' was initially greatest in philosophy proper, not only in the English-speaking world but in Europe too. Bentham and Coleridge were influential rather as theorists of law, politics, or culture than as pure philosophers. Moreover their ideas were assimilated and rethought by later men, who have eclipsed them in contemporary influence. The philosophy of common sense, on the other hand, reached a certain perfection of statement in the writings of the Scots who formulated it and it remained (and continues to remain) a challenging presence in philosophy.

Thomas Reid was born a year before Hume and died twenty years after him. His first fifty or so years were spent around Aberdeen—he was born near it, studied in it, became Presbyterian Minister of a village by it, and in 1752, Professor of Philosophy at King's College, Aberdeen. Eleven years later he moved to the Chair of Moral Philosophy at Glasgow, succeeding Adam Smith; he died in Glasgow in 1796.

He thought the chief merit of his own philosophy lay in its

refutation of what he called the 'Ideal System'—a more usual name is the theory of ideas. This was a way of thinking about the operations of the mind which had, he believed, been made pernicious orthodoxy in the time of Descartes and Locke—though he traced its origin back much further. In the dedication of his first major work, *An Inquiry into the Human Mind on the Principles of Common Sense* (1764), he describes it as the 'hypothesis . . . That nothing is perceived but what is in the mind which perceives it' (R 96).

Reid's criticism of the Ideal System emerges from his study of Hume's *Treatise* in 1739. Till then Reid had been a follower of Berkeley. Reading Hume led him to abandon Berkeley and to develop a philosophy of his own.

Both Berkeley and Hume had built on Locke's principles. In Locke 'idea' denotes 'every immediate object of the mind in thinking.' 'Thinking' should here be taken broadly, to refer to any activity of consciousness; it is understood that the immediate object of thought is itself mental. Ideas are given, Locke says, in 'sensation' or 'reflection'—we have no idea which does not ultimately derive from these two sources alone. Ideas of sensation are what I am immediately conscious of when I perceive or seem to perceive the world around me. Ideas of reflection are the immediate objects of my consciousness of thoughts and feelings. (An improper classification, Reid observes, because 'the second member of the division includes the first' (R 208).)

An idea is either immediately given in sensation or reflection, or it is a copy of such an idea or it is a complex, constructed out of such copies. Since in thought proper (according to Locke) the mind always deals in copies and complexes thereof, this amounts to the psychological thesis that all concepts are derived from experience. The division between given ideas and copies corresponds to Hume's later distinction between *impressions* and *ideas,* which are copies of impressions; but Reid uses 'idea' in the inclusive sense of Locke and Berkeley.

This picture Reid seeks to destroy. Berkeley accepted it in full, but he charged Locke with inconsistency in following it through. He argued that there followed from it the unintelligibility of matter conceived as an external cause of ideas. What existed were ideas inhering in spirits—finite spirits and the infinite spirit, God. But he vehemently denied that the resulting metaphysical system was in any way inconsistent with the tenets of common sense. The ordinary world of common-sense objects remained in place; Berkeley thought that his philosophy, unlike Locke's, was able to justify the common-sense view that those objects were directly perceived—they were perceived just because they *were* ideas in spirits—including God. So while it was true that the theory of ideas led in Locke's hands to scepticism, that, Berkeley thought, was only because he had not developed it consistently. When it was properly thought through it revealed the idea of matter as an external cause of ideas to be unintelligible. But that idea was no product of common sense; it was an intellectual fantasy of the seventeenth century's corpuscular philosophers.

There is a much greater difference of intention and mood between Berkeley and Hume than is sometimes brought out. A parson could sympathize with the former much more readily than with the latter. Berkeley had put forward a system of idealism designed to save religion from both sceptical and materialist threat. Hume harnesses sceptical reasoning to a natural science of man. He uses reasoning to demonstrate how limited is the authority of reasoning. In fact its *authority* properly speaking shrinks to zero. But this, Reid thought, was to do no more than take the implications of Locke's principles to their true extent. Hume convinced him that the line of defence which had been constructed by Berkeley could not be held. He gave Reid a rigorous demonstration that from the principles of Locke ('who was no sceptic') there does indeed follow 'a system of scepticism, which leaves no ground to believe any one thing rather than its contrary' (R 95).

It is a very striking move on Reid's part to call the Ideal System a hypothesis, a theory—that is, something which goes beyond the given and is postulated to explain the given. How can the existence of ideas be a hypothesis? Are they not exactly what *is* given?

Reid recognizes that the theory of ideas is 'founded on natural prejudices, and so universally received as to be interwoven with the structure of the language' (R 88). But he undertakes to demonstrate that ideas are fictions by careful scrutiny of the processes of perception and thought. He argues, most elegantly, that the Ideal System is the last dogma to remain unsubverted by the subverters of common sense—and the very one which they could not subvert, without letting common sense escape unscathed. And he takes his stand on a Newtonian view of hypotheses, thereby commanding the attention of any would-be Newton of the moral sciences.

In rejecting the theory of ideas, what does Reid reject? Not that perception and thought involve a mental state which I immediately feel. So his rejection is not as radical as the term 'hypothesis' might make it sound: he is not taking a standpoint on the mind from outside it: he still appeals to the standpoint of consciousness. What he rejects is the conception of those mental states as *objects* which we perceive, and which are *representations* of something beyond themselves.

Consider the case of perception. When I see or touch I have a sensation. But sensations are states of mind not objects. The tendency to reify them is one of the sources of the theory of ideas; in a manner reminiscent of more recent philosophy Reid thinks it arises from a grammatical illusion:

The same mode of expression is used to denote sensation and perception; and, therefore, we are apt to look upon them as things of the same nature. Thus, *I feel a pain: I see a tree*: the first denoteth a sensation, the last a perception. The grammatical analysis of both expressions is the same: for both consist of an active verb and an object. But, if we attend to the things signified by these expressions, we shall find that, in the first, the distinction between the act and the object is not real but grammatical; in the second, the distinction is not only grammatical but real.

The form of the expression, *I feel pain*, might seem to imply that the feeling is something distinct from the pain felt; yet, in reality, there is no distinction. As *thinking a thought* is an expression which could signify no more than *thinking*, so *feeling a pain* signifies no more than *being pained*. What we have said of pain is applicable to every other mere sensation. (R 182–3)

Secondly, sensations are in no way resemblances of what is sensed—sensations proper do not have an object, Reid often insists. He takes from Berkeley the point that nothing resembles an idea except another idea; he agrees with him that from the concept of a sensation I could never derive the concept of an external object. But he does not think that this result forces him to idealism. Sensations are 'natural signs'; we pass from them by an original instinct, without inference, to perceptual beliefs.

Perception proper is a relation between perceiver and object. 'Perception is applied only to external objects, not to those that are in the mind itself' (R 222). But Reid's treatment of the term 'perception' is one of the points at which his customary clarity eludes him, for he uses it also in such a way that the mere occurrence of a sensation, giving rise to appropriate perceptual beliefs, counts as an 'act of perception'—that is, to cases where one should more properly say that it *seems* to a person that he perceives something. ('Original perceptions' consist on this usage of sensations triggering appropriate beliefs, where the triggering is innate. 'Acquired perceptions' depend on triggering dispositions which are acquired only through experience. Thus Reid is able to say that there are some features of the world that we 'originally perceive', but that we do not, for example, 'originally perceive' distance. The issue at stake remains a good issue in cognitive psychology, and it leads Reid into fascinating enquiries—notably an account of the non-Euclidean 'geometry of visibles'—but the terminology is highly misleading.)

Reid's analysis of memory is similar: I experience a present state of mind, which naturally prompts me to a memory belief by an original instinct. 'Remember' is a relation between me and the object remembered, not my idea of it (though Reid has the same ambiguity about whether 'remember' is always a relation as he has about 'perceive'). Thought confronts him with a bigger problem. He is clear that thinking of $X$ must be distinguished from thinking of the idea of $X$. But what of cases where the object of my thought does not exist? As usual, Reid robustly sides with 'the vulgar' against 'the philosophers', insisting that is indeed possible. He does not, however, explain *how* it is possible on his principles—that is, without treating thoughts as representational states. The difficulty is that thoughts are *intrinsically* object-directed. Their directedness to an object cannot be explained, in the way Reid attempts in the case of sensations, as consisting in a dedicated tendency to prompt some annexed set of beliefs, since they have no such tendency. Connectedly, I can seem to be perceiving or remembering something, without really doing so, but I cannot seem to be thinking of something while not really doing so. Still, if we point out that Reid fails to explain the directedness of thought, it is only fair to add that no one else has explained it either.

The principles of common sense are in part extracted from Reid's analyses of perception and memory—they include all the innate principles by which sensations and remembrances are originally interpreted. But they also include other principles; most importantly, 'the inductive principle':

It is by this general principle of our nature, that, when two things have been found connected in time past, the appearance of the one produces the belief of the other ... (R 198) Antecedently to all reasoning, we have, by our constitution, an anticipation that there is a fixed and steady course of nature ... We attend to every conjuction of things which presents itself, and expect the continuance of that conjunction. (R 199)

He adds some other interesting principles. For example, we interpret the facial expressions of others as signs of underlying feelings by a natural principle. We naturally incline to tell the truth and to accept what others say on the assumption that they do so too. These are among the rules which guide us in the formation of beliefs: they are 'original principles' derived neither from experience nor from reason. Reid's point is epistemological and not just psychological; he holds these rules to be authoritative—they justify the beliefs formed in accordance with them, though they do so defeasibly.

Reid's treatment of moral and aesthetic principles follows similar lines. He criticizes the school of Francis Hutcheson, David Hume, and Adam Smith which resolves judgements of obligation and value into feelings. He takes it that there are original principles of moral and aesthetic, as there are of common, sense.

Moral and aesthetic judgements are genuinely judgements, objectively true or false, and not merely 'agreeable and uneasy Feelings or Sensations'. On Hume's immensely influential comment that reason is, and ought only to be, the slave of the passions, Reid is characteristic—that is, succinct and deflationary: it at first sight appears 'a shocking paradox', but when its meaning is elicited, it turns out, 'like most other paradoxes', to be 'nothing but an abuse of words'.

For if we give the name of *passion* to every principle of action, in every degree, and give the name of *reason* solely to the power of discerning the fitness of means to ends, it will be true that the use of reason is to be subservient to the passions. (R 572)

How successful is Reid's response to Hume and the other modern philosophers he associates with the Ideal System? One question is whether the System can properly be read into these philosophers, another is whether it is what leads to scepticism.

Though Locke certainly used the term 'idea' loosely, he has often been defended against the accusation of reifying sensations and thoughts. Again, sensations may not be resemblances—but they are, according to Reid, 'natural signs', so they must be intrinsically differentiated in such a way as to prompt the appropriate beliefs. Do we need to attribute more to Locke's ideas or Hume's perceptions than that? And we have seen that in the case of thought proper Reid has no option but to recognize its intrinsic object-directedness.

Scholars, with perfect charity, like to absolve their favourite thinker of confusions or oversights which earlier critics had to labour hard to establish. That devalues the critics' labours. The claim that Reid was attacking straw men was, it is true, already made by some of his contemporaries (Thomas Brown, Joseph Priestley), but it is unfair. It is no small achievement, in philosophy, thoroughly to cleanse an issue of loose and misleading terminology—to eliminate a misleading picture. Reid provides a careful description of how we use some key terms and an identification of principles and beliefs which we do in fact regard as evident—what Wittgenstein would later call descriptive reminders of our practice.

The misleading picture he eliminates, according to which ideas are private image-objects, *is* invoked by the philosophers he criticizes, however clear they may sometimes be that it is only a misleading picture. For example, Berkeley reconciles his idealism with common sense by trading heavily on the claim that we perceive only ideas—in effect reifying them. On the other hand, when arguing for the existence of the self he treats them as states of the self—which cannot exist without the self whose states they are. Hume, in contrast, reifies perceptions when he concludes that they could exist without a self.

Rigorous application of Reid's descriptive reminders is greatly effective in dispelling these excesses. But has he shown that scepticism depends on the Ideal System? On his own showing, what we are conscious of is sensation or feeling. We are not in the same sense *conscious* of what we perceive or remember— that is, the *objects* of perception and memory are not to be confused with states of our mind, sensings or feelings. To perceive or remember an object is to be conscious of a present sensation or a remembrance, which is caused by the object, and which gives rise by a natural disposition to appropriate beliefs concerning that object.

But the sceptic can now ask what gives this natural disposition its authority. Reid holds that the perceptual belief is (defeasibly) warranted in the presence of the sensations. 'I shall take it for granted that the evidence of sense, when the proper circumstances concur, is good evidence, and a just ground of belief' (R 328). The critical question is why this normative principle, which he takes for granted, is authoritative; and this seems not to turn at all on the theory of ideas.

The real challenge to its authority is posed by a thesis which will be with us throughout this book and which we shall call *epistemological empiricism*. It is the thesis that any proposition which has genuine content—which is not an empty tautology— can only be justified a posteriori. An a posteriori proposition cannot be justifiably asserted except on the basis of evidence drawn from experience. In Hume the thesis is not yet very clearly formulated; it appears as an exhaustive dichotomy between propositions which correspond to matters of fact—these are the ones with genuine content—and propositions which simply express abstract relations of ideas. Belief in any proposition of the former kind, says Hume, is justified only on possession of appropriate evidence.

This is 'Hume's fork'. When the fork is applied to the inductive principle there is a débâcle. For this principle is not a mere abstract relation of ideas. It follows that acceptance of it is justified only on appropriate evidence—but any such evidence would rely on induction. It could indeed *raise* our confidence in induction if we had some justification for holding to induction in the first place—but such original justification is just what, by Hume's fork, we do not have. In the theory of value, it is again the fork which does much of the damage. Notably, it is used by Hume to force the conclusion that reason is the slave of the passions, that is, that there are no rational norms of action. For any such putatively rational principle of action is empty if a mere abstract relation of ideas, and otherwise stands in need of a justification which it cannot in principle have.

What is the source of this potent thesis? The weakness in Reid's response to scepticism is that he does not identify the threat, provide any diagnosis of it, or suggest a way of avoiding or dissolving it.

In fact it is surprisingly easy to make the difference between Hume and Reid on real fundamentals come to seem much smaller than Reid makes it appear. Reid, as we have seen, provides a powerful criticism of the theory of ideas. But both he and Hume approach the study of the human mind naturalistically. They disagree on the respective role of instinctive belief, which is promoted by Reid as the 'principles of common sense', and custom and feeling, the categories favoured by Hume—but each of them distinguishes between these operations on the one hand and those of reason on the other.

Reid typically contrasts common sense and reason. Common sense, he says, 'declines the tribunal of reason' (R 127). 'To reason against [its principles] is absurd; nay, to reason for them is absurd. They are first principles; and such fall not within the province of reason, but of common sense' (R 108).

All reasoning must be from first principles; and for first principles no other reason can be given but this, that, by the constitution of our nature, we are under a necessity of assenting to them. Such principles are part of our constitution, no less than the power of thinking: reason can neither make nor destroy them; nor can it do anything without them: it is like a telescope, which may help a man to see farther, who hath eyes; but, without eyes, a telescope shews nothing at all. (R 130)

Here Reid seems to confine 'reason', as Hume does, to demonstrative reasoning, the analysis of abstract relations of ideas, which can carry us forward from first principles which have real content, but cannot provide such content itself ('shews nothing at all'). Or again here: 'We agree with the author of the 'Treatise of Human Nature', in this, That our belief of the continuance of nature's laws is not derived from reason' (R 199).

On the other hand, Hume agrees that the fundamental principles which Reid ascribes to common sense—such as the belief in continuing, independent bodies, in a continuing self, in causal connexion, or the very disposition to argue inductively, are natural to us and wholly irresistible. Philosophy, he agrees, cannot undermine them or forbid us to hold them. Hume labours to show that they cannot be justified by reason—but Reid does not disagree with this. Moreover, Hume's purpose in showing that reason fails to justify them is not to reject them— on the contrary, he continues to hold them. His purpose is to clear the ground for his own psychological analysis of how they arise—and he provides that analysis from a standpoint which takes their truth for granted.

It is true that Reid appeals to belief where Hume appeals to feeling, and that Reid is an innatist where Hume is an associationist. Thus if Hume's fork is taken as a psychological thesis about the innate 'powers' of the understanding, Reid certainly disagrees with it. It is also true that Reid makes less of a fuss over the contrast between reason and common sense than Hume does over the contrast between reason and custom and feeling. In later writings he makes it clear that common sense is 'only another name for one branch or one degree of reason', the branch which judges 'of things self-evident' (R 425). But this can have a bearing on the sceptical challenge only if Reid is able to show how it is that an instinctive and irresistible belief can thereby get a *rational* warrant.

It is important to reiterate the naturalism of Reid. He does not hold that first principles are 'self-evident' in the sense in which that doctrine was later held (Chapter 4)—i.e. that they are the deliverances of a rational faculty which discerns or perceives an independent domain of Platonic entities and objective relations between them. His claim is simply that these principles are original—innate in their own right, not the product of associative processes working on simpler dispositions—and that they are irresistible.

'For first principles no other *reason* can be given but this, that, by the constitution of our nature, we are under a necessity of assenting to them' (my emphasis). They are, Reid thinks, 'the inspiration of God Almighty'. But he does not claim that belief in God is itself a principle of common sense, still less that reason alone can demonstrate His existence—so he is right to say that 'no other reason can be given'.

He says nothing to show why the constitutional necessity of assenting to them *is* a reason. Why, that is, should the putative fact that a belief or a principle of reasoning is innate in me and unalterable confer on it a rational warrant? I would have to have reason for inferring from its constitutional necessity to its reliability. But what would justify that inference? Not God or the theory of evolution—unless these can be demonstrated by reason alone, without relying on the original principles they are meant to vindicate.

A great commentator has written that Hume's 'entire philosophy is built around the view of Nature as having an authority which man has neither the right nor the power to challenge'. But then so is Reid's. Seen thus, the disagreement between them is an in-house controversy among enlightened Scottish naturalists. However, unlike Reid, Hume deploys sceptical arguments as a tool for his naturalistic analysis of the human understanding. He deploys them with such force and lucidity that they start up from their intended employment and subvert the whole programme of which they were meant to be a part. We are left by Hume with no account of how the phrase 'There is reason to hold that' can be prefixed to any assertion—including the assertions Hume makes about what we naturally and inevitably hold.

It is naturalism as such that leads to epistemological empiricism: for how can propositions corresponding to states of affairs external to the mind be known by thought alone? It does not affect the question whether we explain thought by innate mechanisms or by association or by a combination of the two. This connexion between naturalism and epistemological empiricism was perceived by Kant. But it also seems, as Kant insisted, that epistemological empiricism must collapse into scepticism. For unless, at the very least, some norms of evidence are a priori, then there is nothing to rule what datum supports what proposition. This critical point will recur again and again. It underlies Kant's claim that knowledge is possible only if some 'synthetic' propositions—propositions which have genuine content—are nevertheless a priori.

How are synthetic a priori propositions possible? To answer this question, Kant held, required nothing less than what he called 'transcendental idealism'. *There must be a point of view from which the mind is seen to be placed outside nature.* From this point of view, we are able to see that certain principles, deployed in the construction of our knowledge of nature, are synthetic and yet a priori. They have that status because they are the principles by which the mind *constitutes* nature, receiving as its materials inputs from things-in-themselves. It could not have this constitutive role, were it simply a part of what is constituted. So we are forced to distinguish two perspectives on the mind, the transcendental and the empirical. Empirically, the mind appears simply as a set of causal processes in a real world of space and time. Transcendentally, it is seen as the active principle which constitutes that world of space and time. Space, time, and their contents, Kant says, can be defended as empirically real only if they are recognized as transcendentally ideal. With the formulation of this view, as we noted earlier, naturalism itself comes sharply into focus. It can now be stated as the doctrine that the only tenable point of view is the empirical point of view—that the Kantian idea of distinguishing from that view another, transcendental, point of view, is unintelligible.

This way of defining naturalism, it may fairly be objected, is unhelpful in defining naturalism by reference to another doctrine, which is at least as obscure. One may try another definition, such as: Whatever exists, exists in space and time, or at least in time. Or more primitively still: Whatever exists comes under causal relations. In Kant's view all of these, space, time, causation, are ingredients which the mind imposes in its constitution of nature. So there cannot be spatio-temporal or even causal relations between things-in-themselves, and thus Kant would reject a thesis defined in these alternative ways. But one trouble with these definitions is that a naturalist may wish to leave it possible that empirical enquiry in natural science itself may lead us to reject the reality of space or time—or even of causation as we currently think of it, for example, through the revisions of causal determinism which seem to be implied by quantum physics. Furthermore, these alternative definitions do not capture the historical significance of naturalism—the aspect of it which from the enlightenment on made it the centre of controversy. The controversy centred on the doctrine that there can be a fully comprehensive natural science of man—one which leaves nothing out.

One thing threatened by this is supernaturalism—the idea of an order of reality above natural reality, in which human beings participate. Religion need not be supernaturalist and primitively was not so; the gods existed within a unified natural reality and acted on it by principles proper to it. On the other hand, the conception of God that one arrives at by arguments of natural theology, such as the argument from design, does place God outside created nature as a whole—but still does not put Him into a metaphysical category compared to which nature is mere appearance. The natural creation remains a full and proper part of the total reality of which God is also a part. Thomas Reid may not be a fully naturalistic philosopher, inasmuch as he does not think that nature is all there is, or that the natural man is the whole man; but he does think (after his rejection of Berkeley) that nature is a fully real part of what there is. And the assertion that God exists, understood in Reid's way, seems open to challenge from such hypotheses as Laplacian determinism or Darwinian evolution.

In contrast, in Kant's view of the relation between transcendental and empirical (or natural) realities, nature is demoted from what is absolutely, unqualifiedly, real. Natural science indeed leaves no aspect of empirical reality out—it is fully sovereign in its own domain. In that sense Kant can agree that a natural science of man is possible which 'leaves nothing out'. But in another and more fundamental sense he disagrees—for empirical reality is itself not absolutely real, whereas the mind as transcendentally active principle is absolutely real. Natural science is sovereign in its own domain; but the reasoning and experience which give rise to it have no authority beyond that domain. Thus science cannot undermine the existence of God, but equally, natural theology cannot produce arguments for the existence of God. Kant himself said that he had placed limits on reason to make room for faith. This was one vital cause of his eventual victory over Scottish common sense among those philosophers in the 19th century who were concerned to defend religion.

Indeed these themes are of the greatest importance in nineteenth-century culture. They intercut with religion, romanticism, the relationships between self and world, the meanings of art, the possibility of spiritual life. In more subtle ways, as we shall see, they retain their importance in the twentieth century. Kant first put them irreversibly on the scene by chaining naturalism, through apparently unbreakable links, to the impossibility of knowledge—while affirming knowledge. This was the turning-point to which anti-naturalistic philosophers later in the century would constantly refer, even when they sought to go beyond transcendental idealism in a variety of ways, in particular by rejecting things-in-themselves or by affirming a single Absolute Mind.

Unless some underlying assumption is suppressed in the argument from naturalism to scepticism, we must embrace scepticism or conclude that *something* is right in the Critical Philosophy. The traditional view that Kant's response to Hume supersedes and goes deeper than Reid's remains in this particular respect correct. But it must not diminish a philosopher of great lucidity and flair—a philosopher's philosopher. Reid scores many palpable and enjoyable hits in his criticism of 'ideas'. With 'that capacity of "patient thought" which so peculiarly characterised his philosophical genius' he undermines the reduction of ethics and aesthetics to 'feeling'. It is true that this reduction cannot be fully rebutted without the head-on deflection of Hume's fork which Kant first provides. None the less, it was as much Reid's achievement as anyone else's to eliminate the simple-minded opposition between reason and feeling for the length of the 19th century—only with Hume's twentieth-century successors did it return.

Reid's most penetrating contribution was to vitalize common sense as a natural phenomenon which must occupy a fundamental place in philosophic reflection. It returns again in Sidgwick, Moore, Wittgenstein, and 'ordinary language philosophy'. Central to it is the idea that a certain system of fundamental principles is warranted by nothing other than human obviousness, an obviousness which survives critical scrutiny. It is an idea of capital importance for naturalism, but Reid has not the materials for vindicating it naturalistically. Kant saw that—but did he provide a credible alternative? Anyone who finds Kant's transcendental idealism incredible or even unintelligible has every reason to seek a deeper defence of Reid. But for that to be possible one must find some way of reconciling the two poles of English-language philosophy—epistemological empiricism and common sense.

German-idealist influence in Britain grew slowly and has always remained at best intermittent. Despite its gorgeous flourish at the end of the century, which we shall come to in Chapter 3, it has made no permanent mark on English-language philosophy. At the beginning it came, mostly in rather muffled form, not through philosophers but through writers caught up in the romantic movement. From among these it sent out one messenger of dazzling brightness and power—Coleridge: extraordinary poet, thinker, man, whose influence was also extraordinary. It is impossible to give a full idea of it here. William Hazlitt called him the only person 'I ever knew who answered to the idea of a man of genius. ... the only person from whom I ever learnt anything. ... His mind was clothed with wings; and raised on them, he lifted philosophy to heaven.' John Sterling, one of John Stuart Mill's closest friends and fellow-spirits, and also one of Thomas Carlyle's, said:

To Coleridge I owe *education*. He taught me to believe that an empirical philosophy is none, that Faith is the highest Reason, that all criticism, whether of literature, laws, or manners, is blind, without the power of discerning the organic unity of the subject.

That was Coleridge's mature influence. But as an undergraduate at Cambridge he had been an enthusiast for the enlightenment, for its belief in man as a natural being and its doctrine of society as progressive and perfectible. He read Hartley and became a necessitarian; he read Locke and Godwin and became a perfectibilist. He was enthused by the French Revolution; he collaborated with Robert Southey on an abortive project for a 'Pantisocracy', a commune of twelve couples to be established in New England on the banks of the Susquehanna.

By 1797 his naturalistic-necessitarian-progressivist phase was over; the reaction against enlightenment naturalism (and the French Revolution) had begun. The following year he went with the Wordsworths to Germany, spending time at the University of Göttingen. In 1799 he returned to England 'with a view to the one work, to which I hope to dedicate in silence the prime of my life' (Cg1 283)—the philosophical *Opus Maximum* which he never completed. There now began a long love-affair with Kant and German romantic philosophy, in particular the philosophy of Schelling.

Coleridge was himself the organic unity he sought—in poetry, philosophy, and life. But he paid a heavy price. His conversation was genial; his writing brilliant but fragmentary. His life was lived for long periods on the edge of breakdown and over. The impulse which drove his thought was the search for spiritual unity of self, nature, and God. He revolted against the passive mind, merely reacting to its environment, which he thought to be the upshot of deterministic associationism. It conflicted with his lived experience of poetic imagination. It did not measure man in either his depth or his height—an alienated, fallen, but authentically creative being. He first found some relief in Berkeley—if ideas are in the mind of God, then finite human minds must somehow participate in that infinite all-creative mind. But it was Kant who provided him with a philosophic framework which seemed to fit his conception.

One seminal distinction in Kant is that between Reason and Understanding. Coleridge, like other post-Kantians, turned it to his own purposes:

by the UNDERSTANDING, I mean the faculty of thinking and forming *judgements* on the notices furnished by the sense, according to certain rules existing in itself, which rules constitute its distinct nature. By the pure REASON, I mean the power by which we become possessed of principle ... and of ideas. (C 4i 177 n.)

Understanding applies rules to experience; it classifies, judges, and generalizes. Reason provides the logical laws and the a priori principles, the Ideas, which Understanding applies. It is the source of all those principles of the Understanding for which an associationist cannot account. Kant's idealism wins the allegiance of Coleridge in a way in which the innatist naturalism of Reid could not do—for it makes Reason transcendentally active:

Supreme Reason, whose knowledge is creative, and antecedent to the thing known, is distinguished from the understanding, or creaturely mind of the individual, the acts of which are posterior to the things it records and arranges. (C 6 18–19)

Reason cannot itself figure among the objects empirically known by a natural science of man, for it constitutes those objects. Coleridge makes parallel distinctions between Imagination and Fancy, Symbol and Allegory, Genius and Talent—in each case naturalistic psychology can accomodate the latter but not the former. Thus poetic imagination synthesizes experience into the organic unity of art. It 'dissolves, diffuses, dissipates, in order to recreate ... it struggles to idealize and to unify. It is essentially *vital*, even as all objects (*as* objects) are essentially fixed and dead.' (C 7i 304) It is a 'shaping or modifying power'—Coleridge calls it an 'esemplastic' power. Fancy in contrast can only rearrange and aggregate already shaped, remembered, 'fixities and definites'. Imagination and Symbol, like Reason, have a creative rather than a merely copying and rearranging function, a function which can only be grasped transcendentally.

To follow Reason and Imagination to their sources is to go beyond the 'natural consciousness'—and thus into a region in which most men are not at home:

It is neither possible nor necessary for all men, or for many, to be PHILOSOPHERS. There is a *philosophic* (and inasmuch as it is actualized by an effort of freedom, an *artificial*) *consciousness*, which lies beneath or (as it were) *behind* the spontaneous consciousness natural to all reflecting beings. As the elder Romans distinguished their northern provinces into Cis-Alpine and Trans-Alpine, so may we divide all the objects of human knowledge into those on this side, and those on the other side of the spontaneous consciousness: citra et trans conscientiam communem. . . . The first range of hills, that encircles the scanty vale of human life, is the horizon for the majority of its inhabitants. On *its* ridges the common sun is born and departs. From *them* the stars rise, and touching *them* they vanish. By the many, even this range, the natural limit and bulwark of the vale, is but imperfectly known. Its higher ascents are too often hidden by mists and clouds . . . But in all ages there have been a few, who measuring and sounding the rivers of the vale at the feet of their furthest inaccessible falls have learnt, that the sources must be far higher and far inward; a few, who even in the level streams have detected elements which neither the vale itself nor the surrounding mountains contained or could supply. (C 7i 236–9)

This Caspar David Friedrich-like metaphor (of which I have quoted only a part) marvellously conjures up the solitude of the transcendental philosopher. Plumbing the torrents of the plain, he recognizes their mountainous source ('trans conscientiam communem') and raises his thoughts to the heights, beyond the enclosing hills, which he cannot see.

Yet so far he remains, with the common-sense philosopher, an inhabitant of the plain—and that is where Kant must leave him. But Coleridge could not find final satisfaction, any more than other romantics could, in the dichotomies and limits imposed by the Critical Philosophy. He wanted the philosopher to *climb* the highest ascents—so that 'to these thoughts, these strong probabilities, the ascertaining vision, the intuitive knowledge, may finally supervene' (C 7i 239). By penetrating to '*the other side* of our natural consciousness' (C 7i 243), Coleridge thinks—and in this departs from the 'venerable sage of Koenigsberg'—the philosopher can reach the *immediate* consciousness of true Being.

There is in Romanticism more than one impulse; one may say the heroic—active, voluntaristic—and the mystical. The Critical Philosophy caters for the first—the Mind as active, and perhaps in particular the Artist and Genius as God-like, productive, imposing order on unshaped given material. But by imposing limits on the knowable, it cannot cater for the second. For the mystical impulse requires that one should somehow achieve a consciousness in which Self and World are no longer distinct, but merge in the unity of Being; in which Nature is but the self-alienation of mind itself, grasped under the categories of causation, space, and time. Or rather the opposition between nature and mind must itself merely be the polarization of an underlying unity, the Unconditioned. 'Reason *is* Being, the Supreme *Reason*, the Supreme Being ... the antithesis of Truth and being is but the result of the *polarizing* property of all finite mind, for which Unity is manifested only by correspondent opposites' (C 4i 515 n. 3). 'The ground of existence, and the ground of the knowledge of existence, are absolutely identical' (C 7i 275).

Coleridge feels the mystical as well as the heroic impulse (the ascent of the mountain is also a journey to the interior, and then in turn an identification with the Whole). He thus becomes an exponent of the Identity-Philosophy, whose preoccupation with the ground of being is as old as Parmenides and as new as Heidegger, but sounds out in English-language philosophy only rarely. 'Great indeed are the obstacles which an English metaphysician has to encounter' (C 7i 290). It is a sad fact that a good deal of his purely philosophical exposition is

taken almost word-for-word from Friedrich Schelling (1775–
1854). He acknowledges in *Biographia Literaria* that he
sometimes uses Schelling's words; anticipating a charge of
plagiarism, he claims that he had reached the same thoughts
by the same route—which was critical meditation on Kant—
before he ever encountered Schelling. Yet when the scale of his
borrowings was made known, initially by de Quincey and then
in detail by the Scottish philosopher James Ferrier, it caused
something of a scandal.

But what matters for us is that the romantic transcendence of
naturalism should have had in England in this period a representative of great brilliance, gifted with the poetic and philosophic power to graft German idealism onto that tree of English
tradition whose roots lay in firm Reformation spirituality and
the contemplative reading of the Bible. Often Coleridge brings
its eloquence into play:

Hast thou ever raised thy mind to the consideration of EXISTENCE, in
and by itself, as the mere act of existing? Hast thou ever said to thyself
thoughtfully, IT IS! heedless in that moment, whether it were a man
before thee, or a flower, or a grain of sand? Without reference, in
short, to this or that particular mode or form of existence? If thou hast
indeed attained to this, thou wilt have felt the presence of a mystery,
which must have fixed thy spirit in awe and wonder. The very words,
There is nothing! or, There was a time, when there was nothing! are
self-contradictory....

Not to BE, then, is impossible: TO BE, incomprehensible. If thou hast
mastered this intuition of absolute existence, thou wilt have learnt
likewise, that it was this, and no other, which in the earlier ages seized
the nobler minds, the elect among men, with a sort of sacred horror.
This it was which first caused them to feel within themselves a something ineffably greater than their own individual nature ... (C 4i 514)

The notion of knowledge as identity of subject and object is
closely related to mysticism proper, which had also influenced
Coleridge greatly. But though Coleridge responds to the mystical
impulse, he still wishes to retain a Christian dualism between a
personal creator and the souls he places in the world. This
dualism is a source of Coleridge's very English conservatism.

Philosophy does not transcend religion. Religion, understood as worship, remains the highest exercise of the human spirit, philosophy a rational preparation for it. In the British revival of idealism which takes place at the end of the century, this question of the relationship between religion and philosophy will return.

For good and ill, but mainly for good, Coleridge's most widely influential contribution was to social and political thought rather than to metaphysics—through his discussion of the role of culture and cultivation (the German *Bildung*) in the shaping of nations.

Nations are animated by two essential principles of 'permanence' and 'progression'. These Coleridge identified with the landed and the mercantile class. But civilization is grounded in the cultivation of the people, cultivation being 'the harmonious development of those qualities and faculties that characterize our *humanity*' (C x. 42–3) For the due maintenance of this cultivating function, Coleridge thought, a 'permanent class, or order' was needed, whose explicit task would be the security and improvement of the Nation's culture—he called it a 'clerisy' or 'National Church'. It would be an endowed estate of the realm, consisting of 'the learned of all denominations . . . all the so called liberal arts and sciences, the possession and application of which constitute the civilisation of a country, as well as the Theological' (C x. 46–7).

The conception of culture as a historically flexible mould, shaping and shaped by the dialectic of permanence and progression, seemed to many of Coleridge's readers to be the most significant way in which the German thought he and others brought to England yielded a higher standpoint on politics and society than had the Enlightenment. It greatly influenced many eminent Victorians, among them John Stuart Mill, who saw in it the deep truth which the Conservative philosophy, the 'Germano-Coleridgean school', had to teach to philosophical radicalism—'the school of experience and association'. Mill was no follower of Coleridge or the Germans in his metaphysics; but in his effort to humanize the utilitarian tradition, which we shall come to in the next chapter, he was a Coleridgean through and through.

For Coleridge of course Culture is the domain of Reason and Imagination, and can therefore only be grasped transcendentally. Coleridge could not have accepted Mill's extraction of *Bildung* and historicity from the romantic metaphysics into which they had been stitched. It is transcendental Reason which provides and revises the 'idea' of our practices and institutions, by which Coleridge means 'that conception of a thing . . . which is given by the knowledge of *its ultimate aim*' (C x. 12) and which goes beyond what can be abstracted from its actual forms.

Yet in harnessing culture to one side of these potent dualisms of reason and understanding, imagination and fancy—organic and mechanical—romanticism creates grave danger. For one thing, the dualisms are made to rest on a precarious metaphysical foundation. If culture depends on religion and metaphysical idealism, what happens when there is a collapse of belief in God and in idealism? Then again, if understanding and fancy are cut off from true culture, do we not have the beginnings of two cultures? Will not the priests of high culture, if organized into an estate of the realm, suffer from their own illusions and corruptions? This is the darker side of counter-enlightenment, whose dilemmas were to be a lifelong preoccupation of John Stuart Mill, for whom they often took the form of an opposition between Coleridge and Bentham—'the two great seminal minds of England in their age', he called them (M x. 77). It is to Bentham that we must now turn.

Reid's life spanned the decades of the enlightenment. In His naturalism he belonged to it—to the sober Christian wing which objected to the associationist and sceptical excesses of Hume. Coleridge was born in Reid's sixty-second year. His revolt against the eighteenth-century intellectual avant-garde comes from a much later period than Reid's, a period of high post-Kantian romanticism, several thought-stages on from Reid—even if the stages were stages of a cul-de-sac. In contrast, the chief intellectual continuity between reforming, secular enlightenment and the nineteenth-century's positive spirit of reform is provided in

Britain by another long-lived man (84 years to Reid's 86), Jeremy Bentham.

Bentham is one of the chief exhibits of the European enlightenment (in body he so remains—though with a wax head—embalmed in University College, London, on show in one of the corridors). He was born in London in 1748. He achieved fame in a French translation by a Genevan. He corresponded with the Continental *philosophes*. His major work in English, the *Introduction to the Principles of Morals and Legislation*, appeared in the year of Revolution, 1789. In 1792 he was made a citizen of the French Republic. He died in 1832—the day before the Reform Bill received its Royal Assent. By then a circle of thinkers and politicians had gathered round him—'the philosophic radicals'—who would have an important influence on British political life. To this picture of longevity one must add that he went to Oxford University aged 12 and took his degree (after leaving) at 16; that having been called to the bar he never practised, but devoted his life to study, intellectual production, and reform of law. A speaker at his funeral calculated that for fifty years he had engaged in study eight to twelve hours a day.

Bentham was an empiricist, associationist, utilitarian; he had much in common with Hume, whom he acknowledged among his masters. But Hume was not entirely to the philosophic radicals' taste—his scepticism and his conservatism dismayed them. So Bentham's school effectively marks a new start rather than a direct line from the Scottish school of Hutcheson, Hume, and Smith, whose greatest influence was not on philosophic radicals but on Whigs.

He was, first and foremost, a legal theorist and reformer: disgusted with the practice and theory of English law. He wanted an intelligible and humane legal system; but his exploration of its existing foundations, and their rebarbative legal fictions, led him vastly further afield, to a wide-ranging critique of language and of practical reason. Vigorous opposition to all poisoned speech—whether it resulted from 'sinister' interest or well-meaning cant—was one of his most attractive traits.

The iconoclasm with which he cleanses language makes him one of the great demystifiers of philosophy, and gives him a distinctly twentieth-century forcefulness. Men are caught in 'the shackles of ordinary language'. 'Metaphysical speculations', he said, have as their object 'understanding clearly what one is speaking of':

> the language of plain strong sense is difficult to learn; the language of smooth nonsense is easy and familiar. The one requires a force of attention capable of stemming the tide of usage and example; the other requires nothing but to swim with it. (B ii. 524)

This is from *Anarchical Fallacies*, an attack on the French Revolution's doctrine of natural rights. Bentham's purgation of language is applied in the service of the principle of utility, or as he later preferred to call it, the Greatest Happiness Principle. He states the principle variously. For example, he says that 'the greatest happiness of the greatest number' is 'the measure of right and wrong' and, elsewhere, the 'right and proper end of government'. The phrase itself, 'greatest happiness of the greatest number', is older than Bentham—yet if anyone has a claim to the title 'father of utilitarianism', it is he.

'Greatest happiness of the greatest number' is in fact a strictly meaningless phrase. Bentham means that the happiness of every individual counts equally with that of every other as valuable in itself, and that nothing else does. 'Utility' he uses interchangeably with happiness—which is 'a vain word—a word void of meaning—to him to whose mind it does not explain itself with reference to . . . pains and pleasures' (Bs iii. 308). To maximize pleasure net of pain, by whatever consciousnesses the pleasure and pain be felt, is for him the only axiom of practical reasoning.

Armed with this axiom Bentham approaches the fictions of moral, legal, and political discourse—'Power, right, prohibition, duty, obligation, burthen, immunity, exemption, privilege, property, security, liberty' (Bl 251). To exhibit them as fictions one must show how to frame, for any sentence in which an expression purporting to refer to them occurs, a new sentence, equivalent in meaning, in which no such expression occurs. This process Bentham calls 'paraphrasis'.

His treatment of 'obligation' and 'right' typifies it. These concepts involve, he thinks, the idea of a penalty—a physical or mental pain ('without the notion of punishment . . . no notion can we have of either right or duty' (Bf 495 n.)). To say that a man has an obligation to do a thing is to say that he is liable to a penalty for not doing it. To say he has a right to a thing is to say that all or certain others are liable to penalty if they impede his possession of it, or fail to supply it (depending on the nature of the right). More needs to be said about the phrase 'liable to', and we shall return to it, but we must first dwell on the notion of paraphrasis itself.

It is one of Bentham's most important innovations. In the Lockean view of analysis, a complex term, standing for a complex idea, can be broken down into its constituents—'orange' into 'spherical, orange-coloured fruit', or 'vixen' into 'female fox'. This corresponds to an explicit definition—'$X$' means '$Y$'—where a word or phrase is defined by another phrase which can replace it wherever it occurs (apart from some very specific contexts which need not concern us). But 'duty', 'obligation', etc. resist that kind of explicit definition. Bentham defines them contextually, showing how to rewrite the sentences in which they occur. The sentence that replaces the one in which 'duty' or 'right' occurred has no alternative phrase purporting to have the same meaning.

Such paraphraseable terms are, Bentham thinks, usually associated with an 'image of some real action or state of things'—he calls this process 'archetypation' (B viii. 246). In the case of obligation, for example, 'the emblematical, or archetypal image, is that of a man lying down with a heavy body pressing upon him' (B viii. 247). It is easy to be misled by archetypation—for example into treating the image, or something associated with it, as the real meaning of the term—but paraphrasis shows that the image plays no essential role in the term's actual function, by showing how the same literal communication could be made without using the term at all.

The effect of this doctrine is to bring the sentence, rather than the terms which make up a sentence, to the forefront as the basic unit of meaning. 'The primary and original use of language', Bentham says, is the 'communication of thought' (B viii. 320)—'every man who speaks, speaks in propositions'— 'terms taken by themselves are the work of abstraction, the produce of refined analysis' (B viii. 321). 'No word is of itself the complete sign of any thought'—'it was in the form of entire propositions that when first uttered, discourse was uttered. Of these integers, words were but so many fragments, as afterwards *in written discourse* letters were of words' (B viii. 322). These are striking anticipations of doctrines which a hundred and more years later were to be developed in depth (as we shall see in Chapter 4).

There is a further striking point about Bentham's idea of paraphrasis. Though he talks of the objects apparently referred to by paraphraseable terms as fictions, one must be careful in inferring that he thought paraphrasis demonstrates non-existence. Fictitious entities are not merely 'fabulous' non-entities, such as the devil. They are 'objects, which in every language must, for the purpose of discourse, be spoken of as existing' (B viii. 198). Bentham means that they are practically indispensable; the possibility *in principle* of paraphrasing them out of discourse is what shows them to be fictional. But while it is false that there are centaurs or golden mountains, it is true that there are rights and obligations. They can be properly said to exist, but the statement that they do can itself be paraphrased:

a fictitious entity is an entity to which, though by the grammatical form of discourse employed in speaking of it, existence be ascribed, yet in truth and reality existence is not meant to be ascribed. (B viii. 197)

Thus Bentham is able, quite consistently, to hold that rights are fictional without denying the common-sense observation that people have rights:

from the observation, by which, for example, the words *duties* and rights are here spoken of as names of fictitious entities, let it not for a moment so much as be supposed, that, in either instance, the reality of the object is meant to be denied, in any sense in which in ordinary language the reality of it is assumed. (B viii. 176 n.)

But while Bentham is happy with rights construed as indispensable fictions, he peremptorily rejects *natural* rights. Natural rights, and natural law, confuse is and ought, the descriptive and the prescriptive—Bentham here acknowledges a debt to Hume. The 'pretended law of nature' is 'an obscure phantom, which, in the imagination of those who go in chase of it, points sometimes to *manners*, sometimes to *laws*; sometimes to what law *is*, sometimes to what it *ought* to be' (Bi 298 n.). Why is Bentham so vehement in his rejection of natural law? He himself has the materials for distinguishing positive and ideal law, as we can see if we return to the phrase 'liable to'. It may mean that infringement does in fact produce the liability to penalty. Or it may mean that it should do so. In the first case we have positive morality and law. The obligation or right is moral if the penalty is—in fact—social disapprobation and personal guilt. It is legal only if rule and penalty are duly constituted by a sovereign. Bentham's doctrine of sovereignty holds, like Hobbes's, that a sovereign is a person or body which is habitually obeyed and not habitually obedient to another. The laws are its commands, enforced by punishment. Customary law becomes such only when sanctioned by the sovereign's command.

Yet given Bentham's principle of utility there is obviously room for a normative, as well as a positive, doctrine of morality and law. Normative morality would be that which *should*, from a utilitarian point of view, be sanctioned by the pains of conscience and social disapproval; normative law would be that which *should* be commanded by the sovereign. (There could also be a normative doctrine of sovereignty.)

It can be argued on behalf of Bentham that we ordinarily use the concept of morality normatively, and the concept of law positively. If that is so, then to invoke a natural law or right—understanding it as a department of law, not morality—is either to assume a divine sovereign or to confuse is and ought. This at any rate is the nub of Bentham's position. It is consistent with recognizing normative moral rights and duties. But these on his view are not the business of judges (though they are the business of sovereigns who legislate)—they cannot therefore be interpreted as natural *law*.

Talk of natural rights, Bentham thinks, is a confusion giving rise to anarchy. He similarly rejects the social contract, repeating

Hume's arguments. The idea that what one has not personally assented to one need not obey leads to anarchy. Of the French declaration of rights he famously comments, '*natural rights* is simple nonsense: natural and imprescriptible rights, rhetorical nonsense, nonsense upon stilts' (B ii. 501).

The opposition to 'natural rights' is universal among British philosophers covered in this book. Bentham and Coleridge are entirely agreed in criticizing the 'rights of man' philosophy of Rousseau and Tom Paine; later on in the century John Stuart Mill and Thomas Hill Green are equally agreed in holding that statements about a person's rights cannot be basic. They can only be derived from a more fundamental moral criterion, which will not itself be couched in terms of rights. Mill indeed interestingly distinguished three kinds of radicalism—he called them metaphysical, historical, and philosophical. Metaphysical radicalism appeals to an individual's natural rights and the idea of a social contract, historical radicalism to the rights anciently recognized in his community, while philosophical radicalism—the position of Bentham and of Mill himself—does not *appeal* to rights at all but, where it recognizes them, grounds them in utility. Of the three varieties metaphysical radicalism, unlike the other two, had little influence in Britain after Locke, but it has always remained a lively tradition in America: this is a fundamental difference between the two political cultures which remains noticeable in contemporary political philosophy.

There is indeed a peculiarly English, as against Scottish or American, positivism about Bentham's views on sovereignty and law—an impatience with 'vague' or 'unmeaning' principles restraining government. It may explain why the Scottish and Coleridgean schools had a greater influence in America than Benthamism did. The Scots in particular gave a non-metaphysical content to the idea of a natural principle—it could be a natural instinct, as with Reid, or a natural mode of social interaction, as with Smith and other social theorists of the Scottish enlightenment. But Bentham has no time at all for any notion of natural liberty, or of 'natural' limitation on positive sovereignty. His typical attitude to such ideas is debunking:

I have not, I never had, nor ever shall have, any horror, sentimental or anarchical, of the hand of government. I leave it to Adam Smith, and the champions of the rights of men ... to talk of invasions of natural liberty, and to give as a special argument against this or that law, an argument the effect of which would be to put a negative on all laws. (Bs iii. 258)

This puts him at a distance from the Scottish writers. They were no more friendly to metaphysical ideas of natural law or right than he was, but they saw the need for something subtler than the simple dichotomy of positive custom and command on the one hand, anarchy on the other. In this they were wiser then Bentham, as also were the Coleridgeans with their historicist notions of character and society—Scottish influence on the Whigs, like Coleridgean influence on conservatism, was as much a part of nineteenth-century commerce between politics and ideas as was philosophic radicalism.

But it was not the principle of utility, nor was it empiricist epistemology, nor finally was it associationist psychology, that made Bentham less wise. That was now to be argued, with great eloquence and incisiveness, and in unprecedented depth, by John Stuart Mill.

# 2

# Liberal Apogee: Mill and his Age

Among Jeremy Bentham's closest associates was James Mill (1773–1836), a Scotsman from the county of Angus on the East Coast. He came to London to seek fortune as an author in 1802. His eldest son, John Stuart (1806–73), born in London, was to be the philosopher who brought British empiricism and British liberalism to their classical shape.

James Mill was a philosopher and historian of importance in his own right. He came from a poor family (whose name was originally 'Milne'). His progress through Montrose Academy and Edinburgh University, where he studied Divinity, was owed to the financial support of Sir John Stuart of Fettercairn and his wife. Though licensed as a preacher he never gained a living; but on moving to London he soon achieved comfortable earnings in journalism. There he married an English woman, Harriet Burrow—his son was thus half English and half Scots. James Mill's public reputation was made by his *History of British India* (1817). It led to employment by the East India Company, of which he became a high official—followed in the same post by his son. His most interesting contribution to philosophy (apart from his son)—the *Analysis of the Phenomena of the Human Mind* (1829)—belongs in the associationist school of David Hartley.

No philosopher's childhood is better known than John Stuart Mill's. He describes it in his *Autobiography*. He was taught by his father, beginning with Greek (at the age of 3) and arithmetic in the evenings. Before breakfast the two of them would walk out in the lanes around Newington Green (then largely rural); John would report on the histories and biographies he had read the previous day. He began on logic at 12, and political economy at 13. David Ricardo was a close friend of James Mill,

and John read his *Principles of Political Economy* in the year
they appeared. He edited Bentham's *Rationale of Judicial
Evidence*—a monumental labour—when he was 18. John never
went to university, but by the age of 20 he in effect had a
postgraduate training in logic, political economy, and juris-
prudence.

The rest of his life does not fall short of this turbo-charged
start. In his twenties and thirties he came to know some of the
most interesting younger figures in English politics and culture.
His horizons broadened and his main themes were established.
The *System of Logic*, the product of his thirties, published in
1843, made his reputation as a philosopher. The *Principles of
Political Economy*, of 1848, was a synthesis of classical economics which defined liberal orthodoxy for at least a quarter of
a century. His two best-known works of moral philosophy, *On
Liberty* and *Utilitarianism*, appeared in 1859 and 1861.

A major event in his personal life was an intense—but apparently platonic—affair with a married woman, Harriet Taylor,
who eventually became his wife in 1851 (and whose influence
on him has intrigued scholars ever since). In the 1860s he was
briefly a member of Parliament, and throughout his life he was
involved in many working-class and radical causes, though always in a stubbornly independent way. One of the causes he
supported was women's rights—see *The Subjection of Women*
of 1869. In 1866 he presented to Parliament a petition for
women's suffrage, and in 1867 he moved an amendment to the
Reform Bill of that year, which would have extended the fran-
chise irrespective of gender—'perhaps', he said, 'the only really
important public service I performed in the capacity of a member
of Parliament' (M i. 285).

Mill's presence in nineteenth-century politics and culture is
so immense that it can be hard to focus on him simply as a
contributor to the British philosophical tradition. But there is a
very strong strand unifying his thought—it is his lifelong effort
to weave together the insights of enlightenment and romanticism. This was an opposition which Mill lived through personally, for his childhood was an enlightenment experiment in
education, while the friends of his early manhood breathed

German and Coleridgean romanticism, and the mental crisis and deep depression which afflicted him in his twenties was resolved by his reading of Wordsworth's poetry.

A keynote discussion of the issues is provided in a pair of essays from Mill's early thirties, on Bentham and Coleridge, from which I have already quoted his description of them as the 'two great seminal minds of England in their age' (p. 24 above). The essays address, and attempt to resolve, the dialectic between enlightenment and romanticism in modern philosophy, a dialectic which was then first emerging clearly. Romanticism is represented by the 'Germano-Coleridgean' school, which Mill also describes as being 'intuitional', 'transcendental', or '*à priori*' in its philosophy. The enlightenment is represented by the school of 'experience and association'.

Notice, before going on, that Mill does not treat Scottish common sense as a separate third strand, as was done in the last chapter. He assimilated Scottish common-sensists to Germano-Coleridgeans. The understandable, but misleading, ground for doing so was that both postulated sources of knowledge independent of experience (though hardly in the same sense); the assimilation also, however, reflects the political divide between London Radicals and Edinburgh Whigs. But at this level, too, the effect is misleading: though (by his own account) Mill reached his mature liberalism from a Benthamite start via French and Coleridgean interactions, the result has substantial affinity with the Scottish Whig tradition mentioned at the end of the last chapter. The differences Mill emphasizes between himself and the Scots should not obscure the very real similarities.

Still, the school of experience and association, unlike the schools of Reid and Kant, certainly denies that there is knowledge independent of experience and holds that attitudes and beliefs are the products of psychological laws of association. The full implication of the opposition between them goes, in Mill's opinion, far beyond epistemology and psychology. It lies 'at the foundation of all the greatest differences of practical opinion in an age of progress' (M i. 269–70).

At the level of metaphysics and psychology, Mill belongs

firmly on this radical wing of the enlightenment—his view is naturalistic, associationist, and utilitarian. He did not spend his philosophical life in criticizing these foundations, but in deepening and strengthening them, and restructuring and enlarging the edifice built on them. In particular, he worked into it the new themes of the 19th century, of which he was himself one of the great spokesmen. He has been dismissed on this score as an unoriginal eclectic. That underrates a philosophical quality which typifies much nineteenth-century thought, though it does not typify ours, and which was as strongly developed in its way in Mill as in Hegel: the impulse to see truth in all historically inherited doctrine, to transcend the oppositions within it, to take up its vital legacy into one's own thought and effect the fullest possible synthesis. Yet—when that has been said—the fundamental question undeniably still remains. Is Mill's synthesis possible?

On history and society Mill learned a good deal from Frenchmen, notably from Auguste Comte and Alexis de Tocqueville. It was with these and other Frenchmen, and not with German philosophers, that he was personally acquainted; differing in this respect from Coleridge and Carlyle. But it is to German romanticism—though indirectly through the Coleridgeans—that he owes the regeneration of such ethically crucial notions as character, reason, will, imagination, purpose: notions which had wilted or died in the legacy of philosophic radicalism. And it is likewise to German romanticism that he owes one of his master themes—that of human nature as the seat of individuality and autonomy, capable of being brought to fruition through *Bildung*, the culture of the whole man.

It is not easy to find a suitable term to cover the elusive discourse, essential to humanities—to culture and politics—which Mill brought to his own moral philosophy. 'Philosophical anthropology' is too German to fit him. The old-fashioned term 'moral psychology' better catches what he was good at. He himself coined a term, 'ethology', for a science of the formation of human character by circumstances, which he expected to play something like the essential role. But his plans for it came to nothing. With hindsight this can be seen as a significant failure.

Trying to mould moral psychology into a *science* only clamps irrelevant disciplines onto an understanding which already has its own very real ones. It is clearer now than it was to Mill that a (permeable) frontier lies between moral understanding and scientific psychology. The paradox is that Mill himself—by his utopian account of the scope of psychology—contributed something to undermining in this century precisely the moral understanding which he thought his eighteenth-century forebears lacked.

Moral understanding was what the Germano-Coleridgeans had. Mill witheringly portrays Bentham as the brainy child–adult. His empiricism was that 'of one who has had little experience . . . he was a boy to the last':

Self-consciousness, that daemon of the men of genius of our time, from Wordsworth to Byron, from Goethe to Chateaubriand, and to which this age owes so much both of its cheerful and its mournful wisdom, never was awakened in him. How much of human nature slumbered in him he knew not, neither can we know. He had never been made alive to the unseen influences which were acting on himself, nor consequently on his fellow creatures. Other ages and other nations were a blank to him for purposes of instruction. He measured them but by one standard; their knowledge of facts, and their capability to take correct views of utility . . . (M x. 92)

This is the Germano-Coleridgean picture of the enlightenment *savant*. Nevertheless Mill reserves a place for Bentham among the 'masters of wisdom': 'he is the great *subversive*, or in the language of continental philosophers, the great *critical*, thinker of his age and country' (M x. 79).

By Bentham, beyond all others, men have been led to ask themselves, in regard to any ancient or received opinion, Is it true? and by Coleridge, What is the meaning of it? The one took his stand outside the received opinion, and surveyed it as an entire stranger to it: the other looked at it from within, and endeavoured to see it with the eyes of a believer in it . . . (M x. 119)

The romantics have historical and psychological imagination, but they lack Bentham's analytic power. On metaphysical and moral foundations, Mill remained throughout on Bentham's side.

So *is* the synthesis he seeks a possible one? There could hardly be a more vital question. Reasons for doubt centre on two great issues, which at bottom are linked. Must not naturalism subvert reason, as Kant thought? And must not a natural science of man—a scientific psychology—subvert the understanding, from within, of characters, societies, and their possibilities, which Mill shares with the Germano-Coleridgeans? Both questions lead us to the *System of Logic*: the first to his epistemological analysis of deductive and inductive reasoning, the second (which has already been touched on and will not be taken further) to his conception of psychology and of its role in the 'logic of the moral sciences'. In both cases the possibility of naturalism is what Mill's *Logic* assumed and its critics denied.

It was suggested in the last chapter that Kant's ascendancy over Reid, among philosophers who followed them, lies in his insight into the connexion between naturalism and epistemological empiricism. He is not satisfied to treat the principles by which we synthesize judgements, and reason about the world, as 'innate' or 'original'—where these categories are thought of naturalistically. He considers that they must be epistemologically, and not merely psychologically, independent of experience, and that they can be so only on the basis of transcendental idealism.

Mill perceives the connexion between naturalism and empiricism just as clearly. If the mind is only a part of nature, no real knowledge of the natural world can be a priori. Either all real knowledge is a posteriori, grounded in experience, or there is no real knowledge. Any grounds for asserting a proposition that has real content must be empirical grounds. On all this Mill and Kant could agree. The difference is that Mill thought knowledge *could* be grounded on such a basis; Kant did not. To spell out the full extent of epistemological empiricism, in all its radicalism, is the central purpose of the *System of Logic*.

So Mill shares with Kant the conviction that naturalism as such entails that all justifications are a posteriori. In particular, it must remove all a priori support from the common-sense principles which Reid presents. But Mill, unlike Hume, Kant or even Reid, shows no interest at all in scepticism. He does not unleash a sceptical attack on reason as Hume does, nor does he see any need to defend reason against such an attack. In fact he sees no crisis of reason, and it is this that sets him apart most fundamentally from the Critical legacy.

We saw in the previous chapter that the Benthamites wished to distance themselves from Hume's scepticism just as firmly as the Scottish common-sensists did—unlike the latter, though, they felt no call to respond systematically to it. Mill's attitude belongs in this tradition; in this respect it is English rather than Scottish. More broadly, however, both Mill and Reid belong in the British naturalistic camp, which thinks no serious philosophical moral can be drawn from scepticism. Neither of them thinks—as Hume did—that sceptical arguments are sound and significant, that they show something of negative importance about reason. The difference between them is rather that Reid (wrongly) believes that scepticism stems solely from an erroneous theory of mind, and can be entirely defused by denying the existence of the objects postulated by that theory—ideas—while Mill, in contrast, never engages with scepticism at all.

If one thinks that scepticism is both unanswerable and unserious this may be the highest wisdom. Whether it is wisdom or evasion is a question which keeps on returning in philosophy. But for the moment we must follow Mill's ultra-empiricist argument.

Fundamental to the *System of Logic* is a distinction Mill draws between 'verbal' and 'real' propositions, and correspondingly, between 'merely apparent' and 'real' inferences. He applies it with greater strictness, and addresses his thesis, that merely apparent inferences have no genuine cognitive content, with greater resolution, than anyone had done before.

We can best reconstruct his distinction by starting with the notion of a merely apparent inference. An inference is merely apparent when no real inferential move has been made. For this to be so, the conclusion must literally have been asserted in the premises. In such a case, there can be no epistemological problem about justifying the apparent inference—there *is* nothing to justify. A verbal proposition can now be defined as a conditional proposition corresponding to a merely apparent inference. (This is not the whole of Mill's distinction, for he also counts elementary inferences and propositions concerning identity as verbal; but we can ignore that for the moment.)

The distinction corresponds, as Mill himself notes, to that which Kant makes between analytic and synthetic, when the latter defines analytic judgements as 'adding nothing through the predicate to the concept of the subject, but merely breaking it up into those constituent concepts that have all along been thought in it'. We may call this the *narrow notion of analyticity*. (Kant formulates it for affirmative predicative propositions, and so does Mill, but the version given in the previous paragraph can be used to avoid this limitation).

There is also a *broad notion of analyticity*. It defines an analytic truth as one from whose negation a contradiction can be deduced, with the help (if necessary) of definitional transformations, and using principles of logic alone. We need not enquire whether this broad definition of analyticity can be found in Kant—but we shall see that it assumes central importance in the twentieth century. In the broad sense of 'analytic', it becomes a trivial truth that logical principles are analytic. They are derivable from themselves using no principles that are not principles of logic. But what is no longer trivial is the crucial thesis that analytic (or verbal) propositions have no genuine cognitive content, and hence pose no epistemological problem.

If we keep to Mill's understanding of the distinction between 'verbal' and 'real', pure mathematics, and logic itself, contain synthetic or 'real' propositions and inferences with genuine cognitive content. The clear recognition of this fact is the chief philosophical achievement of the *System of Logic*. For if Mill is also right in holding that naturalism entails that no real proposition is a priori, then he has shown the implications of naturalism to be radical indeed. Not only mathematics but logic itself will be empirical.

To demonstrate that logic and mathematics contain real propositions Mill has to embark on an extensive semantic analysis of sentences and terms (he calls them 'names'), of syllogistic logic, and of the so-called 'Laws of Thought'. His analysis has many imperfections and he never unifies it in a fully general account. But he does supply the foundations of such an account, and in doing so takes the empiricist epistemology of logic and mathematics to a wholly new level.

The starting-point is a distinction between the denotation and connotation of names. Names, which may be general or singular, denote objects and connote attributes of objects. (Attributes may themselves be denoted by 'abstract' names, though the term is misleading, for Mill conceives attributes nominalistically.) A general name connotes attributes and denotes each object which has those attributes. Most singular names also connote attributes, but their grammatical construction indicates that they denote just one object if they denote at all.

There is however an important class of singular names— 'proper names' in the ordinary sense, such as 'Dartmouth'— which denote an object without connoting any property. Identity statements which contain only such non-connotative names, such as 'Tully is Cicero', are in Mill's view verbal. They lack content in the sense that, according to Mill, the only information conveyed is about the names themselves: 'Tully' denotes the same object as 'Cicero' does. But the obvious difficulty about calling them verbal is that knowledge that Cicero is Tully is not a priori knowledge—we cannot know the proposition to be true just by reflecting on the meaning of the names, as we should be able to do if the proposition was verbal. Mill's point is that there is no fact in the world to which 'Cicero is Tully' corresponds; we shall return to that thought when we consider Wittgenstein's *Tractatus* in Chapter 4—but it does not resolve the difficulty.

The meaning of a declarative sentence—'the import of a proposition'—is determined by the connotation, not the denotation, of its constituent names; the sole exception being connotationless proper names, where meaning is determined by denotation. (Again there is something puzzling here, for it needs to be explained how this thesis about the meaning of proper names is to be reconciled with the aposteriority of 'Cicero is Tully.') Mill proceeds to show how the various syntactic forms identified by syllogistic theory yield conditions of truth for sentences of those forms, when the connotation of their constituent names is given.

Armed with this analysis he proceeds to argue that logic contains real inferences and propositions. (He assumes that to assert a conjunction, '*A* and *B*', is simply to assert *A* and to assert *B*. He defines '*A* or *B*' as 'If not *A*, then *B*, and if not *B*, then *A*'. 'If *A* then *B*' means, he thinks, 'The proposition *B* is a legitimate inference from the proposition *A*.')

His strategy is an admirably forceful pincer movement. One pincer is an indirect argument. If logic did not contain real inferences, all deductive reasoning would be a *petitio principii*, a begging of the question—it could produce no new knowledge. Yet clearly it does produce new knowledge. So logic must contain real inferences. The other pincer is a direct semantic analysis of the supposed 'axioms' of syllogistic reasoning and of the laws of thought. It shows them to be real and not merely verbal.

The execution of this strategy is flawed, because Mill mixes it up with an interesting but distinct objective. He wants to show that 'all inference is from particulars to particulars'. The point is to demystify the role general propositions play in thought. He argues that in principle they add nothing to the force of an argument; particular conclusions could always be derived inductively direct from particular premises. Their value is psychological. They play the role of 'memoranda', summary records of the inductive potential of all that we have observed, and they facilitate 'trains of reasoning' (as e.g. in 'This is *A*, all *A*s are *B*s, no *B*s are *C*s, so this is not *C*'). Psychologically they greatly increase our memory and reasoning power, but epistemologically they are dispensable.

As Mill presents it, this thesis is tied in with his rejection of 'intuitive' knowledge of general truths and with his inductivism (which we shall come to shortly). For it assumes the illegitimacy of *hypothesizing* general propositions, as against generalizing to them from observation of singular conjunctions. Beneath this, however, there lies a deeper and obscurer sense in which a radical empiricist must hold that all inference is from particulars to particulars. For consider the inference from 'Everything is *F*' to '*a* is *F*'. Is it a real or merely apparent inference? It is impossible to hold it real if one also wishes to argue that real inferences are a *posteriori*. But the only way of treating it as verbal which is open to Mill is to treat the premise as a conjunction: '*a* is *F* and *b* is *F* and . . .'. If that approach is precluded then all that remains is to deny that 'Everything is *F*' is propositional—it must, rather, express an inferential commitment.

Both approaches are very close to the surface in Mill's discussion of the syllogism, and he comes closest to the latter when he emphasizes that a general proposition is 'a memorandum of the nature of the conclusions which we are prepared to prove'. But these issues about generality (and about conditional propositions) do not emerge clearly in his analysis; like his treatment of proper names and of identity, they were destined to make a decisive appearance on the agenda of philosophical logic only later, with the development of analytic philosophy.

There is some reason to draw the generous conclusion that Mill's treatment of syllogistic reasoning is confused for the most admirable reason—he is sensitive to more and deeper philosophical issues than he can clearly identify. It is also true that the state of logical theory in his time—still dominated by Aristotelian syllogistic—did not allow him to formulate issues in the philosophy of logic with as much clarity as was possible after the revolutionary development of modern logic. To this Mill made no contribution—indeed he failed to see the need for any such development, and was somewhat hostile to the work of Boole and de Morgan in this field (as he was hostile to the work of Jevons in economics). He was interested in the epistemology and metaphysics of logic, and in the use of logic for clear thinking; and he did not think their new ideas advanced either of these.

But though Mill's treatment of the syllogism is muffled and opaque, he is quite clear-cut in holding the laws of contradiction and excluded middle to be real—and therefore a posteriori—propositions. He takes it that 'not *P*' is equivalent in meaning to 'it is false that *P*'; if we further assume the equivalence in meaning of '*P*' and 'It is true that *P*', the principle of contradiction becomes, as he puts it, 'the same proposition cannot at the same time be false and true'. 'I cannot look upon this', he says, 'as a merely verbal proposition. I consider it to be, like other axioms, one of our first and most familiar generalizations from experience' (M vii. 277). He makes analogous remarks about excluded middle, which turns on these definitions into the principle of bivalence, 'Either it is true that *P* or it is false that *P*'.

This is radical empiricism with a vengeance! After this it is not surprising to find the same broad strategy applied to mathematics. If it was merely verbal, mathematical reasoning would be a *petitio principii*. Moreover, a detailed semantic analysis shows that it does contain real propositions.

Mill provides brief but insightful and radical sketches of geometry and arithmetic. On geometry he is particularly good. The theorems of geometry are deduced from premises which are real propositions inductively established. (Deduction is itself, of course, a process of real inference.) These premises, where they are not straightforwardly true of physical space, are true in the limit. Geometrical objects—points, lines, planes—are ideal or 'fictional' limits of ideally constructible material entities. Thus the real empirical assertion underlying an axiom such as 'Two straight lines cannot enclose a space' is something like 'The more closely two lines approach absolute breadthlessness and straightness, the smaller the space they enclose'.

Mill applies his distinction between denotation and connotation to show that arithmetical identities such as '2 plus 1 equals 3' are real propositions. Number terms denote 'aggregates' and connote certain attributes of the aggregates. (He does not say that they denote those attributes of the aggregates, though perhaps he should have done.) 'Aggregates' are natural, not abstract, entities—'collections' or 'agglomerations' individuated by a principle of aggregation. This theory escapes some of the famous but rather unfair criticisms Frege (see Chapter 4) later made of it, but its viability none the less remains extremely doubtful. The trouble is that the respects in which aggregates have to differ from *sets* if they are to be credibly natural, and not abstract, entities are precisely those in which they seem to fail to produce a fully adequate ontology for arithmetic. (One can, for example, number numbers, but can aggregates of aggregates, or of attributes of aggregates, be seen as natural entities?)

However this may be, Mill's philosophical programme is clear. Arithmetic, like logic and geometry, is a natural science, concerning a particular department of the laws of nature—those concerning the compositional properties of aggregates. The upshot is that the fundamental principles of arithmetic and geometry, as well as of logic itself, are real. Given epistemological empiricism, it follows that deductive reasoning, 'ratiocination', is empirical. Mill has provided the first thoroughly naturalistic analysis of meaning and of deductive reasoning itself.

He distinguishes his own view from three others—'Conceptualism', 'Nominalism', and 'Realism'.

'Conceptualism' is his name for the view which takes the objects studied by logic to be psychological states or acts. It holds that names stand for 'ideas' which make up judgements, and that 'a proposition is the expression of a relation between two ideas'. It confuses logic and psychology by assimilating propositions to judgements and attributes of objects to ideas. Against this doctrine Mill insists that

All language recognises a difference between a doctrine or opinion, and the fact of entertaining the opinion; between assent, and what is assented to.

Logic, according to the conception here formed of it, has no concern with the nature of the act of judging or believing; the consideration of that act, as a phenomenon of the mind, belongs to another science. (M vii. 87)

[Conceptualism is] one of the most fatal errors ever introduced into the philosophy of logic; and the principle cause why the theory of the science has made such inconsiderable progress during the last two centuries. (M vii. 89)

He traces its roots to the seventeenth century: it was introduced by Descartes, fostered by Leibniz and Locke, and has obscured the true status of logic—which is simply 'the Science of Science'—ever since.

The 'Nominalists'—Mill cites Hobbes—hold that logic and mathematics are entirely verbal. Mill takes this position much more seriously than Conceptualism and seeks to refute it in detail. His main point is that nominalists are only able to maintain their view because they fail to distinguish between the denotation and the connotation of names, 'seeking for their meaning exclusively in what they denote' (M vii. 91).

Nominalists and conceptualists both hold that logic and maths can be known non-empirically, while yet retaining the view that no real proposition about the world can be so known—but both are confused. But what if one abandons the thesis that no real proposition about the mind-independent world can be known a priori? The realists do that—they hold that logical and mathematical knowledge is knowledge of universals existing in an abstract Platonic domain; the terms that make up sentences being signs that stand for such universals. This is the view Mill takes least seriously. But it was destined, as we shall see in the next chapters, to stage a major revival in philosophy, and semantic analysis was going to be its main source.

In fact, in the contemporary use of the term, Mill is himself a nominalist—he rejects abstract entities. That is why he treats aggregates as concrete objects, and attributes as natural properties rather than universals. But, just as severe difficulties lie in the way of treating the ontology of arithmetic in terms of aggregates rather than classes, so there are severe difficulties in the way of treating the ontology of general semantics without appealing to universals and classes, as well as to natural properties and objects. We can have no clear view of how Mill would have responded to these difficulties had they been made evident to him. But we can, I think, be fairly sure that he would have sought to maintain his nominalism—perhaps by seeking Benthamic paraphrases of the references to universals and classes which semantics seems to require.

However, the central target of Mill's attack is the doctrine that there are real a priori propositions. What, he asks, in practice goes on, when we hold a real proposition to be true a priori? We find its negation inconceivable, or that it is derived, by principles whose unsoundness we find inconceivable, from premises whose negation we find inconceivable. Mill is not offering a definition of what is meant by such terms as 'a priori', or 'self-evident'; his point is that facts about what we find inconceivable are all that lends colour to the use of these terms.

They are facts about the limits, felt by us 'from the inside', on what we can imagine perceiving. Mill thought he could explain these facts about unthinkability, or imaginative unrepresentability, in associationist terms, and spent many pages claiming to do so. They are not very convincing pages, but that does not affect his essential point, which is this: the step from our inability to represent to ourselves the negation of a proposition, to acceptance of its truth, calls for justification. Moreover, the justification *itself* must be a priori if it is to show that the proposition is known a priori. (Thus Mill is prepared, for example, to concede the reliability of geometrical intuition; but he stresses that its reliability is an empirical fact, itself known inductively.)

How, if the mind is simply a part of a larger natural order, could it be otherwise:

> even assuming that inconceivability is not solely the result of limited experience, but that some incapacities of conceiving are inherent in the mind, and inseparable from it; this would not entitle us to infer, that what we are thus incapable of conceiving cannot exist. Such an inference would only be warrantable, if we could know *à priori* that we must have been created capable of conceiving whatever is capable of existing: that the universe of thought and that of reality, the Microcosm and the Macrocosm (as once they were called) must have been framed in complete correspondence with one another ... (M ix. 68)

Once again, Kant could agree: his 'Copernican Revolution' consists precisely in the doctrine that the mind cannot be seen as solely a Microcosm within the larger Macrocosm. To vindicate the possibility of synthetic a priori knowledge calls, he claims, for nothing less than transcendental idealism.

But without synthetic a priori knowledge, according to Kant, scepticism is forced: knowledge as such becomes impossible. The very possibility of knowledge requires that there be a priori elements in our knowledge.

The *System of Logic* in contrast sets out to vindicate in general terms the possibility of a scheme of scientific knowledge which appeals at no point whatever to any kind of a priori principle. Anyone who had imbibed the Critical Philosophy could only find it peculiarly provoking. It ignores the threat of scepticism altogether—and hence from the Critical standpoint it misses out the very thing that matters for a truly philosophical epistemology.

The contrast between the *Critique of Pure Reason* and the *System of Logic* is, one may say, the contrast between *Critical* and *naturalistic* epistemology. Three ingredients characterize naturalistic epistemology: a refusal to take seriously pure sceptical arguments, an appeal to a natural, or in Mill's word 'spontaneous', agreement in propensities to reason, and finally, what may be called an 'internal' vindication of these fundamental reasoning propensities. All these ingredients are present in the *System of Logic*.

For Mill, the basic form of reasoning—epistemologically, historically, and psychologically—is enumerative induction, simple generalization from experience. This is the disposition to infer to the conclusion that all *A*s are *B* from observation of a number of *A*s which are all *B*. (Or to the conclusion that a given percentage of all *A*s are *B* from observation of that percentage of *B*s among a number of *A*s.) We spontaneously agree in reasoning that way, and in holding that way of reasoning to be sound. The proposition 'Enumerative induction is rational' is not a verbal proposition. But nor is it grounded in an a priori intuition. All that Mill will say for it is that people in general, and the reader in particular, in fact agree on reflection in accepting it. It is on that basis alone that he rests its claim.

The Critical philosopher will question the coherence of this. But for the moment our task is to explore Mill's naturalistic epistemology more fully. The first thing to appreciate is that Mill's problem of induction, the problem *he* wants to solve, is not Hume's—Hume gets on mention at all. In sidestepping the purely sceptical question about induction, Mill uses the very same analogy of a telescope which Reid had used in a similar context (p. 12 above)—though in Reid the telescope is Reason as against Common Sense, while in Mill it is scientific as against spontaneous induction:

Assuredly, if induction by simple enumeration were an invalid process, no process grounded on it would be valid; just as no reliance could be placed on telescopes, if we could not trust our eyes. But though a valid process, it is a fallible one, and fallible in very different degrees: if therefore we can substitute for the more fallible forms of the process, an operation grounded on the same process in a less fallible form, we shall have effected a very material improvement. And this is what scientific induction does. (M vii. 567–8)

Mill's aim is to provide the telescope. The problem he starts from is not a sceptical but an internal one—why is it that some inductions are more trustworthy than others?

Why is a single instance, in some cases, sufficient for a complete induction, while in others, myriads of concurring instances, without a single exception known or presumed, go such a very little way towards establishing a universal proposition? Whoever can answer this question knows more of the philosophy of logic than the wisest of the ancients, and has solved the problem of induction. (M vii. 314)

Mill's answer takes the form of a natural history of the 'inductive process'. The point is to show how that process is internally vindicated by its actual success in establishing regularities, and how it eventually gives rise to more searching methods of investigation.

Mankind begins with 'spontaneous' and 'unscientific' inductions about particular unconnected natural phenomena or aspects of experience. Generalizations accumulate, interweave, and are found to stand the test of time: they are not disconfirmed by further experience. As they accumulate and interweave, they justify the second-order inductive conclusion that *all* phenomena are subject to uniformity, and more specifically, that all have discoverable sufficient conditions. In this less vague form, the principle of general uniformity becomes, given Mill's analysis of causation, the Law of Universal Causation. This conclusion in turn provides (Mill believes) the grounding assumption for a new style of reasoning about nature—eliminative induction.

In this type of reasoning, the assumption that a type of phenomenon has uniform causes, together with a (revisable) assumption about what its possible causes are, initiates a comparative enquiry in which the actual cause is identified by elimination. Mill formulates the logic of this eliminative reasoning in his 'Methods of Empirical Inquiry'. His exposition is rather garbled but he was right to be proud of it, for it did show how effective eliminative reasoning can be. His picture of the interplay between enumerative and eliminative reasoning, and of the way it entrenches, from within, our rational confidence in the inductive process, is elegant and penetrating.

The improved scientific induction which results from this new style of reasoning spills back onto the principle of Universal Causation on which it rests, and raises its certainty to a new level. That in turn raises our confidence in the totality of particular enumerative inductions from which the principle is derived. In short, the amount of confidence with which one can rely on the 'inductive process' as a whole depends on the point which has been reached in its natural history—though the confidence to be attached to particular inductions always remains variable. The coherentist element in this is often explicit:

We are constantly told that the uniformity of the course of nature cannot itself be an induction, since every inductive reasoning assumes it, and the premise must have been known before the conclusion. Those who argue in this manner can never have directed their attention to the continual process of giving and taking, in respect of certainty, which reciprocally goes on between this great premise and the narrower truths of experience; the effect of which is, that, though originally a generalization from the more obvious of the narrower truths, it ends by having a fulness of certainty which overflows upon these, and raises the proof of them to a higher level ... (M ix. 482 n.)

Mill's naturalism is equally evident in the following passage:

Principles of Evidence and Theories of Method are not to be constructed *à priori*. The laws of our rational faculty, like those of every other natural agency, are only learnt by seeing the agent at work. The earlier achievements of science were made without the conscious observance of any Scientific Method; and we should never have known by what process truth is to be ascertained, if we had not previously ascertained many truths ... (M viii. 833)

Since the fundamental norm of scientific reasoning, enumerative induction, is not a merely verbal principle, it too cannot be a priori. But what can it mean to deny that it is a priori? Mill says that we only learn the laws of our rational faculty, like those of any other natural agency, by seeing the agent at work. He is quite right: we can find out what our most basic reasoning dispositions are, only by critical reflection on our practice. This reflective scrutiny of practice is, in a certain sense, an a posteriori process. It examines empirical dispositions that we have before we examine them; it does not, for example, descry facts in a Platonic domain. Having examined our dispositions, we reach a reflective equilibrium in which we endorse some—and perhaps reject others. We endorse them as sound norms of reasoning.

At this point the sceptic asks by what right we do so—and Mill rules his question out of order. So denying that the fundamental principle of induction is a priori comes down, it seems, to just that ruling. Might it not just as well have been said that the principle is a priori? But that would suggest that there was some further story, Platonic or transcendental, to be had, which explained and legitimated our reasoning practice, and that is what Mill denies.

So too does the sceptic: the fact that the sceptic and the naturalist agree on that hardly shows why it is all right to rule the sceptic's question out of order. Is this not evasion? It seemed obvious to Mill's epistemological critics, whether they were realists or post-Kantian idealists, that it was: naturalism could only seem to differ from scepticism by being uncritical.

Mill's naturalism differs from Reid's not, like Hume's, because it launches a sceptical assault on reason, but because it opens up *all* our beliefs to an empirical audit. Hume and Mill are both naturalistic radicals—but in quite different ways. Mill leaves no real principle of deduction, no common-sense belief entrenched—with one telling exception. The exception is our disposition to rely on the deliverances of memory, which he acknowledges, in Reid-like fashion, to be 'ultimate':

all the explanations of mental phenomena presuppose Memory. Memory itself cannot admit of being explained. Whenever this is shown to be true of any other part of our knowledge, I shall admit that part to be intuitive. (M ix. 165 n.)

This could have been written in the eighteenth century. But with this exception, the only 'original principle' that survives in Mill's science of science is enumerative induction. The whole of science, he thinks, can be built by this single instrument.

This is Mill's *inductivism*—the view that enumerative induction is the only *ultimate* method of inference which puts us in possession of new truths. Is he right in thinking it to be so? In his own time the question produced an important, if confused, controversy between him and William Whewell.

Whewell (1794–1866), Master of Trinity College, Cambridge, was a major force in intellectual Victorian Britain—almost on the extravagant scale of Mill himself. ('Science is his forte and omniscience is his foible,' Sidney Smith said.) The disagreement between him and Mill was thoroughgoing—it ranged not only over the philosophy of science but over moral and social philosophy as well, where Whewell attacked utilitarianism and Mill attacked Whewell's intuitionism.

In the philosophy of science, their disagreement concerned the role of hypotheses. Whewell argued that the Hypothetical Method was fundamental in scientific enquiry: the method in which one argues to the truth of a hypothesis from the fact that it would explain observed phenomena. He documented it copiously in the three volumes of his *History of the Inductive Sciences from the Earliest to the Present Times* (1837), following up with *The Philosophy of the Inductive Sciences Founded upon their History* (1840).

Mill had read Whewell's *History of the Inductive Sciences*, and he could hardly fail to be aware of the pervasiveness of hypotheses in the actual process of enquiry, or of their indispensability in supplying working assumptions—their 'heuristic' value, Whewell called it. The same point—the indispensability of hypotheses in providing lines of enquiry—had been emphasized by the Frenchman, Auguste Comte, with whose *Cours de philosophie positive* (which began to appear in 1830) Mill was also familiar. But what Mill could not accept was that the mere fact that a hypothesis accounted for the data *in itself* provided a reason for thinking it true. He denied that the Hypothetical

Method constituted, *in its own right*, a method of arriving at new truths from experience.

Yet Whewell's appeal was to the actual practice of scientific reasoning, as observed in the history of science. An appeal of that kind was precisely what Mill, on his own naturalistic principles, could not ignore. The disposition to hypothesize is spontaneous, so why should it not be recognized as a fundamental method of reasoning to truth, as enumerative induction is?

Mill's refusal to recognize it is not arbitrary. The essential point underlying his refusal is a powerful one: it is the possibility that a body of data may be explained equally well by more than one hypothesis. What justifies us in concluding, from the fact that a particular story would, if true, explain the data, that it is a true story? Other stories may equally explain the data.

The fluctuating fortunes of the hypothetical method are a major element in the story of philosophy and methodology over the last 200 years. Increasing awareness of the role of hypotheses in science is one of the forces driving philosophy in the last part of the nineteenth century, as we shall see in the next chapter. The debate between Mill and Whewell is a significant passage in that story, and it is worth taking some pains to get the nub of Mill's objection right.

He places great emphasis on the increasingly deductive and mathematical organization of science—that is quite compatible with his inductivism, and indeed central to it. But he takes the 'Deductive Method' of science to involve three steps: 'induction', 'ratiocination', and 'verification'. A paradigm, in his view, is Newton's explanation of Kepler's laws of planetary motion. Induction establishes causal laws of motion and attraction, ratiocination deduces lower-level regularities from them in conjunction with observed conditions, and verification tests these deduced propositions against observation. (Though this was not, and did not need to be, the historical order of enquiry.) Now,

the Hypothetical Method suppresses the first of the three steps, the induction to ascertain the law; and contents itself with the other two operations, ratiocination and verification; the law which is reasoned from being assumed, instead of proved. (M vii. 492)

Mill agrees that it is legitimate to do this when the hypothesis in question is demonstrably the only one consistent with the facts. He also thinks that where the causes of a phenomenon are known or ascertainable, a hypothesis concerning the form of the law relating them can be legitimate—as with Kepler's hypotheses about the relation between the lines of incidence and refraction of light passing through a medium. In such cases verification is proof. He further permits postulation of causes too distant in space or time to be observable. Theories of this kind can in his view properly be termed 'inductive' rather than merely 'hypothetical'—he has in mind the geological and cosmological theories which formed such an important part of the nineteenth-century's intellectual climate. But his point applies generally to any historical enquiry which postulates causes in the distant and unremembered past. Such explanations, he thinks, involve only 'the legitimate operation of inferring from an observed effect, the existence, in time past, of a cause similar to that by which we know it to be produced in all cases in which we have actual experience of its origin'. (M vii. 506)

When all these cases have been taken into account, we are left with pure cases of the Hypothetical Method, in which the causes postulated are not directly observable, and not simply because they are assumed to operate—in accordance with known laws, inductively established—in regions of time or space too distant to observe. What are we to say of such hypotheses? For example of the 'emission' theory, or the 'undulatory' theory of light? They cannot be accepted as inductively established truths, not even as probable ones:

an hypothesis of this kind is not to be received as probably true because it accounts for all the known phenomena; since this is a condition sometimes fulfilled tolerably well by two conflicting hypotheses; while there are probably many others which are equally possible, but which from want of anything analogous in our experience, our minds are unfitted to conceive. (M vii. 500)

Such a hypothesis can suggest fruitful analogies, Mill thinks, but cannot be regarded as yielding a new truth itself. The data do not determine a unique hypothesis: it is this possibility, of underdetermination, which stops him from accepting hypothetical reasoning as an independent method of achieving truth, even though it is a mode of reasoning as spontaneous as enumerative induction.

Whewell thought that the process of scientific enquiry must eventually converge on a body of knowledge which, once it had been discovered, would be recognizable as necessary. Its categories would be 'the Ideas of the Divine Mind'. But if we do not think we have any such guarantee of convergence, the objection to accepting the hypothetical method as a fully general and independent method of discovering truth is indeed potent. There are subtle responses to it, which give rise to deep questions about the nature of truth; we shall encounter them when we discuss pragmatism and verificationism in Chapters 3 and 5. But in seeing the difficulty Mill is certainly on sound ground.

What he does not see, and this is one of the great points of weakness in his philosophy, is how much must be torn from the fabric of our belief if inductivism is applied strictly. Thus, for example, while his case for empiricism about logic and mathematics is very strong, it is his methodology of science which then forces him to hold that we know basic logical and mathematical principles only by an enumerative induction. And that is desperately implausible.

So it is an important question whether the difficulty can be resolved—and whether it can be resolved within a naturalistic framework, which does not yield to idealism. The status of hypothesis is another point at which the contest between naturalistic and Critical philosophy takes place. If naturalism can endorse the hypothetical method, it can develop a more plausible empiricism about logic and mathematics than Mill's. But the importance of the issue is even wider, as becomes apparent if we turn to Mill's general metaphysics.

He sets this out in his *Examination of Sir William Hamilton's Philosophy* (1865). Sir William Hamilton (1791–1856) was a Scotsman (Professor of Logic and Metaphysics in Edinburgh, 1836) who sought to moderate the views of Reid and Kant. He was a philosopher of subtlety and erudition, or even pedantry, the last eminent representative of the school of Scottish common sense, and a ferocious controversialist. Mill deemed him a pillar of the right-thinking intellectual establishment, ripe for demolition. But by the time the *Examination* appeared Hamilton was in no position to reply—a fact which caused Mill some regret. ('I feel keenly, with Plato, how much more is to be learnt by discussing with a man, who can question and answer, than with a book, which cannot' (M ix. 2–3).) For the present-day reader, what is more regrettable is that Mill's discussion of general metaphysical issues should be cast in so polemical a form. It means that important issues, particularly on the nature of logic and thought, remain shrouded in obscurity. He does however give himself space to develop his view of our knowledge of the external world.

He begins by expounding a doctrine which he rightly takes to be generally accepted (in his time) on all sides. It affirms

that all the attributes which we ascribe to objects, consist in their having the power of exciting one or another variety of sensation in our minds; that an object is to us nothing else than that which affects our senses in a certain manner; that even an imaginary object is but a conception, such as we are able to form, of something which would affect our senses in some new way; so that our knowledge of objects; and even our fancies about objects, consist of nothing but the sensations which they excite, or which we imagine them exciting, in ourselves. (M ix. 5–6)

This is 'the doctrine of the Relativity of Knowledge to the knowing mind'. We will call it *phenomenalism*, since the relativity it asserts is phenomenal relativity. But there are two forms in which it may be held.

According to one of the forms, the sensations which, in common parlance, we are said to receive from objects, are not only all that we can possibly know of the objects, but are all that we have any ground for believing to exist. What we term an object is but a complex conception made up by the laws of association, out of the ideas of various sensations which we are accustomed to receive simultaneously. There is nothing real in the process but these sensations. (M ix. 6)

[According to the other] there is a real universe of 'Things in Themselves' and . . . whenever there is an impression on our senses, there is a 'Thing in itself,' which is behind the phaenomenon, and is the cause of it. But as to what this Thing *is* 'in itself,' we, having no organs except our senses for communicating with it, can only know what our senses tell us; and as they tell us nothing but the impression which the thing makes upon *us*, we do not know what it is *in itself* at all. We suppose (at least these philosophers suppose) that it must be something in itself, but all that we know it to be is merely relative to us, consisting in the power of affecting us in certain ways ... (M ix. 7)

This latter version we will call *weak phenomenalism*, the former version (but without including in it the appeal to laws of association), *strong phenomenalism*. Thus strong phenomenalism roughly corresponds to what is meant by 'phenomenalism' as the term is often used by philosophers today—but it was not so used in Mill's time. It should also be kept in mind that 'phenomenon' is here used to refer to subjective appearances: these may be treated, as they are by Reid, Hamilton, and Mill, as the experiences of a conscious subject, or they may be thought of as the contents of those experiences, the contents being still thought of as in some sense mental items. In any case they are not *objective* appearances, which more than one individual may perceive or misperceive—such as the appearance of a comet at a particular latitude or longitude, or the appearance of a cathedral from its south-west side.

Reid's point, that sensations are not representative mental images but 'modifications'—states—of mind, does not contradict the phenomenalist doctrine, any more than his thesis that we perceive physical objects does. For on his account sensations, states of sensory consciousness, do mediate between the objects that excite them and the beliefs about those objects which are prompted by them—they are themselves distinct from both the objects and the beliefs. I cannot perceive without sensing. But I can sense without perceiving. For example, I may have a visual sensation which prompts me to believe that I am seeing a red triangle on a green field. It is then apparently true to say, in an obvious and legitimate sense, that what I am immediately aware or conscious of is my visual sensation. That remains true even if I am perceiving no red triangle because no red triangle exists. Or, if one objects to talk of consciousness *of* a state of consciousness, one may simply say that my immediate visual consciousness is of a red triangle on a green field—in a sense in which that can be true though there is no such triangle.

This is already enough to make epistemology, in Mill's phrase, the 'Interpretation of Consciousness'. The very fact of consciousness seems to impose weak phenomenalism at least. To escape it something more counter-intuitive would be required than the sensible points Reid makes about perception and sensation—a denial that sensation, subjective experience, constitutes an ontologically distinct category at all. Mill questions the irreducible status of sensation no more than Reid did. But he thinks it must follow that—whether or not we *actually* make an inference from sensations to objects beyond sensation—such an inference is, epistemologically speaking, *required*.

Is this too hasty? Is it dogmatism on Reid's part simply to point out that we do form particular beliefs prompted by particular sensations, beliefs which we just do regard as rational? Cannot these specific cognitive dispositions be defended naturalistically, if the general disposition to make enumerative inductions can? But there is a difference. If we are immediately aware only of states of affairs of one kind (our own sensory states), and on that basis form beliefs about states of affairs of a quite distinct kind (states of external physical objects), then some warrant is required. Reid needs to show why such a warrant does not have to rely on inductive inference—even though it licenses a belief in a state of affairs on the basis of immediate consciousness of a quite distinct state of affairs. He must call on warrants which are neither deductive nor inductive. And this requires support from ideas in the philosophy of language which had not yet been formed.

Mill sets about the notion of an 'external' object in great style:

What is it we mean, or what is it which leads us to say, that the objects we perceive are external to us, and not a part of our own thoughts? We mean, that there is concerned in our perceptions something which exists when we are not thinking of it; which existed before we had ever thought of it, and would exist if we were annihilated; and further, that there exist things which we never saw, touched, or otherwise perceived, and things which have never been perceived by man. This idea of something which is distinguished from our fleeting impressions by what, in Kantian language, is called Perdurability; something which is fixed and the same, while our impressions vary; something which exists whether we are aware of it or not, and which is always square (or of some other given figure) whether it appears to us square or round—constitutes altogether our idea of external substance. Whoever can assign an origin to this complex conception, has accounted for what we mean by the belief in matter. (M ix. 178–9)

To assign this origin, Mill postulates

that after having had actual sensations, we are capable of forming the conception of Possible sensations; sensations which we are not feeling at the present moment, but which we might feel, and should feel if certain conditions were present, the nature of which conditions we have, in many cases, learnt by experience. (M ix. 177)

These various possibilities are the important thing to me in the world. My present sensations are generally of little importance, and are moreover fugitive: the possibilities, on the contrary, are permanent, which is the character that mainly distinguishes our idea of Substance or Matter from our notion of sensation. These possibilities, which are conditional certainties, need a special name to distinguish them from mere vague possibilities, which experience gives no warrant for reckoning upon. Now, as soon as a distinguishing name is given, though it be only to the same thing regarded in a different aspect, one of the most familiar experiences of our mental nature teaches us, that the different name comes to be considered as the name of a different thing . . . (M ix. 179–80)

The critical ingredients in this account are *sensation conditionals* of the form, 'If such and such sensations were to occur, then such and such other sensations would occur with a given degree of probability.' (It need not always be certainty.) They express Mill's famous 'Permanent Possibilities of Sensation'— 'Permanent ' is slightly misleading, for there is of course a change in the 'Permanent' possibilities of sensation whenever there is change in the world. Mill also uses other terms—'certified', 'guaranteed'.

We regularly find that whole clusters of sensation conditionals are true together, whenever some other sensory condition obtains. Thus whenever we experience that condition, we are justified in forming all the conditional expectations expressed in that cluster of conditionals. Moreover, as well as finding simultaneous correlations between certified possibilities of sensation, that is, between the truth of any sensation conditional in a set and the truth of any other in the set, we also find 'an Order of succession'. Whenever a given cluster of certified possibilities of sensation obtains, then a certain other cluster follows—a certain other set of sensation conditionals *becomes* true. 'Hence our ideas of causation, power, activity, . . . become connected, not with sensations, but with groups of possibilities of sensation' (M ix. 180–1).

But though 'the belief on which all the practical consequences depend, is the belief in Permanent Possibilities of Sensation', we also, at least in moments of philosophical reflection, believe in more than this—namely, in the existence of a cause of all our sensations which is not itself sensation:

familiarity with the idea of something different from *each* thing we know, makes it natural and easy to form the notion of something different from *all* things that we know, collectively as well as individually. It is true we can form no conception of what such a thing can be; our notion of it is merely negative; but the idea of a substance, apart from its relation to the impressions which we conceive it as making on our senses, *is* a merely negative one. There is thus no psychological obstacle to our forming the notion of a something which is neither a sensation nor a possibility of sensation, even if our consciousness does not testify to it; and nothing is more likely than that the Permanent Possibilities of sensation, to which our consciousness does testify, should be confounded in our minds with this imaginary conception. (M ix. 185)

Mill means to undermine the claim that the reflective idea of matter is 'intuitive'—but he does not take the further step of dismissing it as wholly empty of content. Here, as elsewhere, his pragmatic approach to the role of concepts in thinking stops short of taking off into a pragmatist account of concepts and meaning as such.

But even if our reflective concept of matter—as the external cause of sensations—can be explained on psychological principles, it remains open for someone to accept the proposed *origin* for the concept, while also holding that good grounds can be given for thinking it to have instances. He will say that a legitimate inference can be made from the existence of the Permanent Possibilities and their correlations to the existence of an external cause of our sensations. It is at just this point that Mill's inductivism comes in. Such an inference would be a case of hypothetical reasoning, to an explanation of experience which transcended all possible data of experience; and that is just what Mill rejects:

I assume only the tendency, but not the legitimacy of the tendency, to extend all the laws of our own experience to a sphere beyond our experience. (M ix. 187)

The conclusion that matter is the permanent possibility of sensation is not forced by associationist psychology: it follows rather from the combination of weak phenomenalism and inductivism.

If matter is the permanent possibility of sensation, what is mind? Mill considers that 'our knowledge of mind, like that of matter, is entirely relative.' Can the mind then also be resolved into 'a series of feelings, with a background of possibilities of feeling' (M ix. 193)? He finds in this view a serious difficulty:

The thread of consciousness which composes the mind's phaenomenal life, consists not only of our present sensations, but likewise, in part, of memories and expectations. (M ix. 193–4)

But to remember or expect a state of consciousness is not simply to believe that it has existed or will exist; it is to believe that *I myself* have experienced or will experience that state of consciousness.

If, therefore, we speak of the Mind as a series of feelings, we are obliged to complete the statement by calling it a series of feelings which is aware of itself as past and future; and we are reduced to the alternative of believing that the Mind, or Ego, is something different from any series of feelings, or possibilities of them, or of accepting the paradox, that something which *ex hypothesi* is but a series of feelings, can be aware of itself as a series. (M ix. 194)

Mill is unwilling to accept 'the common theory of Mind, as a so-called substance' (M ix. 206): nevertheless, the self-consciousness involved in memory and expectation drives him to 'ascribe a reality to the Ego—to my own Mind—different from that real existence as a Permanent Possibility, which is the only reality I acknowledge in Matter' (M ix. 208).

He overlooks that our knowledge of mind is not relative in the way that our knowledge of matter is. The ego is not an external cause of sensations. To say that I only know myself by my conscious states is more like saying that I only know a thing by its properties. So to deny the existence of the self on the basis that we are conscious only of our mental states is not like the inductivist's refusal to postulate a non-phenomenal cause of phenomena. Moreover, Mill's own statement of the difficulty is gratuitously paradoxical because he has not thought through the paraphrasis which is required. If we do endorse the view that the mind is only a 'series' of feelings, we are not committed to holding that 'a series of feelings can be aware of itself as a series': a series cannot of course be aware of anything. But it is no implication of the 'series' view that it can. It does not identify selves with series: it paraphrases talk of selves in term of talk of series: for *me* to *remember* a previous conscious state is for a certain *series* of conscious states to *include* a consciousness of some previous state, together with the belief that that previous conscious state is a part of the same series as the present one.

Ultimately, on Mill's view, and discounting his uncertainty about what to say of the self, all that exists are experiences in a temporal order. Yet he claims, like others before and after him, that this metaphysics is consistent with common-sense realism about the world. Strong phenomenalism, he thinks, leaves common sense and science untouched. In particular, minds and experiences are still properly to be seen as a part of the natural order.

But are the experiences referred to, in the strong phenomenalist's analysis, the very same as those referred to in common-sense and scientific talk (call this 'naturalistic' talk)? If they are not, then we have yet to be told *what* they are. Then suppose they are the same. In naturalistic talk, we make reference to subjects and their experiences—and also to physical objects and their properties. Psychology, including Mill's psychology, seeks to establish causal correlations between experiences and their physiological antecedents and consequents.

But if strong phenomenalism is right, only the experiences are real. Mill thinks we are led to that by the very standards of reasoning recognized in a naturalistic 'science of science', or 'system of logic'. If he is right, then the naturalistic vision of the world, which sees minds as part of a larger causal order, is self-undermining. For if we are led to the conclusion that only states of consciousness are real *by an application of naturalism's own standards*, then that conclusion has to be understood *on the same level* as the naturalistic affirmation that states of consciousness are themselves part of a larger causal order external to them—and therefore as inconsistent with it. Causal relations cannot exist between fictional entities which are mere markers for *possibilities* of sensation.

So either naturalism undermines itself, or there is something wrong with Mill's inductivist analysis of our natural norms of reasoning, or with his endorsement of weak phenomenalism—or both. If it is possible to make sense of strong phenomenalism at all, it would have to be along the lines of transcendental idealism. Consciousness becomes a timeless presentation. Nature is a construction within consciousness. Minds, considered as empirical objects within nature, are part of the construction, and so is the relation of causation. But in that case it no longer makes sense to suppose that Consciousness—understood transcendentally—might not have existed. And so *it* cannot be identified with any empirical item in the world—in particular, with the thread of consciousness of an empirical individual—since any such object most certainly might not have existed, its existence being causally dependent on the contingent dispositions of the physical world.

The pure experience which seems to confront me when I take the standpoint of consciousness, precisely *because* it is conceived as intrinsically phenomenal, cannot be thought of as something which is also characterizable in a radically different, objective-naturalistic way. So, if we accept the conception of our own experience which offers itself when we take that standpoint, we are left with a category of pure consciousness which cannot be identified with anything within the objective world. And precisely because it is not *in* the world, it cannot be explained by its relation to something outside of itself and in the world. That is why the position of a philosopher who postulates the objective world as an inference to a supposed explanation of pure experience is—as Sir William Hamilton said—radically superficial.

If this is right, then phenomenalism itself—and not just strong phenomenalism—is incompatible with naturalism. We see again how incoherent Mill must have appeared to philosophers who took Kant's Critical Philosophy seriously. He fails to see the need for a synthetic a priori to render any knowledge possible, even though he gives an account of real propositions and inferences which agrees in essentials with Kant. On top of that, in accepting phenomenalism he accepts a doctrine which must lead to a transcendental view of consciousness, yet he remains determinedly naturalistic in his view of the mind. The extraordinary developments in metaphysics after Mill, which spring in part from this criticism, will occupy us in the next chapter.

In their naturalism, Mill's epistemology and metaphysics are entirely of the progressive and humanist enlightenment. With ethics and politics it is more complex. His premises remain those of the philosophic radicals. Value resides within individual lives; the proper end of human life is happiness. The interests of every individual make an equal claim on the consideration of all; but general happiness is most effectively attained when society leaves people free to pursue their own ends subject to rules established for the general good. A properly developed science of man will ground rational policies for social improvement.

Mill thought that these honourable and down-to-earth doctrines, which he fully accepted, needed to be rethought—invested with greater depth and authority through more adequate conceptions of human nature, of human ends, and of social life. He wanted to infuse into them ideas of the early nineteenth century which lay close to his own heart—the freedom, sponta-neity, and progressiveness of the individual, the historicity and holism of social facts. He needed to rethink the moral psychology and the historical sociology of utilitarian liberalism.

This synthesis is worked out in many places, but it is classi-cally stated in two short works—*On Liberty*, which appeared in 1859, in the same year as Darwin's *Origin of Species*, and *Utilitarianism*, of 1861. In the latter work Mill gave a compre-hensive but succinct—in many ways too succinct—account of the utilitarian foundations of his thought.

Its fourth chapter makes a case for the utility principle. It is an ultimate principle, so it does not admit of proof, in the normal sense of the word. But 'considerations may be pre-sented capable of determining the intellect either to give or withhold its assent to the doctrine; and this is equivalent to proof' (M x. 208). In fact Mill's argument is mainly for hedonism, the view that happiness is the sole human good. His method is noteworthy:

> the sole evidence it is possible to produce that anything is desirable, is that people do actually desire it. If the end which the utilitarian doc-trine proposes to itself were not, in theory and in practice, acknowl-edged to be an end, nothing could ever convince any person that it was so. (M x. 234)

This appeal to reflective endorsement, agreement 'in theory and in practice', is exactly the same naturalistic appeal that we have already seen Mill making in defence of another ultimate principle, the principle of enumerative induction. Here again the appeal is to reflective scrutiny of our spontaneous disposi-tions—in this case our dispositions to desire, rather than to believe.

Certainly we often desire a thing under the idea that it will be enjoyable or pleasant. An appeal to agreement in theory and practice can show that happiness is something desirable, part of a person's good—but it cannot yet show that it is the *only* good. So Mill claims further that *whenever* we desire something for its own sake, we desire it under the idea of it as enjoyable or pleasant. He thinks it a matter of 'fact and experience' that people 'desire nothing for itself but that which is a pleasure to them, or of which the absence is a pain'.

On Mill's own test, does happiness turn out to be the only end? Or are there other ideas—categorial ends other than happiness—under we which desire things? This is like the question posed by his claim about enumerative induction. The question there was whether there are other spontaneous modes of reasoning, which ought to be recognized by the test of agreement in theory and practice, such as hypothetical reasoning. The question here is the same: do we not, in theory and practice, desire things under categorial ends other than the end of happiness, for example under the end of knowledge, or the end of freedom?

Mill's defence of hedonism has strength and subtlety; if we criticize it we must be sure that we are not underestimating its depth. There are two points about it which we must be careful not to ignore. In the first place, he points out himself that it is no part of his argument that every action must ultimately flow from a desire. So one must not read this Humean doctrine, which Thomas Reid had criticized so well (p. 9 above), into Mill. We can will against inclination; 'instead of willing the thing because we desire it, we often desire it only because we will it' (M x. 238). That point about the will Mill fully concedes to his Coleridgean friends. Coleridge had criticized utilitarianism as lacking an adequate conception of personality and will. Mill recognized that there are conscientious actions, flowing not from any unmotivated desire but solely from acceptance of duty. But this was all perfectly consistent with his hedonistic argument, for what mattered for that was only that *when we do* unmotivatedly desire a thing we desire it under the ideas of it as pleasant.

A second carefully considered distinction is between desiring a thing as 'part' of our happiness and desiring it as a means to our happiness. By this distinction Mill hopes to show how the virtues can become a part of happiness.

Consider the difference between a spontaneously generous man and a conscientious giver. The first wants to give because he takes pleasure in giving. The second gives out of duty. If the actions of the first did not spring precisely from the *pleasure* he finds in giving pleasure, he would not be a spontaneously generous man. Both dispositions have moral worth; the first—spontaneous generosity—as well as the second—conscientiousness. It is a strength of Mill's moral psychology (as against Kant's) that he has room for both. The conscientious man acts not from spontaneous desire but from a 'confirmed will to do right' (M x. 238). The generous man acts from a simple desire to give—and he desires to give because giving pleasure to another pleases him.

The spontaneously generous man pursues another's happiness as *part* of his own. He is not thereby pursuing the other's happiness as a *means* to his own. His motivating desire is that he should make the other happy by his gift. Certainly he desires to do that because it is, for him, a pleasant thing to do. But that is not at all to say that he conceives it as a *means* to his own pleasure. The desire to make the other person happy is an unmotivated desire; it is not a motivated desire dependent on the self-centred desire to secure his own happiness.

So Mill can quite consistently hold that happiness is the only human good, while simultaneously acknowledging that other objects are desired for their own sake, and arguing that it is good that they should be so:

The ingredients of happiness are very various, and each of them is desirable in itself, and not merely when considered as swelling an aggregate. (M x. 235)

We pursue them for their own sake—but that is not to deny that we pursue them under the idea of happiness. We do not, by and large, stand back to consider how far the pursuit of any particular desire will contribute to our happiness taken as a whole, nor does Mill think it likely that the happiness of most of us would be greater if we very often did.

The virtues can become a part of our happiness, and for Mill they ideally should be so. That ideal state is not an unrealistic one, for the virtues have a natural basis: they are spontaneously admired, or they can come by a natural process to be admired, as excellences intrinsically worth having—and they are then desired as parts of happiness. Thus a man who admires generosity as an excellence will take pleasure in generous acts. There is an element in his motive different from that of either the spontaneously generous or the conscientious man. He takes pleasure in generous acts inasmuch as he knows them as *generous* acts. A man for whom the virtues have become a part of happiness, through becoming ideals of character, takes pleasure in their exercise: not only does he want to give to others, he also *wants* to be the kind of person who wants to do that.

Mill's case for hedonism, then, is that whenever a person wants something he wants it either as a means to or as a part of happiness. He quite accepts that many of the things which people pursue under the idea of happiness will not make them happy; or not as happy as things for which they have no desire, but which they could have come to recognize as deeply satisfying, through education or experience. Indeed he holds that some forms of happiness are inherently preferred as finer, more deeply satisfying, by those able to experience them fully—but these valuations are still in his view evaluations from within the perspective of happiness, not from outside it.

Hedonism is not utilitarianism. To get to the utility principle, Mill must make the transition from happiness as the sole individual good to aggregate happiness as the criterion of all conduct.

Here his case is unimpressive. For while he transforms Benthamite notions of what utility is and what the springs of action are, he never questions the principle of utility itself. This inheritance he leaves unprobed: it remains a dogma in his thought. It does not follow that it is wrong, of course, but we cannot look to Mill for a penetrating defence of it. What mainly concerned him was to attain a civilized conception of utility, the human individual's good. To question whether *aggregate* utility was indeed the proper test of conduct was simply not on his agenda.

To move to the utility principle we need the principle that a practice can be justified by appeal to the good of individuals, and by appeal to nothing else; and further, that the appeal must be made to the good of all individuals *impartially*. It was not Mill but a philosopher of the generation after Mill's, Henry Sidgwick (1838–1900), who probed these aspects of utilitarianism most deeply.

Like Whewell, Sidgwick was a fellow of Trinity College, Cambridge; he held the Chair of Moral Philosophy at the University and was the first in a remarkable Cambridge run of major philosophers, before and after the turn of the century. But unlike Whewell, he was a utilitarian; his *Methods of Ethics* (1874) is one of the masterpieces of that tradition, and in that respect (though not in others) he belongs in this chapter rather than with his contemporaries in the next.

There is, though, a difference of epistemological *mood* between Mill and Sidgwick. Sidgwick thought that rational ethics must rest on self-evident axioms—this talk of self-evident intuitions is a Cambridge trait which Moore and Russell would take much further, and not something of which Mill would have approved. It is a divergence from the insistent naturalism of Mill's epistemological pronouncements, a divergence in the spirit of a later period of philosophy. But from another point of view, the difference between Mill and Sidgwick is not great. Both think that fundamental principles of reasoning are located by reflective scrutiny, which identifies what our most fundamental commitments are. In both cases there is also an appeal to the systematic coherence a principle can provide, and to the general agreement it can secure. Nor does Mill deny that a fundamental principle, either of theoretical or of practical reason, is a requirement of *reason*: we have seen that his standpoint on reason is naturalistic, not sceptical. And on the other hand Sidgwick does not put his self-evident rational intuitions into an explicitly anti-naturalistic Kantian or Platonic setting.

The real difference lies in Sidgwick's view of what the self-evident axioms of practical reasoning are. He states them in a variety of forms. But for our purpose the important thing is that he thinks two things. He thinks it self-evident that if an action open to me would promote the good of some one or more individuals (whoever they may be), that fact as such gives me a reason to perform the action, a reason whose strength is measured by how much the action would promote the good of all, estimated impartially. He *also* thinks it self-evident that if an action would promote my own good, that fact gives me reason to perform it, a reason whose strength is measured by how much my own good would be promoted. He sees this as an independently self-evident principle, not a corollary of the first.

He concludes that there exists what he calls a dualism of the practical reason. Whether it is a contradiction depends on how precisely the two principles, universalistic and egoistic, are formulated. But at least it is possible that the two requirements may diverge, and Sidgwick finds himself concluding that, barring Divine providence, practical reason itself can make conflicting demands on action.

What is clear to him is that the egoistic principle can be stated in a rational and universal form. Of course an egoist who thinks his own good is the *only* good thing, the only thing that everyone has reason to promote, can be convicted of attaching irrational significance to his good as against that of others. Such an egoist thinks his own good the only thing that is 'agent-neutrally' good, the one thing that provides everyone with reasons for action. (The term is not used by Sidgwick; it comes from more recent moral theory.) But egoism need not appeal to the idea of the *agent-neutrally* good. The egoist may instead hold simply that his own good is the only good relative to him— this is not a tautological doctrine. And he can put this in universal terms by saying that everyone ought to pursue what is good relative to them, namely their own good.

It now becomes clear that hedonism is a doctrine about what a person's good is. To advance from it to utilitarianism we need at least to add that every person's good is *agent-neutrally* good. The rational egoist can block our considerations at this point, unless we can make it plausible that reasons as such are agent-neutral.

It seems that Mill does implicitly make this assumption, but it is to Sidgwick that the credit is due for locating it. His analysis of utilitarianism's foundations is sharper than Mill's—and it leads him to his dualism. As he says himself, others before him had endorsed it; Sidgwick's novelty lies in the logical clarity and the emphasis with which he states it. Yet this very clarity serves to highlight its strangeness. It is one thing to say that the Egoist cannot be vanquished by sheer logic if he plays his cards right, another to find his principle rationally self-evident. If one takes that positive step, will it not block the thesis that the universalistic principle, the principle of 'Rational Benevolence', is self-evident? For the root of the principle is surely the conviction that reasons must be agent-neutral, while the root of egoism is the conviction that they cannot be. If this is right, there is no stable 'self-evident intuition' which *simultaneously* recognizes both agent-neutral and agent-relative reasons: one cannot conjoin them in a single view. Sidgwick tries to do so because he combines Cambridge clarity with Hamlet-like indecision.

Even if we grant that Rational Benevolence is self-evident, that would not yet get us to classical utilitarianism, and this is something which neither Mill nor Sidgwick sees. For utilitarianism holds that the ultimate test of practice must be the *aggregate* good of all. But Rational Benevolence only requires that the good of all be consulted impartially—and it is far from obvious that the only way to implement this requirement of impartiality is by maximizing the sum (or come to that the average) of individual goods.

But since this point does not emerge in the period of philosophy which we are concerned with, we shall not pursue it. We turn instead to Mill's conception of the relationship between an ultimate principle of conduct, and the actual system of norms by which day-to-day social life proceeds. Here Mill is at his most impressive—and, often, least well understood.

Whatever one's view about the ultimate criterion of conduct, there is patently a great distance between recognizing any such criterion and laying down specific institutions for a society or norms of conduct for an individual life. Mill insists that the utilitarian need not and cannot require that 'the test of conduct should also be the exclusive motive of it'. Confusing those two things was, he thought, the error of Auguste Comte. He decidedly does not share Comte's vision of a society permanently mobilized for general good:

Why is it necessary that all human life should point but to one object, and be cultivated into a system of means to a single end? May it not be the fact that mankind, who after all are made up of single human beings, obtain a greater sum of happiness when each pursues his own, under the rules and conditions required by the good of the rest, than when each makes the good of the rest his only object, and allows himself no personal pleasures not indispensable to the preservation of his faculties? The regimen of a blockaded town should be cheerfully submitted to when high purposes require it, but is it the ideal perfection of human existence? (M x. 337)

Rules of conduct cannot be designed into existence—a society's practices at any given moment are a stage in an evolving and constraining tradition, a received fabric of ethical life. In the essay on Coleridge, Mill's criticism of Benthamite radicalism centres precisely on its lack of historical and sociological sense. The *philosophes* of the eighteenth century 'threw away the shell without preserving the kernel; and attempting to new-model society without the binding forces which hold society together, met with such success as might have been expected' (M x. 138).

Those binding forces are education which provides restraining social discipline, shared allegiance to some enduring and unquestioned values, and 'a strong and active principle of cohesion', or mutual sympathy, among 'the members of the same community or state'. They form the substance of society. That can be recognized by a utilitarian: he does not have to be a foundationalist in any sense in which 'foundationalism' should be rejected as a rationalistic dream. One can believe that there are ultimate criteria of the good, without thinking that they should be applied to every action individually, or even that it makes sense to do so—just as one can believe that there are criteria of truth, rules of evidence, canons of good explanation, without thinking that they should be applied to every belief individually, or that it makes sense to do so.

This aspect of Mill's utilitarianism is the key to his way of founding the institutions of justice and liberty on utility. Justice and liberty raise questions of individual right, and the relation between them and utility turns on the analysis of rights. Mill's treatment of rights follows Bentham, though with considerable changes of rhetorical emphasis. He makes nothing of a natural right—a right existing independently of questions of utility. But he does not reject the notion of a *moral* right, that is, a right existing otherwise than by custom or law. He gives an analysis of what it is for a person to have a right to something: a person has a right to a thing, he holds, if there is an obligation on society to protect him in his possession of that thing, or to guarantee the resources which enable him to possess it. But the obligation itself must be grounded in general utility.

The rights of justice correspond to a class of exceptionally stringent obligations on society. They are obligations to provide to each person 'the essentials of human well-being'. The claim of justice is the 'claim we have on our fellow-creatures to join in making safe for us the very groundwork of our existence' (M x. 255, 251) Because justice-rights protect those utilities which touch that groundwork they acquire an exceptional inviolability and overridingness. They take priority over the direct pursuit of general utility as well as over the private pursuit of personal ends.

On the conception of justice which Mill sketches in chapter 5 of *Utilitarianism*, the essentials—food, shelter, security, human solidarity and support—which are requirements of a worthwhile human life must be guaranteed to an individual as of right. What these essentials are will be to some extent relative: it will not be independent of the overall level of well-being achieved in a society. Within this general conception, the important political arguments will be about where that level of support is pitched. But the philosophical question about Mill's position is whether this 'baseline' conception of justice can be grounded, as Mill wishes to ground it, on aggregate utility.

Can the utilitarian recognize rights as trump cards within a system of practices which he underwrites, *as a whole*, on grounds of aggregate utility? It is not in principle impossible. It would be a special case of the fact that aggregate utility may often require moral agents and policy-makers to guide their decisions by principles other than the direct appeal to aggregate utility.

But certainly the criterion of aggregate utility is under strain at this point. It might be better to advance the baseline conception of justice as foundational: instead of arguing for it on grounds of aggregate utility, to present it as directly explicative of what is involved in the idea of general good. After all, that idea must have some distributive structure, and it is not obvious that aggregate utility is the most plausible distributive structure. The baseline conception is just as intuitively impartial as is the criterion of aggregate utility, and it still satisfies what is plausible in Sidgwick's notion of Rational Benevolence. But this suggestion takes us well beyond classical utilitarianism.

Turning from justice to liberty, we find again that Mill's liberalism is grounded on a utilitarian base. The famous principle which Mill enunciates in the essay *On Liberty* is intended to safeguard the individual's freedom to pursue his goals in his private domain:

the sole end for which mankind are warranted, individually or collectively, in interfering with the liberty of action of any of their number, is self-protection. . . . the only purpose for which power can be rightfully exercised over any member of a civilised community, against his will, is to prevent harm to others. His own good, either physical or moral, is not a sufficient warrant. . . . The only part of the conduct of any one, for which he is amenable to society, is that which concerns others. In the part which merely concerns himself, his independence is, of right, absolute. (M xviii. 224)

To define the limits of the private domain, in which the individual's 'independence is, of right, absolute'—or the limits of liberty of expression, which Mill also famously defends in this essay—is of course not easy. The essay says many wise and sensible things about these questions of demarcation, but it is very far from leaving them solved.

What is clear, however, is that Mill proposes to defend individual liberties by appeal to the general good—'utility in the largest sense, grounded on the permanent interests of a man as a progressive being'—though he freely borrows rhetoric from other traditions. In that respect, his liberalism stands opposed both to the classical natural-rights liberalism of Locke, and also to most forms of libertarianism in the twentieth century, which have typically sought foundations in some form of Hobbesian contract.

Can *liberal* principles of politics be grounded on an appeal to the general good? The third chapter of *On Liberty*, 'Of Individuality, as One of the Elements of Well-Being', is a classical passage of liberal theory; among Mill's writings it is, *par excellence*, the place to look for an answer to this question. Mill defends the liberty principle—what is sometimes called 'negative' liberty—on two grounds: it enables individuals to realize their individual potential in their own way, and by liberating talents, creativity, and dynamism, it sets up the essential precondition for rational progress as against stagnation. Yet this chapter is also a place in which the limitations of his Benthamite inheritance constrain him. He could have made his defence of a liberalism founded on general good much stronger, if he had recognized that human goals encompass ends such as autonomy and knowledge as well as happiness.

If, in particular, we recognize that autonomy—the freedom to make one's own decisions in one's private domain—is a categorial human end, one of the essentials of a worthwhile human life, we can defend it as a right, on Mill's own conception of justice-rights. The route to the liberty principle is then short. Of course there will be the question whether Mill's baseline conception of justice can itself be defended on grounds of aggregate utility. But that question would no longer arise if we defined the distributive structure of general good directly in its terms.

Such a position—which takes autonomy and knowledge to be ends co-ordinate with happiness, and the baseline conception as basic—differs from Mill's official commitments by rejecting hedonism and the aggregate utility principle. But its substantive divergence from Mill's general emphases is in fact much smaller than that suggests—small enough for one to think of it still as a Millian form of liberalism. It would be a Millian liberalism purged more thoroughly of the Benthamite legacy than Mill himself purged it, despite all his efforts in that direction. It would be more complex and less tidy than Mill makes out: leaving inevitable disagreement and indeterminacy in the balancing of categorial ends within a life, and in the limitations placed on balances of well-being across lives. But this plurality and indeterminacy may, after all, be authentic features of the ethical and political situation we find.

# 3

## *Fin de Siècle*:
## Idealists, Pragmatists, Scientists

When Mill died in 1873 he already belonged to an earlier intellectual epoch. In the last four decades of the nineteenth century, great changes took place in every subject on which he had thought: logic, metaphysics and psychology, ethics, political philosophy and economy. Changes just as great were taking place in politics and general culture.

Mill's public influence on a younger generation still soared at a dizzy height. A. J. Balfour, many years later, compared the authority Mill had had at this time to Hegel's earlier influence in Germany, or Aristotle's in the Middle Ages. Dicey noted that *On Liberty* 'was to the younger body of Liberal statesmen a political manual'.

The comparison with Aristotle and Hegel was apt, at least so far as both were synthesizers whose influence depended on their wholeness and many-sidedness. Mill's *summa* for secular humanist liberalism has those same virtues; it also has bell-like clarity. But the balance and authority were just what irritated counter-suggestible philosophers in the younger generation, who recognized unresolved problems and wanted to think for themselves. The list of those born in 1835–50 is intriguing: Green in 1836, Brentano, Mach, and Sidgwick in 1838, Peirce 1839, James 1842, Nietzsche 1844, Bradley 1846, Frege 1848. Not all of them were hostile to Mill's outlook—James and Mach, for example, in many ways shared it. But all felt the need to put Mill away. Even Sidgwick, one of the friendliest to Mill's thought, concluded that Mill 'will have to be destroyed, as he is becoming as intolerable as Aristeides, but when he is destroyed, we shall build him a mausoleum as big as his present temple of fame.'

Exactly—Mill was ostracized because he was famous for

goodness and wisdom. The ostracizers wanted to acknowledge other philosophers (Hume's rise dates to this time); they minimized any area of agreement with Mill. His public apotheosis had become a barrier to new thinking. So much was felt even by those whose disagreement with him was on technical questions in logic or in political economy. It was felt very much more violently by those who disagreed with the Millian vision as such; who thought he had given to some of the best and brightest a flawed and superficial humanist synthesis, which diminished the spiritual depth and the grandeur or tragedy of life.

Despite the best efforts of Coleridgeans, popular philosophical orthodoxy in the mid-century continued to lie along the spectrum of naturalism. At one end was religious and Whiggish common sense—the equivalent in France was the philosophy of the 'juste milieu'. At the other was philosophic radicalism, agnostic and utilitarian, along with other forms of atheistic 'materialism'. (This term is rather loosely used in the nineteenth century; nineteenth-century materialists were typically epiphenomenalists.) Thomas Hill Green traced out the spectrum from its enlightenment origins in an essay published in 1868 in the *North British Review*, under the title 'Popular Philosophy in its Relation to Life'. Its relation to life was that it accentuated selfish individualism and suppressed spiritual self-realization.

Mill of course had himself been a fierce critic of bourgeois orthodoxy—a critic from within, taking weapons from Coleridge and others outside. But, as always, the popular version was the vulgar version. It was also in the opinion of Mill's critics the consistent version. Mill's vision of an elevated human nature freely expressing itself, in all its diversity, through liberal and just institutions, could not be sustained by the secular naturalism on which he sought to base it. Critics as mutually opposed as Green on the one hand and Nietzsche on the other could agree on that.

The assault on the 'popular philosophy' was gathering pace throughout Europe. There was a revival of Kant. His doctrine, that the subject constitutes the objectivity of any domain of which it has possible knowledge, was again taken seriously. There was also a thorough rethinking of the nature of science by a series of distinguished philosopher-scientists and mathematicians. It led to a new positivism, or 'empirio-criticism' as one of them, Richard Avenarius, called it. Empirio-criticism had more than a little in common with the revival of Critical Philosophy proper—in its view of the constitution of objectivity and in locating science within the horizon of a purified, de-psychologized conception of experience. In America the philosophical developments were parallel, but America also contributed something really distinctive and new in the form of pragmatism.

In Britain the German-idealist critique of naturalism triumphed for a generation as it had never triumphed before. The collapse of idealism, which followed its sudden triumph, was just as dramatic. This brief and gorgeous flowering of absolute idealism in a distant and hostile climate was certainly a curious thing. The roots and original stock were undoubtedly German, yet the resulting plant was profoundly and paradoxically British. The successful transplantation was largely the product of the character of one man—Thomas Hill Green (1836–82).

British idealism was a reforming philosophico-social movement, rather as philosophical radicalism had been, though its philosophic spirit could hardly have been more different. Its intellectual leaders taught at universities (Oxford, Glasgow, St Andrews), and its philosophy was deeply religious in inspiration; but like philosophic radicalism it sent out reforming agents into public and civic life. Not all the philosophers who made up this close-knit idealist resurgence were political liberals—F. H. Bradley, who made the greatest impact in the world of academic philosophy itself, was not. But it was the fusion of idealism with liberalism which gave the movement its remarkable, and remarkably brief, power.

The founder and leader—though his life was far briefer than Bentham's—was Green. He came from a family of solid Puritan and Evangelical Midland stock. He was educated at Rugby (with Henry Sidgwick—who remembered him as having a 'certain solid wilfulness, a certain grave rebelliousness') and at

Balliol College, of which he became a Fellow. He became, like Sidgwick, a Professor of Moral Philosophy—he held the Chair at Oxford from 1878 to his death in 1882.

The éclat of idealism was the product of three factors at work in the 1860s. The first of these, wholly internal to philosophy, was the resurgence of Critical Philosophy which we have already noticed. This was a wholly expectable revival of fundamental philosophical questions about the coherence of naturalism. There had indeed been earlier flirtations with German idealism in Britain—for example by Hamilton, Whewell, and James Ferrier of St Andrews (the scourge of Coleridge's plagiarism). But now Green provided a fully thought-through native statement of the Kantian critique, and an assimilation (in no way uncritical) of Hegelian philosophy and theology, which he studied in the early 1860s as a fellow at Balliol. The upshot was a potent revival of the Coleridgean conception of philosophy, as 'the effort towards self-recognition of that spiritual life of the world, which fulfils itself in many ways but most completely in the Christian religion' (G iii. 121).

The time was ripe. The two other factors at work were the crisis of religious faith and the political emergence of the working classes. It turned out that German idealism had something to say to both of these—it provided a defence of religion and a philosophical incorporation of the working class into the moral community of the state. The key notions for Green—but they warred with each other—were the (initially) Kantian idea of autonomy, and the Hegelian idea of Absolute thought realizing itself in individual minds.

The immensity of religion in the intellectual as well as the middle-class world of nineteenth-century Britain is hard to re-imagine. In philosophy, religion is at present almost wholly ghettoized, a subject of special options on the syllabus, in no way a source of legitimation—while the naturalism which Green dreaded holds full sway. Then too, British religion partook of the British naturalistic temper; it sought an accommodation and partitioning of territory with science, when others—particularly in Germany—had long since felt a need to 'demythologize' Christianity on philosophical and historical-critical grounds. But the space for natural theology was fast shrinking. The Newtonian universe had long ceased to require divine correction, and now evolution removed the need of an intelligent designer of life. (As late as 1868–70, when Mill wrote his essay on Theism, he took the argument from design very seriously, as lending some probability to a powerful but not omnipotent designer. But he pointed out that evolutionary theory, which he took to be still uncertain, would if admitted 'greatly attenuate the evidence' for Creation, though it would not be inconsistent with it. (M x 450))

If religion was central, doubts about religion were central. 'The forties', it has been said, 'was the time of doubts, in the plural and with a small d; . . . In the sixties Britain and France and Germany entered the age of Doubt, in the singular and with a capital D.' A similar sea-change was making its way in America. Oliver Wendell Holmes was in the early 1870s a member of the Metaphysical Club at Harvard, which we shall return to when we consider Pragmatism. He wrote:

My father was brought up scientifically—i.e. he studied medicine in France—and I was not. Yet there was with him as with the rest of his generation a certain softness of attitude toward the interstitial miracle—the phenomenon without phenomenal antecedents, that I did not feel. The difference was in the air, though perhaps only the few of my time felt it . . . I think science was at the bottom.

One possible response to the crisis of faith was to attack religious liberalism, which Newman described as

the mistake of subjecting to human judgement those revealed doctrines which are in their nature beyond and independent of it, and of claiming to determine on intrinsic grounds the truth and value of propositions which rest for their reception simply on the external authority of the Divine Word.

But many, such as Matthew Arnold, thought that this was to adopt 'for the doubts and difficulties which beset men's minds to-day, a solution which, to speak frankly, is impossible'. Green agreed:

Once let the conflict be presented as one between reason and authority, and just those nobler elements of character which it is feared that
popular materialism will undermine will be enlisted in its defence . . .
(G iii. 223)

The real need was to rethink the scope and ontological foundations of reason itself. The men who turned to German thought
had a very clear strategic vision of what was required. It was
nothing less than rejection, root and branch, of that naturalistic
temper which Britain brought to religion. One could not hypothesize God from data within the regular phenomenal order.
One must rethink the metaphysical status of the phenomenal
order as such and as a whole:

No longer is it possible as it once was, to intercalate the ideal, the
divine, as it were surreptitiously, as one existence in a world otherwise
secular and natural . . . we can find the ideal anywhere, only by finding
it everywhere.

As important to the mental transitions of the *fin de siècle* as
its religious crisis was the progressive political emancipation of
the working class. In idealist terms, this was an expansion of
spirit into new centres of self-consciousness and autonomous
reason, which had hitherto been dormant. Those centres must
now be incorporated in the kingdom of ends, guided to conscious existence as free citizens. It required moral regeneration,
in part at least through interventionist legislation designed to
develop autonomy ('positive freedom'). Green seemed to many
specially fitted for the task; 'he was [as Edward Caird put it]
specially characterised by the intimate blending in him of idealism and practicality . . . an intensely democratic or Christian
tone of feeling that could not tolerate the thought of privilege,
and constantly desired for every class and individual a full share
in all the great heritage of humanity' (Gp p. vii).

The connexion between left liberalism or liberal socialism
and a rejection of naturalism or 'materialism' was not restricted
to Britain. German philosophers in the liberal and social-
democratic camp—they also were university professors—showed
the same tendency to revise their politics onto a Kantian and
idealist foundation. This realignment contrasts notably with the

connexion the enlightenment had made between naturalism in metaphysics and social and political reform—a connexion which had been continued by Mill. But now naturalism became identified with crass and exploitative selfishness—bourgeois hegemony, or empty external reformism.

Green's liberalism, as we shall see, is far closer to Mill's in its recommendations of policy than has sometimes been thought. But its metaphysical foundations differ utterly. By Green the central Kantian argument is at last rethought in Britain from the inside, and laid out with full force. It is beautifully presented in an extended essay published in 1882 under the title 'Can there be a Natural Science of Man?' (The essay also forms the first, metaphysical, section of his *Prolegomena to Ethics*.) In words echoing the contemporaneous German cry of 'Back to Kant!', he writes,

We have to return once more to that analysis of the conditions of knowledge which forms the basis of all Critical Philosophy, whether called by the name of Kant or no, and to ask whether the experience of connected matters of fact, which in its methodical expression we call science, does not presuppose a principle which is not itself any one or number of such matters of fact, or their result.

If the answer is 'No',

we shall at least have satisfied ourselves that man, in respect of the function called knowledge, is not merely a child of nature. We shall have ascertained the presence in him of a principle not natural, and a specific function of this principle in rendering knowledge possible. (Gp 12)

And his answer is indeed 'No':

in a man, who can know a nature—for whom there is a 'cosmos of experience'—there is a principle which is not natural and which cannot without a ὕστερον πρότερον be explained as we explain the facts of nature. (Gp 14)

If this negative result holds, naturalistic philosophies after Kant can be dismissed wholesale as anachronism. Whatever the relation of mind and nature may be, the utterly intuitive naturalistic view of it—Coleridge's 'natural consciousness', Green's 'popular philosophy'—must be wrong, and so something counter-intuitive to popular philosophy must be right. Kant's negative result opened up a new world in which the relations of self, God, and nature could be conceived afresh, even if the result of such rethinking took one beyond Kant.

It was pre-eminently Green who laid down the Great Tradition of modern philosophy which is still with us in our syllabuses. According to this canon, the advance locomotive of philosophy was switched by Kant onto a new main line (through the Channel Tunnel), leaving the whole British debate between common-sense and radical-empiricist forms of naturalism stranded on side rails. In his 'Introduction to Hume's "Treatise of Human Nature"', Green presents a brilliantly sustained criticism of Locke, Berkeley, and Hume, in terms of their own assumptions. Of the naturalistic debate after Hume he takes a very lofty view:

the method, which began with professing to explain knowledge, showed knowledge to be impossible. Hume himself was perfectly cognisant of this result, but his successors in England and Scotland would seem so far to have been unable to look it in the face. They have either thrust their heads again into the bush of uncriticised belief, or they have gone on elaborating Hume's doctrine of association, in apparent forgetfulness of Hume's own proof of its insufficiency to account for intelligent, as opposed to merely instinctive or habitual, experience ... (G i. 2)

Thus the 'Treatise of Human Nature' and the 'Critic of Pure Reason,' taken together, form the real bridge between the old world of philosophy and the new. They are the essential 'Propaedeutik,' without which no one is a qualified student of philosophy. (G i. 3)

This approach has the advantage of getting Green speedily out of mere trench warfare with contemporaries, and onto commanding high ground. But it has a corresponding and serious weakness—he is able to ignore the very real development in naturalism produced by Reid's criticism of ideas, and (with particular damage to his own ethics) Mill's rethinking of utilitarian moral psychology. He fails, in consequence, to separate incidental difficulties from those inherent in the naturalist project. The fact remains that his definition of the canon had an influence lasting well beyond his idealist construction. The cloud of mediocre obscurity into which it cast the naturalism of the 19th century remained in place during the modernist phase of philosophy—even when Green's idealist critique, which gave the canon its rationale, had collapsed.

In his rethinking of the Kantian critique Green focuses on our grasp of relations. Without such a grasp, no thought, no 'intelligent experience' of 'connected matters of fact' is possible. But the world of nature cannot transcend intelligent experience. Here Green invokes the doctrine of phenomenalism. which holds that all our knowledge is phenomenally relative (see p. 55 above). It follows that the objects of science—in particular matter and motion—must be known objects, related to experience—*they* cannot therefore be things in themselves lying beyond its bounds:

> matter and motion, just so far as known, consist in, or are determined by, relations between the objects of that connected consciousness which we call experience. (Gp 13)

With this of course Mill and the positivists could have agreed. But from it, Green thinks, the Critical conclusion must follow.

> If nothing can enter into knowledge that is unrelated to consciousness; if relation to a subject is necessary to make an object, so that an object which no consciousness presented to itself would not be an object at all; it is as difficult to see how the principle of unity, through which phenomena become the connected system called the world of experience, can be found elsewhere than in consciousness, as it is to see how the consciousness exercising such a function can be a part of the world which it thus at least co-operates in making; how it can be a phenomenon among the phenomena which it unites into a knowledge. (Gp 14–15)

Mill too drew an ontological conclusion—it was that empirical objects have to be analysed as possibilities of sensation, possibilities whose existence is simply a brute fact about the series of sensation, requiring no constitution by a transcendental self. But Green introduces an all-important change of register at this point, by stamping onto the discussion a distinction between the series of mere sensations—'feelings'—and intelligent experience proper. The empiricist's term 'idea', he says, 'stood alike for feeling proper, which to the subject that merely feels is neither outer nor inner, because not referring itself to either mind or thing, and for conception, or an object thought of under relations' (G i. 141). But feeling is transmuted into intelligent experience only when it becomes conceptual, that is, when it is worked up into judgements through relations. Without relations we have no objects of experience; feeling alone cannot give us relations.

If relational concepts are not drawn from sensation, but are constitutive of empirical objects, then the constitution of objects and facts must be the work of a knowing subject—which cannot be annulled without annulling the natural or empirical world as such, and so cannot be a part of that world. This gives Green the desired conclusion, that the world itself is constituted by active thought.

So there are two premises. One is phenomenalism—in effect it is, as in Mill, *strong* phenomenalism, which holds that the application of our concepts cannot transcend our experience. The other is provided by Green's critique of the Lockean-empiricist tradition, according to which concepts are entirely derived from sensation or 'feelings'. In reply, Green argues that intelligent experience presupposes relational concepts which could not be derived from feelings. (His thesis here is Kantian, or constitutive, rather than Reidian, or innatist.) Both premises are essential—for if one rejected strong phenomenalism one might be able to agree with Green on his critique of Lockean empiricism, without being forced to his idealism—or at any rate to his form of it. This point will return in Chapter 5. In the period covered by this chapter, however, rejection of strong phenomenalism is not on the agenda.

It is the other premise which requires more scrutiny. The notion that there is something terribly important about relations comes up in this period again and again. But what is Green claiming about relations? Why cannot ideas of relation be derived from experience? Why must sensations be related by a relator, a unifying non-empirical principle?

One line of argument here is that there are no *impressions* of relation of which ideas could be copies (using 'idea' here in the

Humean rather than the Lockean sense). This, Green thinks, simply carries through consistently the very principles which underlie the empiricist's assault on such notions as substance, causation, and the self. But is he right? Even if Locke thinks relations to be the work of the mind, or Berkeley considers them 'neither a feeling nor felt' (G i. 149), why cannot a new empiricist accept that ideas of relation are derived from experience? Can it not be given in experience that this shade is bluer than that? That this edge is longer than that? Green emphasizes that the cosmos of experience essentially includes the experience of succession—why cannot the empiricist hold that we have an impression of succession? It is true that empiricists have often felt some discomfort in countenancing such impressions. But the claim that we have 'impressions' of such relations none the less remains much more plausible than would be a claim that we have impressions of substance, causation, or the self. Green's response would be that an alleged 'impression' that $X$ is longer, or bluer, than $Y$, or that $X$ precedes $Y$, is already *conceptual experience*, judgmental in content, and not, as it would have to be in the empiricist concept of experience, pure sensation or feeling.

He also highlights the problem of general ideas, which Berkeley had discussed. It is a feature of the theory of ideas that what ideas are *of* is always particulars—particular objects, events. (Note that this thesis is distinct from and even incompatible with the conception of experience as pure feeling, which we have just seen Green criticizing.) How then is it possible to have a thought? On Berkeley's view, when I deploy the predicate 'triangle' in general reasoning about triangles, I have in mind a particular image of a fully determinate triangle which is taken as standing for triangles in general. As Green says, this story requires that I be capable of recognizing other ideas as resembling my paradigm image in the relevant respect of triangularity. He concludes that to have general concepts I must have the concept of resemblance, which can derive from nothing in feeling since relation is 'neither a feeling nor felt'. But this means that even a singular thought, such as 'This is a triangle', requires me to have the concept of resemblance:

Hume must be met *in limine* by the question whether, apart from such ideas of relation as according to his own showing are not simple impressions, so much as the singular proposition is possible. (G i. 186)

The Locke–Berkeley–Hume–Mill treatment of generality must lead to the conclusion that what, according to them, is 'really existent'—that is, particulars—is

the unmeaning, and that any statement about it is impossible. We cannot judge of it without bringing it into relation . . . if we say that it is the mere 'this' or 'that,' as such—the simple 'here' and 'now'—the very 'this,' in being mentioned or judged of, becomes related to other things which we have called 'this,' and the now to other 'nows'. Thus each acquires a generality and with it becomes fictitious. (G i. 36)

We have arrived again at the problems about generality which we have seen troubling Mill in the previous chapter, but now in more generalized form. It is certainly entirely plausible to make a link between the grasping of general concepts and the ability to recognize similarities. But cannot the naturalist reply that possessing a general idea *just is* having the capacity to recognize the similarity which all instances of the idea share? Thus, for example, the resemblance of this patch of colour to that one causes me to call them both green, whether or not I have the relational *concept* of resemblance. So I can have the concept *green* without having a relational concept.

But while the resemblance may be what *causes* me in both cases to utter the word 'green', the question can still be raised, what makes it *right* for me to predicate of each object the word 'green'? Must I not grasp a principle or criterion of application which determines when it is right? The question remains at the centre of philosophy. Intelligent experience requires possession of concepts; to possess concepts is to respond to norms. What, at the naturalistic level, could deliver such norms? It seems that naturalism must leave out rationality—it cannot deliver the crucial point that experience and action is a continuous response to *reasons*.

Experience *is* intelligent experience. Feeling, Green stresses, is something other than thought, but it would be a misunderstanding to think that something called 'feeling' could exist without something called 'thought', grounding, in the Millian manner, a sensationalist construction of the physical world irrespective of thought. The antithesis of thought and feeling, or thought and object, is dialectical, not ultimate: thought must posit something other than itself to be conscious of itself.

Subject and object, thought and its ετερον [other], are correlative or complementary factors in the whole of self-consciousness, or (which is the same) together constitute the reality of the world. Each is what it is only *in relation to* the others. (G ii. 181–2)

When the antithesis between thought and feeling is overcome, so also is the antithesis of mind and nature. (This point in the idealist dialectic is not reached by Kant, who retains, against the implication of what Green considers his best doctrine, an antithesis between concept and intuition, knowing subject and things in themselves.)

It follows also that Self-consciousness, or Thought as such, is not to be identified with this or that empirical thought, since all such particular thoughts are within experience. Self-consciousness is rather a single, actively self-distinguishing spiritual principle: which expresses itself in temporal human intelligence, in something like the way that the whole meaning of a text is potentially present throughout the temporal act of reading. That active principle is God.

Our formula then is that God is identical with the self of every man in the sense of being the realisation of its determinate possibilities ... that in being conscious of himself man is conscious of God, and thus knows that God is, but knows what he is only in so far as he knows what he himself really is. (G iii. 227)

A contemporary Balliol rhyme summed it up—

> I am the self-distinguishing
> consciousness in everything;
> the synthetic unity
> one in multiplicity,
> the unseen nexus of the seen
> sometimes known as TOMMY GREEN

—though 'sometimes' hardly catches the mystifying dialectical relation of Thought to the empirical Tommy Green.

But despite his closeness to Hegel, Green's attitude to Hegel's method and reasoning was wary:

That there is one spiritual self-conscious being, of which all that is real is the activity or expression; that we are related to this spiritual being, not merely as parts of the world which is its expression, but as partakers in some inchoate measure of the self-consciousness through which it at once constitutes and distinguishes itself from the world; that this participation is the source of morality and religion; this we take to be the vital truth which Hegel had to teach. It still remains to be presented in a form which will command some general acceptance among serious and scientific men. (G iii. 146)

The last sentence epitomizes Green's understanding of his task in speaking to a British audience, and the nonconformist background which was his strength.

This independent-mindedness, a kind of probity or solidity in Green, belongs to the recognizably British mode of philosophizing. Green recast one side of the most important metaphysical debate of the nineteenth century in indigenous form, applying much more philosophic power than Coleridge before him, but drawing support from many of the same strands in their native culture. This last certainly cannot be said of the other leading British idealist, Francis Herbert Bradley (1846–1924). He is not a man of roots as Coleridge and Green are. But he *is* eminently a man of the last years of the nineteenth century, and one can learn a lot about the spirit of that period by studying his philosophy.

They were both at Oxford (Bradley at Merton, holding a fellowship which did not require him to teach), but they had very different personalities and they led very different lives. Bradley's was much longer than Green's—this was one reason why he eventually built a greater influence in the world of academic philosophy. He was somewhat reclusive, and very often ill—he suffered from chronic kidney trouble. Perhaps that should be remembered if one is put out by his quite extraordinary vituperativeness and unfairness to opponents. Bradley's edge, his liking for unremitting dialectics, has an appeal to fundamentalists, of whom there will always be plenty in philosophy. One can admire Mill and Green as men who unified their life and thought in a peculiarly English way. But this is also what puts some people off them: their stiff sobriety, active citizenship, public manner, lack of specialist dedication and skill. In contrast, Bradley can seem pleasingly knowing and at the same time informal, sophisticated, and cosmopolitan, as he seemed to T. S. Eliot, who contrasted him with 'the crude and raw and provincial' utilitarians. But Bradley's thrusts are effete and his style ingratiates to a coterie. A comparison with his close contemporary Nietzsche, a philosopher at the opposite extreme to English sobriety, and whose hostility to the liberal-orthodox has real power to disturb (though from a very different angle), immediately reveals Bradley as the cloistered insider.

Bradley has the same, or an even greater, horror of commonsense naturalism that Green had. But his impulse is mystical rather than religious; not the redemption of Christianity but the Eleatic craving. He seeks self-transcendence along with the transcendence of all distinctions, in an all-inclusive, selfsubsistent One. This is his Absolute, and he arrives at it by arguing, like the Eleatics, that all mere appearance is selfcontradictory.

It is a *fin-de-siècle* Absolute:

its contents are nothing but sentient experience. It will hence be a single and all-inclusive experience, which embraces every partial diversity in concord. (BRa 147)

Again, one premise for this is strong phenomenalism. It is true that Bradley has a withering chapter on 'Phenomenalism'—but what he there opposes is a view of phenomena as a series of particulars possessing qualities and relations, stretched out in time. Immediate experience is prior to such appearance, and immediate experience is all there is. He takes this as evident: 'to be real, or even barely to exist, must be to fall within sentience' (BRa 144). But he proceeds to put a case for it:

When the experiment is made strictly, I can myself conceive of nothing else than the experienced. Anything, in no sense felt or perceived, becomes to me quite unmeaning. And as I cannot try to think of it without realizing either that I am not thinking at all, or that I am thinking of it against my will as being experienced, I am driven to the conclusion that for me experience is the same as reality. The fact that falls elsewhere seems, in my mind, to be a mere word and a failure, or else an attempt at self-contradiction. It is a vicious abstraction whose existence is meaningless nonsense, and is therefore not possible. (BRa 145)

Like Berkeley, this argues directly to the unintelligibility, and not merely the unknowability, of unexperienced objects, and does so by the same curiously powerful fallacy, below which there always seems to lurk something plausible which stubbornly escapes formulation. You cannot think of something without thinking of it as experienced; so 'nothing else than the experienced' is thinkable, hence, possible.

But unlike Berkeley, Bradley denies the ego. Can we then still talk of experience at all, since this seems intelligible only as the activity of an ego, or the content of that activity? What drives Bradley further is his unusually pure reliance on immanent critique: that is, criticism by the detection of internal contradictions. The real is what we arrive at when all appearances have been purged of the contradictions which result from their one-sidedness, their lack of comprehensiveness. The real is the whole, the self-subsistent. Whatever is conditioned, dependent on something else, is not real. 'The character of the real is to possess everything phenomenal in a harmonious form' (BRa 140).

In particular, the motor of Bradley's dialectic is the alleged contradictoriness of all relations. Where Green thinks them the work of Thought, Bradley denies their reality altogether. This theme is deployed in the first part of *Appearance and Reality* to show that Substantive and Adjective, Space and Time, Motion, Change, Causality, Activity, Things, the Self, are all unreal. Any plurality is unreal; Reality is one.

His arguments are striking both for their abstract purity and their badness. Such flagrance silences a merely rational response. But the focus, again on relations, is significant. Bertrand Russell later claimed that Bradley's denial of the reality of relations rested on the assumption that all propositions are subject–predicate in form. It is certainly true that the new logic, which was at that time emerging from more than one source, was particularly concerned to develop a formal treatment of arguments turning on the logic of relations, arguments with which syllogistic theory could not properly deal. And once such a theory of relations had been developed, relations acquired an ontological respectability which they had not previously had.

Nevertheless, the central issue underlying Bradley's arguments is a different one; it is the problem of the unity of the proposition as such. If relations are admitted as real alongside what they relate, how can they do the relating? The question extends to how qualities inhere in objects, for inherence is a relation; so it is really the problem of understanding predication as such. There is a vicious regress—further relations are at every stage needed to relate the relation to its *relata*:

we are forced to go on finding new relations without end. The links are united by a link, and this bond of union is a link which also has two ends; and these require each a fresh link to connect them with the old.

Now this implicitly assumes that to be real is to be a substantive, particular, individual; an assumption obscured by Bradley's loose language:

If you take the connection as a solid thing, you have got to show, and you cannot show, how the other solids are joined to it. (BRa 33)

If every term in a sentence signifies something real, why is a sentence not a list of names? The answer seems easy—relations are real but they are not particulars: they are *relations*. But how can we know or even think of such non-particular reals—how can we make them the object of our thought? The assumption that whatever we are conscious of (whatever we 'grasp') is particular, which Green exploited in criticizing British empiricism from within, is evidently a deep-laid one. One might state it as: whatever is given is particular. From that together with *the real is the given* we reach the conclusion that the real is the particular. Of course neither Green nor Bradley would accept these formulations. But they do have something in common with them. Green holds that relations are thought-induced, not given. For Bradley experience is not 'given' to any ultimate subject, being itself the only reality. But he also implicitly assumes that experience cannot itself be relational, and thus, given that it is the only reality, implicitly assumes his conclusion, that relations are not real. We shall see in the next chapter that rejection of the thesis that the real is the particular was central in the early development of modern logic.

Since relations are contradictory, and any judgement is a related complex, it is an immediate consequence that no judgement can represent Absolute reality. A judgement can only be true relatively, true of more or less one-sided appearances:

to be more or less true, and to be more or less real, is to be separated by an interval, smaller or greater, from all-inclusiveness or self-consistency. Of two given appearances, the one more wide, or more harmonious, is more real ... the truth and the fact, which, to be converted into the Absolute, would require less rearrangement and addition is more real and truer. And this is what we mean by degrees of reality and truth. (BRa 364–5)

The Absolute itself is immediate and non-relational. Relations being ultimately unreal, there remains no route to an ultimate relating Agent. There is only Experience in its unity-in-diversity.

Undoubtedly Green's doctrine that the only final reality is Thought—active and personal Self-Consciousness—is hard to defend by his own principles. He himself argues, in reconciling his idealism with the natural realism of common sense, that the very concepts used in expressing this realism have 'no meaning except such as is derived from experience' (Gp 42). This pushes the concept-empiricism of British philosophy beyond its naturalism, and that line of thought remains deeply interesting. But where then does Green's own conclusion, that there must be a self-alienating, relation-constituting principle, come from? It is supposedly deduced as a necessary condition of experience. But what justifies applying, to the transcendentally deduced principle, such empirically determinate concepts as 'thought' or 'person'?

Green's religious starting-point drives him, as it drove Coleridge before him, to think of that principle as God, a principle to which finite creatures can stand in a personal relation. But most other idealists could not accept this as the final truth. Green raises the question himself (G iii. 142–3), but he does not solve it. Personality reduces itself for him to 'the quality in a subject of being consciously an object to itself' (Gp 208)—hardly enough to satisfy ordinary Christians, too much to satisfy philosophical critics. J. H. Muirhead put it neatly:

The completeness and self-consistency which our ideal requires can be realised only in a form of being in which subject and object, will and desire, no longer stand as exclusive opposites, from which it seemed at once to follow that the finite self could not be a reality or the infinite reality a self.

Bradley was clear. 'If you identify the absolute with God, that is not the God of religion.' The God of religion 'is but an aspect, and that must mean but an appearance, of the Absolute' (Ba 447, 448).

This is a convenient point to stand back and review what the idealists shared with their empiricist forebears. They obviously did not share Mill's epistemological empiricism. But they did (like Kant) accept a certain concept-empiricism, which in turn flows from phenomenalism. In a Kantian formulation, the latter doctrine may be said to hold that *any objective item* is knowable only by experience. Kantians will of course argue that this leaves open the possibility of arguing to necessary *subjective conditions* of experience. However, it certainly rules out the doctrine Mill calls 'Realism', since that doctrine holds that concepts are both objectively real *and* known independently of experience, that is, known non-phenomenally.

It is this anti-Realism which in turn gives rise to concept-empiricism, that is, to the view that (in Kantian language) concepts applicable to objective items—empirical concepts—must have their conditions of application given in experience and hence cannot be applicable beyond experience. The empiricist thinks empirical concepts are the only concepts we have, the Kantian thinks we have concepts expressing, at least negatively, the subjective conditions of experience. But he cannot consistently apply empirical concepts to those subjective conditions—the problem we have seen Green running up against.

Concept-empiricism is related to the rejection of a metaphysically real self: the most obvious link is by means of the doctrine that no such self is given in experience. Mill, as we saw, feels some pull along these lines towards denying the self's reality; in the *fin de siècle* the self is rejected unambiguously, and not only by Bradley, but also by James and Mach, whom we have not yet discussed. A Kantian might argue for a transcendental subject as a condition of experience; in contrast these three philosophers make a very determined effort to overcome the subject–object dichotomy completely.

Concept-empiricism is also related to another very important doctrine that comes into view in this period: the doctrine that the true, the real, is that which manifests greatest comprehensiveness and coherence. It is a major element in Bradley's philosophy, and it is upheld by other idealist philosophers associated with Bradley. But, again, we shall see that it is propounded not only among idealists but among pragmatists and empirio-critics too. Can sense be attached to a question about what there is, other than by reference to the most economical and comprehensive explanation of experience? Can we have any other notion of the true? To answer in the negative is to adopt— at some level (there are many subtleties here)—a coherence conception of truth, or perhaps of meaning. It is not obvious that this conception must be allied with strong phenomenalism, or that if not so allied, it must lead to idealism. But in the *fin de siècle* the combination of strong phenomenalism with a coherence conception of truth was so widely influential as to be a dominant orthodoxy.

Before we pursue these themes in the work of pragmatists and philosophers of science we must take some account of the idealists' moral and political philosophy. Green's thinking on these subjects was as distinguished as—and perhaps more lastingly influential than—his quixotic effort to plant absolute idealism in British soil.

Just as he sought to rethink the philosophical foundations of religion, so he sought to rethink the foundations of liberalism. He wanted to purify and regenerate its individualism. To regenerate it—not to replace it by collectivism. This point comes at a number of levels. He certainly believed in the sovereignty of individual, personal good:

there can be nothing in a nation however exalted its mission, or in a society however perfectly organised, which is not in the persons composing the nation or the society. Our ultimate standard of worth is an ideal of *personal* worth. All other values are relative to value for, of, or in a person. To speak of any progress or improvement or development of a nation or society or mankind, except as relative to some greater worth of persons, is to use words without meaning. (Gp 210)

This is one deep line of continuity between Mill and Green. Typically, though, Green's goal is to transcend the distinction between individual and collectivity rather than to identify with one side of it. The higher the development of the self the more universal and thus the more identified with other selves it becomes. Of course here too there is something with which Mill would have agreed, though he would not have attempted to phrase it in idealist terms.

At a less philosophical, more proximately political level, Green remained a firm believer in the voluntary principle. Nonconformism and Manchester liberalism were his background. State action was 'necessarily to be confined to the removal of obstacles' (G ii. 514–15). His rationale for this was characteristically moral; rights are earned by the individual's 'capacity for spontaneous action regulated by a conception of a common good', and legal compulsion would interfere with that spontaneity and check its growth. Green's support for the newer, more interventionist liberalism with which he is often associated is genuine, but it is defined in those enabling terms—the removal of impediments to individuals' moral growth. It has been said that he 'gave to the idea of positive liberalism its letters of credit'. But it is questionable how far he would have approved of the use to which they were later put.

What is true is that he gave a new kind of emphasis to the idea of 'positive freedom'. He said, in an influential lecture delivered in 1881 to the Leicester Liberal Association,

freedom, rightly understood, is the greatest of blessings; . . . its attainment is the true end of all our efforts as citizens. But . . . we should

consider carefully what we mean by it. We do not mean merely freedom from restraint or compulsion. We do not mean merely freedom
to do as we like irrespectively of what it is that we like.... When we
speak of freedom as something to be so highly prized, we mean a
positive power or capacity of doing or enjoying something worth doing
or enjoying ... (G iii. 370–1)

He does *not* mean that your freedom is measured by your
ability to get whatever you want, or to get the enjoyable things
in life. Positive freedom for him includes that quality of a person
captured by Kant's notion of rational autonomy—the ability to
recognize good reasons for action and the capacity to act on
them. It is in this sense that he speaks of the 'capacity of doing
or enjoying [i.e. experiencing, under-going] something worth
doing or enjoying'.

It is not, however, Green's recognition of the ideal of 'positive freedom' that was new in English liberal philosophy, it is
rather the interpretation he gave of its implications for legislation. The positive notion of moral freedom is also present in
Mill. Moral freedom for Mill is a character-ideal, and an important part of happiness in the highest sense, though not an end
of life separable from the end of happiness. No doubt Green
would have said that Mill had provided no satisfactory metaphysical basis for moral freedom, or rational autonomy; that
any appeal to it on his part was inconsistent with his naturalism.
But in political terms the divergence between the two great
liberals lies rather in the way they connect the positive concept
of moral freedom, which refers to a quality of character—one
which a person may logically have or fail to have in any social
circumstance (including the concentration camp)—with the
negative concept of social and political liberty—freedom from
impediment or restraint by others. Moral freedom is as much
deployed in Mill's argument for negative liberty as is his more
famous invocation of spontaneity. Both—moral freedom and
spontaneity—are in his view best strengthened by social ar-
rangements which observe negative liberty. It is here that Green
takes a new tack.

The lecture from which I have just quoted was on 'Liberal

Legislation and Freedom of Contract'; it was a defence of legislation on factory safety, tenancy, temperance, education —legislation which was being opposed on the grounds that it weakened people's ' "self-reliance, and thus, in unwisely seeking to do them good ... lowers them in the scale of moral beings" ' (G iii. 365). Green was not objecting to the high moral value placed on self-reliance. His point was that it was only by means of constructive legislation that the development of self-reliance could be secured for all citizens. They must be supported on their feet while they were becoming able to stand on them. Self-reliance involves both moral freedom and the absence of intrusive provision by others. The disagreement between Mill and Green was not on its value but on whether, for example, temperance legislation, which infringes Mill's principle of liberty, is nevertheless justified—because it helps people to develop and retain positive freedom. Green thought it was, but he also thought that the role of the state should be limited by this enabling criterion: it should strengthen, not substitute for, self-reliance, and it should never undermine 'the self-imposition of duties'.

We have said that Green wanted to regenerate, rather than simply to reject, the individualist dimension of liberalism, and noted that he, like Mill, held to the sovereignty of personal good. But if idealism means denying the ultimate reality of distinct personal selves, how can the sovereignty of personal good survive? Is there not a problem here analogous to the problem Green has in recognizing the final reality of God?

This has often been suggested. Put so simply it implies a closer tie between idealist metaphysics and the doctrine of the State than could be expected or than Green ever proposed; but it remains true that he has great difficulty in giving the sphere of individuality its due. This is where the philosophical difference between Mill and Green in respect of that diffuse notion, 'individualism', lies. For if individualism is belief in the axiomatic rationality of self-interest, or in the natural rights of the individual, they were both, the utilitarian and the idealist, opposed to it.

The difference is really a matter of Green's excessive moralism, which blends Hegelian idealism into his own background and dispositions. He always strives towards the mirage of an all-embracing community of interest, which metaphysical idealism certainly helps to sustain. The 'Common Good' must be non-competitive and nothing else is truly good. Thus 'the only true good is to be good', because this is 'the only good in the pursuit of which there can be no competition of interests, the only good which is really common to all who may pursue it' (Gp 288). Freedom in the positive sense is freedom to make the best of oneself—but to make the best of oneself, it turns out, is to contribute single-mindedly to common good, and to one's own self-perfection as a harmonious part of common good. It is a freedom for which only active citizens need apply. Even to have a right is only to have a claim on society 'in respect of a capacity freely . . . to contribute to its good' (G ii. 463).

The obsession with transcending all distinctions, Green's fatal inheritance from Hegel, undermines his moral psychology —and the 'common good' is the point of collapse. Two critical distinctions resist all Green's dialectical massaging: between self and others, and between reason and desire. As to the first— individuals *are* separate. This, often puzzlingly advanced as an objection to utilitarianism, is a literal objection to the ethics of Hegelian idealism, whose fantasy it is that self-realization is identity with a rational community. Of course there *is* very real fufilment in discharging a worthwhile role; and there are things which cannot be properly enjoyed unless shared, or if others lack them. But other goods are enjoyed at least in part because they are competitive achievements, and others again are neither competitive nor common but quite simply private. The sense of human diversity and individuality, which Mill fully registers —with its acceptance of irreducible public-collective, social-competitive, and private domains—receives only notional recognition from Green.

He also removes the distinction observed by Mill between pure conscientiousness, and pursuit of virtue as part of one's good. For Mill, as for Green, others' good can and should become genuinely a part of one's own, and spontaneously desired as such; but one has reason to promote it even when it is not so. He is not a rational egoist, in however 'high' a sense. But Green, following Hegel's criticism of Kant, refuses to acknowledge any final distinction between reason and desire. Moreover, though a motive for him is a self-conscious desire, as against a simple animal impulse, it is always a desire involving an idea of the agent's *own* personal good. Rationality is self-satisfaction. The conflict between will and desire becomes the conflict between a desire with which I identify and one with which I do not. What then is the distinction between good and bad will? It lies in the aspect of the self under which self-satisfaction is sought:

sin consists in the individual's making his own self his object, not in the possible expansion in which it becomes that true will of humanity's which is also God's, but under the limitation of momentary appetite or interest. (G iii. 73)

Realizing the self is achieving that expansion to its fullest possible extent. Self-realization turns out to be self-transcendence—one of the deepest *fin de siècle* themes.

This holds also for Bradley; but it is not so moralized as it is in Green. Bradley is more consistently a Hegelian in his ethical outlook (though not his metaphysics) than Green is. His influential volume, *Ethical Studies*, appeared in 1876—the first statement published by the idealists on ethics, for although Green's moral and political philosophy had been developed earlier, it only appeared posthumously.

Having criticized utilitarianism and Kant (they are travestied unmercifully under the guise of 'Hedonism' and 'Bare Duty'), Bradley moves on to his famous ethic of 'My Station and its Duties'. Here the individual realizes himself in his concrete social relations and the obligations encountered in his actual social setting. But this is not the final stopping-place in Bradley's dialectical ascent. There are higher forms of self-realization. Morality must transcend simple social morality—in Ideal Morality there is 'no limit to the moral sphere' (BRe p. xii). Ideal Morality transcends the ethic of My Station, which it retains 'in the main' but corrects and supplements. Self-realization is now no longer a matter of realizing the ideal given to me by my actual society, with its imperfections, but of striving towards an ideal of the self which encompasses the perfection of social being but also those aspects of full self-realization which go beyond the social.

Ideal Morality itself is not the stopping-point, for it does not overcome the bad self. It is indeed a condition of its character as morality that it should not do so, since morality always posits an ideal against the actual—'the moral is what it is only in asserting itself against its opposite' (BRe 233). Success in the moral quest would annul the contradiction between the bad and the good self, between the ought which is not, and the is which ought not to be, and would thus overcome morality as such. The point of view which overcomes the contradiction of morality, and in which morality ceases as such to exist, is religious. Yet even the religious consciousness remains, as we have already seen from *Appearance and Reality*, appearance (though not illusion). Full self-realization would be self-dissolution in absolute experience.

Let us return finally to the idealists' critique of individualism, for it was that as much as anything which captured their *fin de siècle* contemporaries, and which now again interests many political philosophers. In later reflections on his *Ethical Studies*, Bradley commented: 'It was Individualism, much rather than Hedonism, on which really I was making war' (BRp 386). And the essay on 'My Station and its Duties' has many forceful statements of his hostility to it:

The 'individual' man, the man into whose essence his community with others does not enter, who does not include relation to others in his very being, is, we say, a fiction . . . the 'individual' apart from the community is an abstraction. (BRe 168, 173)

Bradley claims this to be evident 'without aid from metaphysics'—but how are we to understand such terms as 'essence' and 'abstraction' non-metaphysically? In contrast, Green remarks of Burke that he

almost alone among the men of his time caught the intellectual essence of the system which provoked him. He saw that it rested on a metaphysical mistake, on an attempt to abstract the individual from the universal essence, i.e. from the relations embodied in habitudes and institutions which make him what he is; and that thus to unclothe man, if it were possible, would be to animalise him. (G iii. 116–17)

This is from his essay on 'Popular Philosophy in its Relation to Life'. Green does not make it clear what exactly the system that provoked Burke was. Sometimes it seems to be Jacobinism and a belief in natural right, sometimes the Humean notion that feeling is the sole principle of action, sometimes the idea that freedom is doing what one likes.

If we do bring in the aid of absolute-idealist metaphysics, then of course there is a clear sense in which Green and Bradley deny individualism. But if we leave that metaphysics to one side, it becomes much harder to specify what they oppose. A utilitarian (as Sidgwick noted in his very hostile review of *Ethical Studies* in *Mind*, vol. 1) could agree with them in scouting the social contract. And we have seen that Mill would have joined with Burke in denying the various doctrines mentioned in the previous paragraph. Nor need Mill deny that being rooted in locality, tradition, and community, and having a function therein, is a pressing need for most human beings—though he also, and importantly, sees the danger of communal suppression of individuality.

It would not be fair to the idealists, however, to leave the impression that they were demolishing straw men. For in the first place, it was primarily a popular and blinkered individualism they were attacking—and one which keeps on coming back. And in the second place, there are more difficult metaphysical questions involved in understanding the relation between individual and community than we have been able to bring out—just as there are more difficult issues involved in understanding the relation between thought and reality than we have yet been able to bring out. Perhaps they do not force us to absolute idealism. But they will never be absent for long in what follows.

We must leave the idealists and turn to America, where an authentically American philosophy was in process of being forged: pragmatism, whose conceptions of meaning and truth are still shaping philosophical thought today. They have probably never been more influential.

The influences on American philosophy in the first half of the century had come predominantly from Scottish Common Sense and German Romanticism—philosophic radicalism had had relatively less effect. There are, though, evident continuities between Mill and pragmatism; some of pragmatism's fundamental themes are implicit in the *System of Logic*—the rejection of Cartesian foundationalism, the fallibilistic view of knowledge, the functional view of reasoning.

Not that the acknowledged founder of pragmatism, and coiner of the word, Charles Sanders Peirce (1839–1914), was a great admirer of Mill. William James, the other pragmatist we shall consider, dedicated his lecture series, *Pragmatism*, to Mill's memory—'from whom I first learned the pragmatic openness of mind and whom my fancy likes to picture as our leader were he alive today'. But Peirce's philosophical provenance was very different—German idealism and medieval scholasticism.

He was born in Cambridge, Massachusetts. His father, Benjamin Peirce, was Perkins Professor of mathematics and astronomy at Harvard, from which University Peirce received a degree in chemistry. Peirce was a difficult man, who found it hard to get on with others—university authorities in particular. Though his intellectual stature and integrity were recognized he never built a university career; he gave occasional series of philosophical lectures at Harvard, and from 1879 to 1884 was lecturer in logic at Johns Hopkins. In 1887 he inherited a small bequest and retired to Milford, Pennsylvania, where he lived and died in considerable poverty and isolation.

As a philosopher he had wonderful gifts. He was a lucid, succinct, and lively writer. He had great scientific and mathematical ability; and a brilliant feeling for history, particularly the history of science and philosophy. He became very interested in logic and made important technical advances in the theory of relations. This logical interest was one of the things which led him to his long-lasting and profound interest in the medieval scholastics. One might say that he was part of the 19th century's Gothic revival. What he particularly admired in the philosophers of the Middle Ages was their realism about general concepts—which Mill had dismissed as dead—and (like other Gothic revivalists, and with the idealists) their innocence of the individualism of the bourgeois.

Peirce draws wide connexions between nominalism, individualism, and both 'sensationalism' and 'materialism'. In contrast, the philosophy of thought and, in particular, of science which he sought to develop was always anti-nominalistic and social. His kinship with the Middle Ages is clear in a passage such as this:

if anyone wishes to know what a scholastic commentary is like, and what the tone of thought in it is, he has only to contemplate a Gothic cathedral. . . . Nothing is more striking in either of the great intellectual products of that age, than the complete absence of self-conceit on the part of the artist or philosopher. That anything of value can be added to his sacred and catholic work by its having the smack of individuality about it, is what he has never conceived. His work is not designed to embody *his* ideas, but the universal truth . . . there is nothing in which the scholastic philosophy and the Gothic architecture resemble one another more than in the gradually increasing sense of immensity which impresses the mind of the student as he learns to appreciate the real dimensions and cost of each. (P viii. 12–13)

In the 1860s Peirce, like Green (who was just three years older) was preoccupied with the Kantian point that knowledge must be expressed in judgements. Those judgements must be constituted from signs which represent something to somone in some respect; hence, Peirce thought, knowledge presupposes three irreducible categories—things constituted in experience, mentality, and abstractions; the 'It', the 'Thou', and the 'I', Peirce called them. The 'I', or Firstness, was God: for the *abstracta* in virtue of which signification is possible were universal forms in the mind of God. (The tripartite categorization would always remain with Peirce, being later called 'Thirdness', 'Secondness', and 'Firstness', but its significance was repeatedly and thoroughly transformed. Firstness became Felt Quality, Secondness, External Reaction, Thirdness, Habitual Law. But the large and fascinating topic of Peirce's speculative metaphysics, a major part of his thought, in which chance, evolution, faith, and objective idealism are intertwined cannot be further pursued here.)

It was in this framework that Peirce sought a phenomenalist analysis of the objectively real. In some ways his idea is cognate to Mill's permanent possibilities of sensation. But there are vital differences. Peirce's view denied the possibility of any reality which transcended experience. But it allowed the reality of generals. It allowed that methods of science encompass 'abduction', or 'retroduction'—that is, hypothetical reasoning —as well as induction. And it made experience and enquiry intersubjective. There is a *community* of enquiry. Individual thought itself is only internal dialogue, presupposing standards and norms for discourse embodied in a community.

We can follow the connexion between phenomenalism, Peirce's notion of the real, and his realism about universals, as it emerges in his important critical review of a new edition of Berkeley's works. (The same edition, incidentally, which was by Fraser, was also reviewed by Mill; the two reviews appearing in the *North American Review* and the *Fortnightly Review*, in October and November of 1871 respectively.) 'Are universals real?', Peirce asks:

We have only to stop and consider a moment what was meant by the word *real*, when the whole issue soon becomes apparent. . . . The real is that which is not whatever we happen to think it, but is unaffected by what we may think of it . . . (P viii. 15)

This is reminiscent of Mill's invocation of the Kantian notion of Perdurability (p. 58 above). Peirce now suggests that 'there are two widely separated points of view, from which *reality*, as just defined, may be regarded'. On the first view the idea of the real, of something independent of our thought which constrains it, is equated with the idea of a thing existing out of the mind, which constrains our sensations and by means of them our thoughts. From this point of view, he thinks, in which reality is equated with externality, 'it is clear that the nominalistic answer must be given to the question concerning universals'.

But the other conception of reality, the 'realist conception, if less familiar, is even more natural and obvious'. It holds that the real is that on which opinion finally converges. Peirce explains that the 'catholic consent which constitutes the truth is by no means limited to men in this earthly life or to the human race, but extends to the whole communion of minds to which we belong, including some probably whose senses are very different from ours' (P viii. 18). Final convergence captures the core notion of Perdurability just as well as Externality does.

This final opinion, then, is independent, not indeed of thought in general, but of all that is arbitrary or individual in thought; is quite independent of how you, or I, or any number of men think. Everything, therefore, which will be thought to exist in the final opinion is real, and nothing else. (P viii. 17)

The resulting theory of reality is 'instantly fatal to the idea of a thing in itself—a thing existing independently of all relation to the mind's conception of it'. For the real is just what all minds arrive at as coherently ordering their diverse experience. But the theory is also 'inevitably realistic',

because general conceptions enter into all judgements, and therefore into true opinions. Consequently a thing in the general is as real as in the concrete. It is perfectly true that all white things have whiteness in them, for that is only saying, in another form of words, that all white things are white; but since it is true that real things possess whiteness, whiteness is real. It is a real which only exists by virtue of an act of thought knowing it, but that thought is not an arbitrary or accidental one dependent on any idiosyncracies, but one which will hold in the final opinion. (P viii. 18)

This argument of Peirce's remains classical. (He also presents it elsewhere, for example, in 'What Pragmatism is', (P v. 287–8).) We earlier, in discussing Green and Bradley, said that phenomenalism entails concept-empiricism, and that, in turn, a denial of the doctrine Mill calls 'Realism', the doctrine that concepts are both objectively real and known independently of experience, that is, known non-phenomenally. Now we see Peirce *using* phenomenalism, in combination with the pragmatist notion of reality, precisely to deduce the reality of concepts—in a way which in no way militates against concept-empiricism, since he does not claim that concepts are known by a non-phenomenal faculty of intuition.

But the foundation which would legitimate this conception of the real had not yet been fully laid. In 1871 Peirce started one of those small discussion groups which have always been so important for innovation in philosophy. Its members were Peirce himself, William James, Chauncey Wright, Oliver Wendell Holmes, and Nicholas St John Green:

a knot of us young men in Old Cambridge, calling ourselves, half-ironically, half-defiantly, 'The Metaphysical Club'—for agnosticism was then riding its high horse, and was frowning superbly upon all metaphysics . . .

St John Green was a lawyer and disciple of Bentham who

often urged the importance of applying Bain's definition of belief as 'that upon which a man is prepared to act'. From this definition, pragmatism is scarce more than a corollary; . . . I drew up a paper expressing some of the opinions that I had been urging all along under the name of pragmatism. This paper was received with such unlooked-for kindness, that I was encouraged, some half-dozen years later . . . to insert it, somewhat expanded, in the *Popular Science Monthly* for November, 1877 and January, 1878. (P v. 7–8)

What he inserted was the 'Fixation of Belief' and 'How to Make our Ideas Clear', the first two of six famous papers which appeared in *Popular Science Monthly* in 1877 and 1878.

Alexander Bain was a friend and close associate of Mill's. His definition of belief, connecting it with the disposition to act, was an attempt to solve a problem which had caused considerable difficulty to the associationists—the problem of what converts ideas which are associated, however strongly, into a *judgement*. The importance of the problem is recognized, and Bain's solution to it treated sympathetically, in Mill's review of *The Emotions and the Will* (1859) (the book in which Bain makes his proposal). We have also seen the tendency in Mill's *System of Logic* to treat a general belief as a conditional expectation, or a standing preparedness to infer, and, in the *Examination*, to adopt a functional view of the concept of an object.

But it is Peirce who makes the step of connecting the dispositional view of beliefs with what he calls a theory of meaning—by basing his account of what it is to possess the concept of a type of object, or a property of an object, on the dispositional view of belief. To have such a concept is to have a set of habits of inference involving that object, expectations about its behaviour; 'our idea of anything *is* our idea of its sensible effects' (P v. 258). This new view of the concept of an object was also facilitated for Peirce by his development of a logic of relations; that made it plausible to think of relations between objects—their interactions and effects on each other— as being just as real as their qualities, and indeed to analyse those qualities in terms of relations, rather than the other way round. A substance is hard, for example, if many other substances fail to scratch it. Peirce's general rule is:

consider what effects, that might conceivably have practical bearings, we conceive the object of our conception to have. Then, our conception of these effects is the whole of our conception of the object . . . (P v. 258)

there is no distinction of meaning so fine as to consist in anything but a possible difference of practice. (P v. 257)

This rule is from 'How to Make our Ideas Clear', of 1878. He held to it throughout his life, keeping up the search for decisive arguments for it. An alternative formulation, from more than twenty-five years later, is:

The entire intellectual purport of any symbol consists in the total of all general modes of rational conduct which, conditionally upon all the possible different circumstances and desires, would ensue upon the acceptance of the symbol. (P v. 293)

This account of meaning and concepts, applied to the concept of reality itself, provides an argument for Peirce's theory of the real. To say that a conception stands for something real just is to commit oneself to holding that enquirers who sought stable practices of inference—*and used the methods of science*—would inevitably converge on that conception of it. For those effects on enquirers *are* the observable effects of being real. Note that the argument does not force a *definition* of 'real', or 'true', in terms of ideal convergence—with all the difficulties such a definition entails. This is because pragmatism is a method of clarifying concepts by the norms which constitute them, not a recipe for analytic definitions. The argument simply identifies a norm governing use of 'true' (or 'real')—to *hold* something true is to commit oneself to holding that ideal enquirers would converge on it.

However, a pressing question arises—particularly when we remember that Peirce includes the method of hypothesis among the methods of science. We saw in the last chapter that Mill rejected that method as an independent mode of discovering truth, on the grounds that more than one hypothesis could account for all the data. What guarantee is there that enquirers using the methods of science will indeed converge on the same results? If there is none, how can we ever be justified in holding that an opinion 'is fated to be ultimately agreed to by all who investigate' (P v. 268), and thus, ever justified in holding it true?

Once he admitted that the notion of a universe within which scientific methods did not guarantee convergence was not self-contradictory, Peirce had to face this problem. He sought ways of solving it by appealing to the idea that the universe itself was in process of evolution, and that the logic of that process could be thought of as corresponding to the logic of scientific enquiry. Another challenge he faced was to give an account of what it is for a possibility to be real. For subjunctive conditionals, which are appealed to when we analyse the concept of an object into the observable effects it would have in a certain possible cir-cumstance, or when we commit ourselves to holding that scien-tific enquirers would finally reach a particular result if they applied themselves to a question, express 'permanent possi-bilities' just as the conditionals invoked in Mill's analysis of objects do. The difficulty of making sense of brute possibilities therefore arises for Peirce too, in so far as he is claiming that reality is not the thing-in-itself which categorically *underlies* these possibilities of experience and gives rise to them—but that it is *constituted* by them. But of course Peirce does not approach this problem with Mill's nominalist assumptions.

To give any adequate idea of Peirce's bold and extraordinary attempts to deal with these questions is impossible here. Nei-ther question is factitious; both remain central in philosophy. The first problem in particular, that of reconciling a pragmatist conception of truth with the possibility that evidence under-determines theory, remains crucial for any philosopher who is attracted to something like the pragmatist conception of truth and yet is unconvinced by attempts to rule out in advance the possibility that there is a plurality of optimal theories of the world. It seems he is forced either to instrumentalism about science, or to relativism about truth. We shall take up the issue again in Chapter 5, when we come to the Vienna Circle.

Peirce and William James (1842–1910) were as different in their personalities as Green and Bradley. In each case there was a puritanism, a dedication to serious sustained argument, in the older man that the younger seemed to lack. 'Peirce was above all a logician,' said John Dewey, whereas James' interest was in the human significance of philosophical questions. The real difference is that James did not give undisputed sover-eignty to reason, any more than Bradley or Nietzsche did. Peirce dismissed all 'methods' of fixing belief other than the scientific method. But Nietzsche transferred sovereignty to the will to power, James to the will to believe. In Bradley the liberation from reason takes the form of a mysticism of Experience; in James, of a certain genial or even at times farcical playfulness, a tendency to see philosophy and philosophers from sideways on, from the psychological point of view, and an openness to the interplay of thoughts and feelings or wishes which produces his notorious theory of truth.

William James was born in New York, the elder brother of the novelist Henry James. His father, Henry James Sr., was a Swedenborgian. William attended schools in New York, Paris, Boulogne, Rhode Island, Geneva, Bonn. Like John Stuart Mill he suffered a mental crisis in his twenties which centred on the problem of free will. In 1880 he became Professor of Philosophy at Harvard; but he was as much a psychologist as a philosopher. One of his happiest and best-known insights was that very perceptive distinction between tough and tender-minded people and their philosophies.

It was James who made Peirce's pragmatism famous, by adapting it to his own purposes and giving a set of lectures on its implications for life (*Pragmatism*, 1907, delivered at the

Lowell Institute in Boston; these were the lectures published with the dedication to Mill). But we shall begin by considering James's 'radical empiricism'.

He gives this doctrine its name in the preface of his book *The Will to Believe* (1897). In the preface of another collection of essays, of 1909, *The Meaning of Truth*, he says that radical empiricism consists of a postulate, a statement of fact, and a generalized conclusion. The postulate is that:

the only things that shall be debateable among philosophers shall be things definable in terms drawn from experience. (Jp 172)

'Things of an unexperienceable nature may exist ad libitum', he somewhat formally concedes—for in fact it turns out that he is unambiguously committed to strong phenomenalism. The statement of fact is that:

the relations between things ... are just as much matters of direct particular experience, neither more so nor less so, than the things themselves.

And the conclusion is that:

the parts of experience hold together from next to next by relations that are themselves parts of experience. The directly apprehended universe needs, in short, no extraneous, trans-empirical connective support, but possesses in its own right a concatenated or continuous structure. (Jp 173)

This strikes to the heart of Green's case against empiricism. He, says James, realized 'more than anyone else ... that knowledge *about* things was knowledge of their relations; but nothing could persuade him that our sensational life could contain any relational element' (Jpl 278). That relations *are* given in our sensational life was just what James now affirmed. In this he differed from the older empiricists, or 'sensationalists' as he called them, whose own views in this matter had been seized on by Green. (Though they too, James thought, had accepted the experiential givenness of at least some relations, such as similarity and distinctness.) But with 'intellectualists' like Green, who thought that relations could be known only through an 'Actus Purus of Thought, Intellect, or Reason, all written in capitals' (Jpr i. 245), he disagreed completely.

After Green had turned back the older empiricists' weapons on themselves, it was obviously opportune for a new empiricist to come along and question whether those weapons were at all essential to empiricism. Yet what is finally at stake is not easy to see. In opposition to an atomistic view of experience James wanted to affirm its continuity. (The mathematical concept of continuity and its general metaphysical significance was also a great preoccupation of Peirce's.) In the *Principles of Psychology* James quotes Alexander Bain:

The stream of thought is not a continuous current, but a series of distinct ideas, more or less rapid in their succession. (Jpr i. 245n.)

He disagrees, and if his point is phenomenological he is on firm ground. (If Bain is not doing bad phenomenology, what *is* he doing?) The causal, spatial, and temporal relations indicated by such particles as *because*, *against*, *from*, *toward*, *through*, *before*, *after*, are, he holds, phenomenologically given in experiences of continuous transition. Why then should their concepts not be generated from experience in any sense in which the concept of a colour is?

In the same vein he quotes Hume's famous remark that:

All our distinct perceptions are distinct existences, and ... the mind never perceives any real connection among distinct existences. (Je 103)

Epistemology and psychology here pass each other by, true though it is that Hume himself did not labour to distinguish them. The epistemological point, which is of great importance for empiricism, is that the *necessity* of causal connexions cannot be observed. That is quite consistent with it being true, in a psychological sense, that we have 'impressions' of a distinctive sort when we observe some kinds of singular sequences. It is also consistent with it being true that our concept of causal necessitation *originates* in these impressions. On the other hand, if the questions at stake are what it is to *possess* any general concepts at all, or how we can have knowledge—and those are the essential questions in Green's Kantian critique of naturalism—then James has not touched them. In short, though it is clear that questions about the reality and givenness of relations were much in the air, it is far from clear that the questions Green, Bradley, Peirce, and James are talking about are the same questions.

Apart from affirming the phenomenological continuity of experience, radical empiricism at first sight adds nothing further to strong phenomenalism. But in fact it transmutes that doctrine into something strange and new—'neutral monism', a thesis which had remarkable influence in this period and into the early twentieth century. Like so much else it is already adumbrated by Peirce. In his review of Berkeley he derives it from his realism:

The realist will hold that the very same objects which are immediately present in our minds in experience really exist just as they are experienced out of the mind; that is, he will maintain a doctrine of immediate perception. He will not, therefore, sunder existence out of the mind and being in the mind as two wholly improportionable modes. . . . For he does not think of the mind as a receptacle, which if a thing is in, it ceases to be out of. To make a distinction between the true conception of a thing and the thing itself is, he will say, only to regard one and the same thing from two different points of view; for the immediate object of thought in a true judgement *is* the reality. (P viii. 19)

This doctrine as developed by James teaches that the division between mental and physical is a purely functional one. There is just 'one primal stuff or material in the world, a stuff of which everything is composed'. James calls it 'pure experience':

thoughts and things are absolutely homogeneous as to their material, and . . . their opposition is only one of relation and of function. There is not thought-stuff different from thing-stuff, . . . but the same identical piece of 'pure experience' (which was the name I gave to the *materia prima* of everything) can stand alternately for a 'fact of consciousness' or for a physical reality, according as it is taken in one context or in another. (Je 69)

when we call an experience 'conscious', that does not mean that it is suffused throughout with a peculiar modality of being ('psychic' being) as stained glass may be suffused with light, but rather that it stands in certain determinate relations to other portions of experience extraneous to itself. These form one peculiar 'context' for it; while, taken in another context of experiences, we class it as a fact in the physical world. (Je 61)

This is to apply the new freedom afforded by full recognition of relations with a vengeance! The items called 'pure experiences' are mental or physical only under a relation. When picked out by one subclass of their relations to other items, they are characterized as mental states of an ego. When picked out by another subclass of their relations, to another class of items, they are characterized as a physical thing or attribute. The distinction of representing 'idea' and represented 'thing' is functional: knowing consists in 'a particular sort of relation towards one another into which portions of pure experience may enter'.

*And so too for the division between subject and object.* That this itself is simply a functional distinction, of no ultimate ontological significance, is the distinctive contribution of neutral monism, for it offers a solution, however bizarre, to two fundamental questions—the relation between subject and objective world, and the relation between distinct subjects and their experiences.

James thinks the philosophy of perception has been dogged by 'the paradox that what is evidently one reality should be in two places at once, both in outer space and in a person's mind'. But he refuses the solution offered by representative theories of perception, for 'they violate the reader's sense of life, which knows no intervening mental image but seems to see the room and the book immediately just as they physically exist'. Radical empiricism, he says, 'has in fact more affinity with natural realism than with the view of Berkeley or Mill'. He follows here Peirce's comment in the passage quoted above, in which Peirce says that the realist adopts a doctrine of immediate perception.

It is worth trying to see where the contrast lies. Berkeley himself claimed to save natural realism; he too held that we 'immediately perceive' objects. Objects are not on his view constructs, possibilities of sensation, as in Mill (though he does flirt with this view in his private Commentaries). They are made up of ideas—when not perceived by finite human minds they are perceived by God. Moreover, supposedly distinct minds in some sense nevertheless perceive the same idea/object, and so must somehow finitely partake of the Divine mind. But Berkeley did not abolish the distinction between a substantive self and the ideas it knows; he took the latter to be states of the former— so here there is a clear-cut difference between him and neutral monism.

Mill on the other hand at least tends to dismiss the reality of a substantive self, though we saw that he leaves the problem unresolved. But for him it seems that the streams of consciousness constituting separate minds are fully distinct; there is no one item of which two different minds can be immediately aware, or which can figure in two separate streams of consciousness. The pressure to escape such a conclusion is obvious. James asserts that the very same experience can occur at two minds:

Can we see, then, any way in which a unit of pure experience might enter into and figure in two diverse streams of consciousness without turning itself into the two units which, on our hypothesis, it must not be? (Je 63)

It is, indeed, 'mine' only as it is felt as mine, and 'yours' only as it is felt as yours. But it is felt as neither *by itself*, but only when 'owned' by our two several remembering experiences, just as one undivided estate is owned by several heirs. (Je 66)

It is worth stressing—given the extraordinariness, even unintelligibility, of this doctrine—how widespread it was and how inevitable it seemed. We shall see below that it is shared by Mach. It is also true that James's Pure Experience has a very striking resemblance to Bradley's Absolute Experience. He regards it as 'the immediate flux of life which furnishes the material to our later reflection with its conceptual categories' (Je 46). And he emphasizes that

It is only virtually or potentially either object or subject as yet. For the time being it is plain unqualified actuality or existence, a simple *that*. (Je 13)

Bradley similarly affirms that in immediate experience there is no distinction between my awareness and that of which it is aware. There is an immediate feeling, a knowing and being in one, with which knowledge begins ... (BRk 40)

'Nothing bars you', James wrote to Bradley, 'from believing in our humanism bag and baggage—you need only throw your absolute round it ... ' (Jm 320). 'Humanism'—the term was F. C. S. Schiller's—was used by James to refer to his own pragmatist and coherentist neutral monism. He wrote again to Bradley that they differed only on the Absolute, 'and surely such a trifle as that is not a thing for two gentlemen to be parted by'. When Bradley rebuffed these irenic advances, James was hurt. For they *were* irenic, not ironic. Unfortunately the reconciling spirit, so strong in James, called for an interpretation of pragmatic truth which very few of James's allies, let alone his opponents, could go along with.

In his lectures on pragmatism James generously acknowledges his debt to Peirce. But when he has settled into the driving-seat of Peirce's revolutionary vehicle he slams down gleefully on the accelerator and streaks off into wild country. (There are some post-modernists on whom pragmatism's dizzying insights have recently had the same effect.) The great attraction of pragmatism for James is its promise of mediating between tough- and tender-mindedness; it will allow him to find pragmatic truth in metaphysical and religious doctrines yearned after by the tender-minded, while still holding to the doctrine of the tough.

But the promise arises only through a development in the theory of truth which is not at all Peircean, though it does start from Peirce's notion of belief as the satisfying resolution of doubt. For James, truth is *whatever* provides satisfaction—James means emotional, as well as intellectual, satisfaction—to the *individual*. Since what satisfies can change, truth itself can change—it is plural and mutable.

To Peirce this view of truth was 'suicidal'. It falls into individualism. To make truth mutable is to infect pragmatism with 'seeds of death'. His own view, he pointed out, was that though 'Truth consists in satisfaction, it cannot be any actual satisfaction, but must be the satisfaction which *would* ultimately be found if the inquiry were pushed to its ultimate and indefeasible isssue' (P vi. 331).

Nor did he think it possible to reach finally satisfying convergence by any means other than scientific reasoning. True pragmatism was a cleansing and revitalizing instrument which showed that 'almost every proposition of ontological metaphysics is either meaningless gibberish ... or else is downright absurd' (P v. 282)—though by this he did not mean to rule out the speculative, logic-and-science based cosmology which he himself sought. After 1905 he called his doctrine 'Pragmaticism', to distinguish it from that of James.

Of course we have seen the difficulties in Peirce's own view. Does anything guarantee ideal convergence, and can that notion in any case be given pragmatic meaning? In fact James does not quite eliminate the Peircean notion of 'absolute' or 'abstract' truth:

if you take the satisfactoriness concretely, as something felt by you now, and if, by truth, you mean truth taken abstractly and verified in the long run, you cannot make them equate, for it is notorious that the temporarily satisfactory is often false. Yet at each and every concrete moment truth for each man is what that man 'troweth' at that moment with the maximum of satisfaction to himself; and similarly, abstract truth, truth verified in the long run, and abstract satisfactoriness, long-run satisfactoriness, coincide. (Jp 220)

This passage is an example of how difficult it is to make out quite what James means. He says that truth can be 'taken' concretely or abstractly, but he generally emphasizes the concrete notion. Yet how it can still be possible to 'take' truth concretely —when the intelligibility of abstract truth has been conceded, and without mere verbal evasion—is obscure.

On either reading however, abstract or concrete, one can let the satisfactoriness with which truth is identified include satisfaction of all kinds—emotional as well as intellectual. On this James is clear. He does not try to idealize or refine the inclusive notion of satisfaction in any way. He wants to make it as inclusive as possible. In *all* beliefs it is the *widest* notion of satisfaction that determines truth. By this conception he hopes to mediate between 'materialism, which may better be called naturalism and '"theism", or what in a wider sense may be termed "spiritualism"'' (Jp 49).

Since the 'actually experienced world' is the same on either view it seems, at first, that the pragmatist principle dismisses the dispute between them as verbal. But in practice, they produce wholly different outlooks on life; theism giving hope of, and striving towards, an eternal moral order. It is the more satisfactory, because the more useful for life:

On pragmatistic principles, if the hypothesis of God works satisfactorily in the widest sense of the word, it is 'true'. (Jp 143)

What particular theology one should adopt, however, will also turn pragmatically on which provides the widest satisfaction. For James, it will be a 'pluralistic and moralistic religion', between 'the two extremes of crude naturalism on the one hand and transcendental absolutism on the other' (P 144).

All of this is attractive to some, outrageous, or just plain impossible, however attractive, to others. The trouble is that what James gives with one hand he takes away with another. So long as his thesis is that the emotional and intellectual strands of satisfaction are inextricably intertwined, it is challenging and suggestive to claim that both enter into the determination of truth. But we have just seen, in the debate between naturalism and spiritualism, that James himself extricates them.

How can spiritualism offer an emotional satisfaction that naturalism fails to supply, if intellectually the two are identical? Of course if one overcame that problem, it would immediately become a real question what justifies belief in the former. W. K. Clifford, in a paper of 1877 entitled 'The Ethics of Belief', argued that it was morally wrong to hold beliefs without intellectual warrant. James's reply was that when an option between beliefs was 'live', 'forced', and 'momentous', then it was proper and inevitable to opt on emotional grounds. But there is an option in the first place only if there are two distinct beliefs; to mark the difference between them *just* by their differing emotional satisfactions is to turn the option into a mystery.

This is not to dispute the interest of James's inclusive notion of satisfaction; only his way of pressing it into service in defence of spiritualism. What is really impressive is the wonderful feeling for religious experience which James shows in his writings; and the evident liveness, forcefulness, and momentousness the religious question had for him and his contemporaries—rather than his breezy effort to resolve it.

Meanwhile scientists interested in methodology were also putting their weight behind phenomenalist or outright positivist interpretations of science. Among them too (in Germany, France, and Britain) it became something of an orthodoxy that scientific knowledge is exclusively of phenomena and of correlations between them. Scientific explanation and causal law were reduced to descriptions of regularity, or denied.

This could be a doctrine restricted to science; it need not be held of knowledge in general. Such was the position of Pierre Duhem, a French physicist, who combined a phenomenalist view of scientific knowledge with Catholic metaphysics. (He is also known for his emphasis on the point that evidence underdetermines theory—which, as we noticed in Chapter 2, can easily be given an instrumentalist twist.) But even if phenomenalism was adopted overall and not only as an epistemology of science, it need not be strong phenomenalism. And again a Kantian could be a strong phenomenalist overall at the empirical level, while still endorsing things-in-themselves transcendentally. These latter two positions shaded into each other, for Kant's distinction of the transcendental and the empirical is decidedly elusive— neo-Kantian influences of the resulting rather ambiguous kind were strong.

One may indeed wonder how to distinguish positivism from neo-Kantianism. It is not easy to reach an answer, certainly not without longer discussion than is possible here. One point to remember is that positivism is an intellectual tradition with cultural and political dimensions, and not just a strictly epistemological thesis. (This is why, for example, one hesitates to call Mill a positivist, even though his purely epistemological positions are entirely positivistic. He came to have strong reservations about Comte, and particularly about the illiberal tendencies of the early positivists—see his *Auguste Comte and Positivism*.)

The word 'positivism' is Comte's, and for him it was associated with a three-stage theory of intellectual evolution; according to which thought passes historically from religious postulates to metaphysical ones, and, finally, to the stage of positive knowledge—in which *all* postulates as to what underlies the phenomena are abandoned and enquiry is restricted to establishing phenomenal correlations. (This grand historical picture greatly impressed Mill.) Comte was not a strong phenomenalist; he simply believed that it was definitively unwarranted to indulge in any speculation at all about the underlying, real nature of things.

One may suggest that positivism rejects any notion of the synthetic a priori, and rejects any transcendental foundation for such a notion. Both points are true of nineteenth-century positivists. Perhaps the key point, though, is the second. For when we come to the logical positivists in Chapter 5 we shall see that though they too rejected both, they so reinterpreted the notion of analyticity that it becomes debatable whether they really were rejecting the synthetic a priori, or only the transcendental underpinnings Kant provides for it.

It is also true that though Comte was not a strong phenomenalist, positivism in the later part of the century certainly was strong phenomenalist, and strong phenomenalist about all (non-verbal, non-analytic) knowledge, not just about science. Or better, it held that all genuine knowledge *was* scientific knowledge. This of course distinguishes it from someone like Bradley, who in other respects shared so many *fin-de-siècle* themes with it. But it is not in itself enough to make one a *positivist*, since one can combine the view that science provides the only genuine knowledge with a non-positivistic view of science.

Another way of characterizing *fin-de-siècle* positivism is by the tenet that the real or factual is the observable—or better, the 'given'. (This distinguishes it from Peirce, in view of his theory of the real.) For Comte, facts were *positive* if verifiable by observation and induction. For *fin-de-siècle* positivism there *are* only such facts and they are facts about the 'given'. But here too there remain possibilities of variation, depending on what interpretation a positivist gives of 'given'. Are facts which would have been observable at spatio-temporal locations inaccessible to the enquirer, 'given'?

To a neutral monist, the given is pure experience. Combine this with the positivist view that the real is the given, and the enquirer becomes a fictional construct. (In contrast, on the Peirce/James account of 'real', there is no need to regard the enquirer as *fictional*.) So for *fin-de-siècle* positivism—which was neutral-monist—what is 'observable' to a particular 'enquirer' becomes a subordinate question of no ontological significance. There is also another way in which it differs from earlier positivism, and this brings it closer to neo-Kantianism: it lays great emphasis on how much the fabric of belief is *constructed*, by free hypothesis, rather than 'positively' given or directly generalized from the given. In this respect it deserved the name 'empirio-criticism', given to it by one of its proponents, Richard Avenarius.

One remaining point to be emphasized is that the tradition of positivism proper was always naturalistic or, in the popular sense we have noticed, 'materialist'. Of course there is a real question about the compatibility of positivism with naturalism, exploited by such critics as Green. (It was, curiously, also what led to Lenin's attack on it, from the opposite end of the spectrum, in his *Materialism and Empirio-criticism* of 1908.) But certainly the spirit of positivism is strongly anti-spiritualistic.

Positivism of the *fin de siècle* neutral-monist kind—'empirio-criticism'—was most influentially represented by Ernst Mach (1838–1916), though Richard Avenarius has often been held to be the more rigorous thinker. Mach was professor of the history and theory of inductive science at the University of Vienna from 1895 to 1901, and an important figure in Austrian public life. By training a mathematician and physicist, his interests in science itself, as well as in its logic, history, and applications, were polymathically wide. As a philosopher he was penetrating and vivid, though not rigorous; he described himself as a 'weekend huntsman' (*Sonntagsjäger*) for philosophical quarry, and he insisted that there was '*no* Machian philosophy, but at most a scientific methodology and a psychology of knowledge'.

Mach's best-known statement of his view is in his *Analysis of Sensations* of 1886. 'The world consists only of our sensations' (Ma 12), or as he elsewhere puts it, 'Nature is composed of sensations as its elements' (Ms 579). These are the 'colors, sounds, temperatures, pressures, spaces, times and so forth' (Me 209) which are immediately given to us in experience. Body and soul are alike economical constructs. The ego is not a transcendental principle of unity; its only unity is an 'ideal mental-economical' one.

He sometimes prefers to speak simply of elements, and not 'sensations, nor phenomena, because in either term an arbitrary, one-sided theory is embodied' (Me 209). There *is* reason for thinking of them as sensations, he says, but it is not that they are, in their very essence, states of a subject of experience. For Mach as for James, the distinction between subject and object, and with it the distinction between objective sensible quality and sensation understood as a mental state, is simply functional. What is true though is that the elements as a whole have a specific 'functional dependence' on a particular subset within them—namely those which constitute the ideal unity I call 'my' body; it is this dependence that provides the only objective basis for thinking of them as sensations. For when I am doing psychology I am interested in the laws which constitute that dependence. But when I am doing physics I am considering functional relations which can be discovered to obtain between ideal, thought-economical unities in general—not just my body but all material bodies. As physicists,

we investigate the change of the red colour of a body as produced by a change of illumination. But the moment we consider the special influence on the red of the elements constituting our body, outlined by the well-known perspective with head invisible, we are at work in the domain of physiological psychology. We close our eyes, and the red together with the whole visible world disappears. There exists, thus, in the perspective field of every sense a portion which exercises on all the rest a different and more powerful influence than the rest upon one another. With this, however *all* is said. In the light of this remark, we call *all* elements, in so far as we regard them as dependent on this special part (our body), *sensations*. That the world is our sensation, in this sense, cannot be questioned. (Me 209–10)

We are able to form the notion of object or substance only because we find stable relationships in experience. 'All our efforts would be futile if we found nothing permanent in the varied changes of things' (Me 199).

Take sodium. When warmed, the white, silvery, mass becomes a liquid, which, when the heat is increased and the air shut out, is transformed into a violet vapor, and on the heat being still more increased glows with a yellow light. If the name sodium is still retained, it is because of the continuous character of the transitions and from a necessary instinct of economy. By condensing the vapor, the white metal may be made to reappear. Indeed, even after the metal is thrown into water and has passed into sodium hydroxide, the vanished properties may by skilful treatment still be made to reapppear; just as a moving body which has passed behind a column and is lost to view for a moment may make its appearance after a time. It is unquestionably very convenient always to have ready the name and thought for a group of properties wherever that group by any possibility can appear. But more than a compendious economical symbol, that name and thought is not. (Me 202)

Some of the turns of phrase which I have quoted already indicate the other main thrust in Mach's philosophy: his 'economical' view of science—in general, of all generalizing thought. As with Comte and Mill—or Marx—*homo faber*, the historically evolving concrete agent of his own history, takes centre stage. Much of *The Science of Mechanics* (1883) is a history of the evolution of science; the concrete origins of science in 'the manual arts' are emphasized, and an effort is made to demystify false abstraction and 'misplaced rigour'. Alleged demonstrative proofs in mechanics rest on 'half-forgotten, largely unappreciated' experiences—'instinctive experiences' which are mistaken for a priori knowledge.

Physics is experience, arranged in economical order' (Me 197). This is from an address entitled 'The Economical Nature of Physical Inquiry', given before the Imperial Academy of Sciences, in Vienna in 1882. Laws summarize past experiences and licence prediction. They 'disburden' memory—examples of this disburdening are the gravitational constant, or the indices of refraction—and facilitate the communication of experience. They are 'succint directions, frequently involving subordinate directions, for the employment of economically classified experiences, ready for use' (Me 204). And the greatest example of economy of thought, of the accumulation of many individuals' experiences and economies, is mathematics.

All of this is strikingly reminiscent of Mill on general propositions, 'ratiocination', and the history of the 'inductive process'. Mach's economical conception of science pushes on this historical-evolutionary and a posteriori approach, strengthening it by placing it in the context of Darwinian, and not merely cultural, evolution, and of a hypothetical, not merely inductivist, view of the unity of science. The simplifying and unifying structure of science as a whole is a device of economy— driving it towards a unitary conception of the world.

'Measurement . . . is the definition of one phenomenon by another (standard) phenomenon' (Me 206 n.), as when distances are laid off against a rigid standard rod, or durations against a repeating standard event, such as a pendulum swing or a planetary rotation. 'For practical reasons we should select that event which best served us as the *simplest* common measure of others' (Me 205 n.). The great source of misconception in philosophy is the tendency to reify these economical devices. This is how we arrive at the 'notion of a substance distinct from its attributes, of a thing-in-itself':

our sensations are regarded merely as symbols or indications of the properties of the thing-in-itself. But it would be much better to say that bodies or things are compendious mental symbols for groups of sensations—symbols that do not exist outside of thought. (Me 200–1)

Just as we reify communication-friendly conventions of speech into things in themselves, and concepts like force into anthropomorphic agencies, so we reify spatial and temporal relations into absolute properties. Like Berkeley before him, Mach criticizes Newton's notions of absolute space and time. Motion must always be understood in relation to a materially defined frame of reference; the law of inertia (that a body acted on by no force moves at a constant speed in a straight line), together with laws determining accelerations, should be considered a definition of force. (Peirce produced a similar pragmatist analysis of the concept of force in 'How to Make our Ideas Clear'.)

Theories also extend the economy of thought: they introduce suggestive analogies or pictures, which we are then inclined to reify. But their use is in no way dependent on such reification. Is heat, for example, a substance or a motion? Neither picture is fully supported by the phenomena, both may be heuristically valuable.

So the empirio-critics, like the pragmatists, take the economical view of science (and common sense) much further than Mill. In effect Mill already saw general statements, and physical objects, as successive layers in the economy of thought. These later analysts of science allow the introduction of such economies *wherever* they are useful, and not just where they can be inductively 'proved'. Admittedly, Mill himself goes far in that instrumentalist direction when he discusses hypotheses. But he retains a distinction between generalizations which can be proved by induction and generalizations which are heuristically useful. Mach and Peirce erase that distinction, though in different ways; for Peirce reads truth itself pragmatically. But each represents a further stage than Mill's in the critical analysis of the relation between theory and experience.

Another important scientist–philosopher, whose pedigree was as much Kantian as positivist, was Jules Henri Poincaré (1854–1912). He was a mathematician whose views on the philosophy of mathematics were strongly influenced by Kant. He held that mathematical induction is synthetic a priori; geometrical axioms however are not a priori truths—but they cannot be experimental truths either, because they are exact. They are conventions. That does not make them arbitrary, because we must choose conventions which achieve simplicity, consistency, and predictive adequacy; but they cannot be said to be true or false.

This is a noteworthy distinction. It raises interesting questions which we shall return to in Chapter 5—it is not obvious how to motivate it if one takes an economical view of *all* generalizations. In fact Poincaré makes a number of epistemological distinctions between laws. Some are conventions, to be regarded as disguised 'definitions'—a notion of definition to which we shall return. He thought the principle of inertia, which was initially experimental, had become a disguised definition of 'force', no longer falsifiable by experiment; the same applied to the law of the conservation of energy. It is also a convention that gravitation obeys Newton's law; but it is an empirical statement that gravitation is the only force acting on a particular system, like the stars.

We conduct scientific enquiry in accordance with certain *presuppositions*, of which the most important are that nature is unified—into a single causal system—and that its laws are simple. Within this framework we make hypotheses. Some are 'natural and necessary'—for example, assumptions about what is causally relevant, such as that the effects of very distant events are negligible, or about invariance, as that measuring rods are not deformed by motion. Then there are 'real generalizations' from experience, which always remain open to further testing. And there are also 'indifferent' theoretical generalizations, which are useful for calculating or as pictorial aids to thought. The rival hypotheses that matter is atomic and that it is continuous are examples of this, for nothing could establish the truth of one against the other.

Poincaré agrees with the standard positivist view that science cannot *explain* in any sense other than placing phenomena under predictively sound generalizations; but he was not a strong phenomenalist. Our sensations do in his view result from the properties of external things. His view is describable as 'structural realism': he held that though science cannot teach us what the true nature of those things is, the laws it discovers are nevertheless true reflections of the relations among them.

These Kantian themes in Poincaré do not prevent him from taking a partly instrumental and partly conventional view of hypotheses. There is, however, an obvious attraction in Mach's more thoroughgoingly holistic, 'thought-economical' and neutral-monist view. But there are also pressing questions about its coherence.

In the first place it is not obvious that the old Critical question, of how there can be knowledge without a synthetic a priori, has been laid to rest. How are we justified in adopting generalizations—whether or not they are economical—if there is no a priori base for our inductive practice? If we adopt the evolutionary view of ourselves to which both pragmatists and empirio-critics appeal, then we can argue that our inductive habits, including our preference for economy, are underwritten by the adaptive value of those habits. But the evolutionary view is itself not a priori; it is only a thought-economic device for handling sensations. So the Kantian criticism seems to have the same bite on empirio-critics as it had on Mill.

Can we derive some succour from Peirce's pragmatist theory of concepts? That tells us that to apply a concept in experience is to engage in a set of conditional expectations. But the Critical question asks what warrants us in engaging in such expectations in the first place.

Peirce also argues that the real or the true is that which ideal enquirers are fated to converge on. At first sight this may seem to provide no help either, for what we currently expect ideal enquirers to converge on—what we currently hold to be true—is always based on our experience *hitherto*. Nothing *guarantees* that these expectations will remain stable when our experience is enlarged. At this point, however, Peirce can make a distinction between fallibilism, which he endorses, and scepticism, which he rejects. Fallibilism is the view that further enquiry might lead us to reject any proposition which we currently hold true. Must it collapse into scepticism, according to which we *have* no current grounds for holding any proposition true? Peirce's pragmatism promises to show why it does not. For according to it, the fundamental norms which for us constitute ideal enquiry must have a privileged status—there will be no perspective from which to ask whether they are themselves unsound. If what we currently believe has been arrived at by applying *those* norms, then it is believed on sound grounds, even though further enquiry may overturn it. That is precisely the difference between fallibilism and scepticism.

In making the distinction and basing it in his pragmatist conception of meaning, Peirce foreshadows an answer to the Critical epistemologist which does not blandly ignore his question. From the naturalist's point of view, however, a suspicion must remain—is this answer going to boil down, after all, to the Critical philosophy in a new form? Anyone who wishes to combine pragmatism with naturalism (as Peirce did not) must lay this suspicion to rest. Can the holistic view of knowledge, which became so influential in the *fin de siècle*, be defended without idealism? What norms determine the coherence of a whole system of knowledge—what is *their* status? Peirce does not face these questions squarely; nor does Mach. Green and Bradley of course do, and they return an absolute-idealist answer. The questions will resurface with the Vienna Circle.

Another aspect of *fin de siècle* philosophy, also connected with the question of idealism, is neutral monism. In this case the difficulties of the position seem fatal. What are the relations by which the very same neutral elements or pure experiences are supposedly ordered, on the one hand into distinct minds and on the other into a world of physical objects? It seems imposible to provide a remotely intelligible answer; but if no answer can be given we are returned to Millian phenomenalism and its problems.

There is indeed a fundamental unclarity as to what pure experience *is*. James treats it as the content of consciousness, yet he also refuses to accept the act/content distinction as fundamental. But the effect of that is to reify the content of experience. (It is the cost of refusing to reify 'thought-economical fictions'.) If I sense a red patch when no red patch is there, there is a sensing-redly by me, but there is no red thing. At this point it is tempting to conjure up a neutral something which is red, and then it becomes possible to think of that something as a 'constituent' of a physical object which is red, and also as a content of a sensing by me. But there *is* no such red element. Neutral monism tries to construct the world literally out of nothing.

There is in fact in both James and Mach a strong tendency towards physicalism, which coexists uneasily with their neutral monism. It would be necessary to explore it to get a full sense of the productive and transitional incoherence which prevailed in this period in psychology and the philosophy of mind. These were seeds for the future; but there was undoubtedly something very attractive to the wider culture of the *fin de siècle* about neutral monism and about the holism of the economy of thought. The attractions overlapped with Bradley's Absolute Experience. It was not simply that a deep epistemological doctrine of the phenomenal relativity of knowledge seemed to force one into it; it also spoke to the spirit of the times. There was something liberating to that spirit in any philosophy which dissolved the self, and hard objects set against the self, into the subject-less flux of experience; just as there was also something liberating about Green's dissolution of the self into community. The attraction was felt by those with an interest in art as well as those with an interest in politics, and its root lies in revolt against that burdensome old man of the sea, the liberal-bourgeois self, with its rationally autonomous will, its moral responsibility, and its world-conquering imperative to build permanently in the hard and alien world of things.

Green's liberal idealism did not augur a new world of moralized liberalism. It was the last attempt to reconcile the old world into a new whole, before the collapse of liberalism and the explosion of modernism.

# 4

# Modernism I: Frege and Cambridge

By the end of the nineteenth century philosophical questions about the coherence of enlightenment naturalism had been well mulled over. A consensus had formed against the 'materialism' of the mid-century. Neutral monism, coherentism of various philosophical stripes, evolutionism, had all contributed to the transcending or blurring of distinctions which had previously seemed ultimate. Yet there were already signs of a shift of spiritual mood, which would bring with it a re-imposition of distinctions. The essence of it was a realist impulse, a reassertion of the world's independence of the knowing subject. And with it came a vehement reassertion of the distinctness of logic and fact, value and fact, and reason and feeling.

'Of all silly superficialities,' Bernard Bosanquet, one of the British idealists, protested, 'the opposition of feeling and logic is the silliest.' It was now destined for major revival. The polarization of reason and feeling is, in many forms, a vital strand in modernism, going far beyond philosophy. Bosanquet's comment reflected the idealist vision of logic as transcendental, a dialectical reflection which unifies the totality of feeling and thought, self and world, resolving all into aspects of the concrete universal. But in the 1900s this *fin-de-siècle* obsession with securing meaningful unity—dissolving the world into experience and infusing it with meaning—came to be rejected with scorn. It was bogus, feeble, an unclean mixing of categories. Clarity, sharpness, distinction were now what energized.

What replaced *fin-de-siècle* holism was certainly not the naturalism of mid-century which the idealists had fought. The whole debate between naturalism and idealism now fell into dust. Ditching it (not solving it) was the liberating gift of the new realism. It was linked to another and more lasting enzyme in twentieth-century philosophy—the glorious and unprecedented flowering of formal logic, the very type of logic despised by the idealists. This was a development as momentous as Kant's critique of reason had been, taking philosophy, as he had done at the beginning of the previous century, onto a wholly new level.

The modernist currents on which the flowering of logic had an effect came in two waves, which are the subject of this chapter and the next. They are often called 'analytic philosophy' and conventionally contrasted with other modernist currents called 'Continental philosophy'—the latter covers such movements as phenomenology, Heidegger, Sartre, and so on. The split between the two is really a division within modernism. Both of them are integral to modernist sensibility and thought. Both belong to its complex internal cross-currents. In the *fin de siècle* there was no such split; although earlier there had been a milder but somewhat analogous split between Anglo-French continuers of enlightenment and German philosophers of romanticism. But as modernism recedes into the past it is most doubtful whether the split will survive. It also begins to be clearer what the two sides of philosophical modernism had in common—a rejection of naturalistic ways of thinking, for example,—just as it is possible to see important things—for example, historicism and a preoccupation with the relation between man and society—that the two sides in the earlier nineteenth-century split had in common.

In reality the sources and leading agents of analytic philosophy are at least as much Continental (specifically Austrian and German) as they are Anglo-American. At this point therefore our story inevitably becomes the history of analytic modernism, rather than the history of English-language philosophy as such; but it is an important fact that the great upheavals of Depression, Nazism, and World War drove analytic modernism's most influential Austrian and German proponents into exile in the Anglophone world.

The evolution of modern logic was intertwined with other modernist themes in ways which we can only begin to disentangle. The development of ideas about experience and subjectivity, or about the sources of value, are also of great importance.

Yet it is impossible to get a feeling for twentieth-century philosophy without some grasp of what the advances in logic, semantics, and the foundations of mathematics were. Here as elsewhere, the history of twentieth-century ideas runs up against their technical difficulty and counter-intuitiveness; but some outline of the new logic must nevertheless be made. For, both as a canon and as themselves an object of philosophical reflection, modern logic and semantics bring into focus questions about language, thought, and reality as they could never be brought into focus before. They are the most important source of the idea of philosophy as pure analysis, an idea fundamental to analytic modernism.

We must start not in the Cambridge of Moore, Russell, and Wittgenstein, but in Jena with Gottlob Frege (1848–1925). He was a mathematician whose entire career was spent teaching at the university there, in the mathematics department. His life was devoted to logic and the philosophy of mathematics; his contact with philosophers was small and his engagement with the subject restricted to a narrow and specialized front. Yet he can rightly be described as the father of modern logic—and though it goes too far to call him the father of analytic philosophy too (as some have suggested), his work has been of the utmost importance for it. It greatly influenced both the groups of philosophers which we shall study in these two chapters, in Cambridge and Vienna. And in the last thirty years it has once more been scrutinized with intense care—it is certainly not possible to say that Frege's ideas have yet been fully exhausted.

Frege was two years older than Bradley, and died one year after him, but he belongs as surely to this chapter as Bradley belongs to the last. It is not merely that his innovations in logic and semantics took hold in this century; the logical realism which went with them, like the phenomenological realism of Brentano, only had its effect when the reaction against the *fin de siècle* set in.

Mill and Kant had taken syllogistic theory for granted. Such technical development as the *System of Logic* contained was in the field of inductive logic, where Mill put forward his canons of experimental enquiry. The *System of Logic* was in fact a treatise of philosophical logic and epistemology. There had been technical developments since then—by other writers, most notably Boole, who retains a place of honour in histories of logic. But the real breakthrough for modern logic came with the publication of Frege's *Begriffsschrift in* 1879—'the most important date in the history of the subject', a historian of logic has called it.

The translated full title of the work is *Conceptual Notation: A Formula Language of Pure Thought Modelled upon the Formula Language of Arithmetic*. Frege invents a new formal language designed specifically for purposes of logical analysis. He further provides, using this language, a complete statement of the modern logic of sentences and predicates, treated as a formal system, together with a meta-logical examination of it.

The new notation is to express only the 'conceptual contents' (*begriffliche Inhalte*) of assertions. It is to be like a microscope, inflexible but precise. Frege's main objective is to use it for a completely rigorous analysis of mathematical reasoning. But he hopes it will have a more general philosophical use:

If it is a task of philosophy to break the power of the word over the human mind . . . then my 'conceptual notation', further developed for these purposes, can become a useful tool for philosophers. (Fb 106)

Rarely has a modest ambition been more triumphantly fulfilled.

Frege begins by distinguishing sharply, as Mill did, between an assertion (he calls it a 'judgement') and its content. But unlike Mill, he highlights the crucial point that assertoric contents can occur *unasserted* in discourse. He expresses an assertion by writing the symbol

$$\vdash\!\!\!\!\!-----$$

to the left of the symbol which give the content of the assertion. If the vertical stroke (the assertion stroke) is omitted, we are to understand that the assertoric content (which we shall henceforth call the *proposition*—Frege's term is *Gedanke*, 'thought') is expressed without being asserted. Thus

$$-----A$$

expresses the proposition that *A*, without *asserting* that *A*.

Frege now introduces a very neat notation for conditional propositions. Where *A* and *B* are propositions, there are, he says, four possibilities:

(1) *A* is affirmed and *B* is affirmed.
(2) *A* is affirmed and *B* is denied.
(3) *A* is denied and *B* is affirmed.
(4) *A* is denied and *B* is denied.

The notation

expresses the assertion that 'the third of these possibilities does not occur, but one of the other three does.' Omission of the initial vertical stroke expresses the equivalent proposition. The notation is evidently extendible to express more complex propositions:

denies the case in which *A* is denied and *B* and *C* are affirmed.

It would have been more consistent with Frege's fundamental distinction between assertion and content asserted if he had written 'is true' and 'is false', instead of 'is affirmed' and 'is denied'. For in the conditional proposition, *A* and *B* occur unasserted. If we make this change we can say that Frege has defined the *material conditional* of modern logic, 'if B then A', by its *truth-table*.

'If a small vertical stroke is attached to the underside of the content stroke,' Frege says, 'this is to express the circumstance that the content does not occur.' Here again Frege's informal elucidation is misleading—what

expresses is not the (strictly meaningless) assertion that the content *A* does not occur, but the negation of *A*, that is, the assertion that it is not the case that *A*.

Frege is now able to define 'or' and 'and' in terms of the conditional and negation; though as he points out, conditionality could equally well have been defined by 'and' and 'not'. He next introduces a sign for what he calls 'identity of content', '≡', the need for which arises because the same content can be linguistically expressed in different ways. He treats this as a relation between signs, but it is noteworthy that he nevertheless thinks that a judgement concerning identity of content can be synthetic.

In his preface Frege signals another fundamental innovation: 'the replacement of the concepts of *subject* and *predicate* by *argument* and *function*' (Fb 107). Consider, for example, the proposition

Hydrogen is lighter than carbon dioxide.

If we replace the word 'hydrogen' by 'oxygen' or 'nitrogen', we have a new sentence expressing a new content. Frege now views '. . . is lighter than carbon dioxide' as a function, whose arguments are the expressions 'hydrogen', 'oxygen', 'nitrogen', and so on—singular names which can be fitted into the gap, *the argument place*, supplied by the function. (It is not strictly the quoted expression itself that is the function—we shall come back to this.)

His terminology is drawn from the mathematical theory of functions—this for Frege is no mere analogy; it is, rather, a natural and legitimate generalization of the mathematical concept. Consider, for example, the mathematical function

$$y = x^2 + 5$$

A number substituted for the variable $x$ is known as an *argument* of that function. Thus if the argument is 5, $y = 30$. We say that 30 is the *value* of the function for the argument 5; '$x$' is said to range over possible arguments of the function, '$y$' to range over its values for those arguments. The function is said to 'map' or 'take' its arguments into its values.

Functions need not have just one argument—for example,

$$y = 5x_1 + x_2$$

has two arguments, $x_1$, $x_2$. In general, a function can have any number of arguments, but always has a unique value (where it has a value at all). The same, Frege thinks, holds for logical functions. In '. . . is lighter than carbon dioxide', we may identify 'carbon dioxide' as a replaceable name; viewing it thus we obtain a relational expression with two arguments, '. . . is lighter than——', where the different styles of indicating the gaps show that different names may be inserted into them. Thus '. . . is lighter than . . .' would be a different function, taking a single argument. (We shall use the term 'predicate' to cover relational expressions of any number of arguments as well as one-argument predicates.)

There are in this some areas of unclarity. The most notable is that Frege at this stage does not distinguish sharply between expression and idea: he talks of 'being lighter than carbon dioxide' as a function, and of replacing 'carbon dioxide' by other '*ideas*' like 'hydrogen chloride gas' or 'ammonia'. And what are the values of such functions? The sentence itself, or its conceptual content? Or something else? He soon became much more rigorous on these points.

On the basis of his function/argument analysis of the sentence, Frege could now make one of his most decisive advances. Let the signs $x$, $y$ hold places into which arguments may be substituted, and let $\phi$, $\psi$, etc. hold places for functions; Frege now shows a quite general way of handling generality.

will stand for the assertion 'that the function is a fact whatever we may take as its argument' (Fb 130). Here again there is a touch of confusion: if the function is an expression it cannot be a fact. The assertion should rather be, that for any argument $x$, $\phi(x)$ is true. Or simply, that everything is $\phi$.

The concavity, together with its contained sign, expresses what we now call *the universal quantifier*: it is said to bind all the occurrences of the *variable* within its scope. The use of quantifiers to bind variables is another fundamental advance made by Frege's concept script. It allows us to see how a quantifier can occur within the scope of another, or within the scope of a conditional, or a negation stroke. Thus consider

This tells us that for all $x_1$, if $\phi(x_1, x_2)$ for every $x_2$, then $\Psi x_1$. Or consider

This tells us that it is not the case that everything is not $\phi$; that is to say, it asserts that at least one thing is $\phi$. Nor is there any limit in this notation to the number of places a relation may have, or the number of quantifiers which may be nested within each other. Although Peirce also made great strides towards a theory of relations, developed in a Boolean framework, it is Frege who treats them in a fully general way within a comprehensive logical theory.

Frege's two-dimensional script does have advantages of perspicuity, but it is cumbersome and unwieldy. It greatly held back understanding of the importance and novelty of his ideas and it has not survived. The notations which have come to be standard derive with minor variations from Peano and Russell, so we shall now express Frege's basic logical notions in that notation and use it henceforth.

Propositions are schematized by the letters $P$, $Q$, and so on. The negation of '$P$' is '$\sim P$'. The conditional is '$P \rightarrow Q$'. ('Or' and 'and' are respectively written as '$v$' and '$\&$'.) The universal quantifier is written thus: $(x) (\ldots x \ldots)$. Brackets here and elsewhere are used to eliminate syntactic ambiguities: for example, the difference between $(x) (\phi x \rightarrow P)$ and $(x) (\phi x) \rightarrow P$. ('If anything is $\phi$ then $P$', versus 'If everything is $\phi$ then $P$'.) The 'existential quantifier', $(Ex) (\ldots x \ldots)$, read as 'There is at least one $x$ such that $\ldots x \ldots$', can be defined in terms of these basic notions.

Note that nothing in this more modern notation corresponds to Frege's assertion sign. The issues behind this point form a topic in their own right. A descendant of the assertion sign is made use of in what is called 'natural deduction', but it is commonly granted in modern logic that inference can be made from unasserted premises—which Frege would not have allowed. Note also that the general proposition, 'All $\phi$s are $\psi$s' is read by Frege and modern logic as a universally quantified conditional:

$$(x) \; (\phi x \rightarrow \psi x).$$

There is more to the *Begriffsschrift* than its introduction of a powerful conceptual notation. At the technical level it provided an integrated formal logic of propositions and predicates, with a semantic account (as we have seen) of the fundamental logical constants, and a complete set of axioms and inference rules for first-order logic with identity. In its third and last chapter Frege defines for the first time the ancestral of a relation and gives the first logical analysis of proof by mathematical induction: we shall return to this when we come to his analysis of arithmetic.

Much later, in a note of 1906 headed 'What may I Regard as the Result of my Work?', Frege listed his treatment of concepts and relations as functions, the distinction between assertion and predication, the 'Hypothetical mode of sentence composition', the treatment of generality, and the distinction between sense and reference (Fp 184). The one thing on this list not already present in the *Begriffsschrift* is the distinction between sense and reference. We have noted some unclarity, in that treatise of 1879, as to the relation between an expression, the idea it expresses, and what it stands for or is about—notions which Mill had handled by distinguishing connotation and denotation. There is no comparable distinction in the *Begriffsschrift*. But the defect is powerfully remedied in a series of semantic papers which Frege published in 1891 and 1892. The most famous of them, 'On Sense and Reference', of 1892, introduces a distinction between the 'sense' (*Sinn*) and 'reference' (*Bedeutung*—sometimes translated 'meaning') of expressions.

At first sight this recapitulates Mill's connotation and denotation. Frege considers the case of 'proper names' (these, in Frege's use, correspond to Mill's 'singular names') and he considers such identities as 'The evening star is the morning star.' In the *Begriffsschrift* he had treated identities as relations between names (as Mill had treated 'Cicero is Tully'). But now he observes that the information conveyed, on that construal, would concern the names and their use in the language—whereas 'in many cases' we want to convey 'proper knowledge' (Ft 57) about what they refer to. Such knowledge may be conveyed because one and the same object may be presented in different ways—thus one and the same planet (Venus) is seen in the evening sky, and known as 'the evening star', and in the morning sky, and known as 'the morning star', but it is a real discovery of astronomy that the evening star is the morning star. Different names will have different senses insofar as they correspond to such different 'modes of presentation', even where their referent is the same. The sense determines the reference, but not vice versa, just as the connotation determines the denotation, but not vice versa.

Again, just as Mill was at pains to distinguish the connotation of a name from the ideas associated with it, so Frege distinguishes the sense from the associated idea. Both philosophers are eager to avoid psychologism; but now the first difference appears. For Frege, senses are entities sharply distinguished from merely psychological ideas—and since they are neither mental nor physical they must be abstract. They are *real*—i.e. they exist objectively outside the mind—but not *actual*. ('*Wirklich*'—here translated as 'actual' to constrast with 'real'.) The actual is what 'acts on our senses or at least produces effects which may cause sense-perceptions as near or remote consequences' (Ff 97). But Frege rejects 'the widespread inclination to acknowledge as existing only what can be perceived by the senses' (Fbl 10). Now Mill, as we saw, had not thought through what the status of the attributes which names connote was—but it is hard to think that he would have allowed them to be nonactual abstract entities in Frege's fashion.

The distinction between sense and reference is applied by Frege to predicates and relational expressions, just as Mill applies his distinction to general names. But here there is an even bigger difference, corresponding to Frege's doctrine of functions. For in Frege the reference of a predicate or a relational expression is a function, something incomplete—an abstract entity but not a 'self-subsistent' object—and the same goes for its sense.

Nor is the predicate itself just a proper part of the sentence, if the sentence is considered as an object—as an utterance or an inscription. It too is incomplete, in Frege's peculiar sense, which we must now consider further.

Frege's doctrine of incompleteness is his response to the problem which was already emerging in the last chapter, for example in Bradley's assault on the reality of relations—the problem of the unity of the thought or proposition. Or at least it is a response to one part of that mysterious and somewhat shapeless problem. In Frege's hands this part of it gets a sharp formulation. Consider 'Red Rum is a horse.' On Frege's view this breaks into two: 'Red Rum', a name referring to an object, and the incomplete expression which results from dropping that name from the sentence. This latter expression also refers, to the concept *horse*. But there is trouble here—our last sentence, taken literally, must be false; for according to Frege one cannot *name* a concept—it is a function, not an object. And any name, including the expression 'This latter expression', or the expression 'the concept *horse*', must refer to an object.

This is symptomatic of a deep difficulty. For if we allowed that the expression 'the concept *horse*' did indeed refer to a concept, it would have to refer to just what the incomplete expression contained in the sentence 'Red Rum is a horse' refers to. But it is a fundamental principle of Frege's logic that co-referential expressions can be substituted for each other without change of truth value. Should we not then be permitted to substitute 'the concept *horse*' into 'Red Rum is a horse', producing 'Red Rum the concept *horse*'? Obviously this latter thing is not just untrue, it is not even a well-formed sentence. It follows that we cannot even truly *express* such fundamental Fregean doctrines as: 'Concepts are not objects.' Either this sentence has no meaning or it is false.

Much of Frege's own semantic exposition is afflicted in this way. Frege concedes as much in his paper 'On Concept and Object' of 1892:

I admit that there is a quite peculiar obstacle in the way of an understanding with my reader. By a kind of necessity of language, my expressions, taken literally, sometimes miss my thought; I mention an object, when what I intend is a concept. I fully realize that in such cases I was relying upon a reader who would be willing to meet me half-way—who does not begrudge a pinch of salt.

Somebody may think that this is an artificially created difficulty; that there is no need at all to take account of such an unmanageable thing as what I call a concept; that one might ... regard an object's falling under a concept as a relation, in which the same thing could occur now as object, now as concept ... This may be done; but anybody who thinks the difficulty is avoided this way is very much mistaken; it is only shifted. For not all parts of a thought can be complete; at least one must be 'unsaturated' [incomplete] or predicative; otherwise they would not hold together. (Ft 54)

This is very close to Bradley. Has Frege solved the problem or simply labelled it? Is there indeed a genuine difficulty here in the first place? What is this problem of parts of a thought not hanging together?

A definite problem arose because co-referential expressions were to be freely substitutable, and predicates were held to refer. But should we hold that 'incomplete' expressions *refer*? Why not just hold with Mill that predicates connote properties and denote (i.e. are true of) objects? (They do not, remember, *denote* the class of objects they are true of.) Now that relations, $n$-place predicates, have been introduced, we shall have to say that these denote $n$-tuples of objects. That may give pause to a strict Millian nominalist, for $n$-tuples are most easily thought of as a type of abstract entity, constructed from the objects ordered in the $n$-tuple. But waive that point; at least the problem of the unity of the proposition seems to have been staved off—in so far as it has been made clear. For substitution of co-denoting terms preserves truth value and does not generate nonsense.

A further difference between the two semanticists appears in the fact that Frege, unlike Mill, applies his distinction to whole sentences. The sense of a sentence is the thought (*Gedanke*) it expresses—thought being understood here non-psychologically, and thus better captured by the word 'proposition'. But what then is the sentence's reference? If we delete 'the morning star' from the sentence 'The morning star is a body illuminated by the sun', replacing it by 'the evening star', the new sentence will express a different thought from the old. One may assent to the one without assenting to the other: the two sentences have different senses. Yet the name deleted and the name inserted have the same reference—surely then the reference of the two sentences must be the same. But what is it that remains constant when co-referential terms are substituted? The truth value. Thus Frege concludes that the reference of a sentence is its truth value—a doctrine which is indeed already strongly suggested by the *Begriffschrift* doctrine that predicates are functions, although it is not there announced.

There seem, however, to be exceptions to this rule of substitutivity. Take Mill's example of 'Tully is Cicero', and suppose that to be a truth of which Joe is unaware. Then the sentence 'Joe believes that Cicero was a Roman orator' may be true, while the sentence 'Joe believes that Tully was a Roman orator' may be false. Frege deals with this point in a very beautiful way. Such sentences are complex: they are formed by embedding a sentence in the context 'Joe believes that. . .'. Embedded in such a context a sentence does not take its ordinary reference, that is, its truth value. It takes its *indirect* reference, which is, Frege says, its *sense*.

This Fregean line of thought also generates strong pressure against Mill's very intuitive doctrine that proper names are connotationless tags. For if they are so, how do we explain their failure to substitute smoothly in such contexts? Mill never considered the question, so we cannot know what he would have said. Frege of course holds that *all* terms, including ordinary proper names, have sense as well as reference.

The logical syntax which Frege had outlined in the *Begriffsschrift* was comprehensive, simple, and had great power. Could it perhaps be retained without his semantic doctrines—his troublesome view that 'incomplete expressions' refer to functions, or his account of sense and reference? One route would be to combine it with something like Mill's account of connotation and denotation for singular terms and predicates, allowing oneself, however, as above, the notion of an *n*-tuple; and then to give an account of the meaning of connectives and quantifiers which did not rely on the connotation/denotation distinction at all. There are detailed problems in plenty for this semantical framework, (for example, how to cope in general with instances of '*X* believes that *P*'), but it does represent one broad church among contemporary semanticists—though a more purely Fregean approach also retains its vitality.

However, neither this route nor the Fregean route was followed in Cambridge. Neither Russell nor Wittgenstein thought that semantics needed *two* primitive semantical concepts—as both Mill and Frege in their different ways did. The immense influence of Frege on Cambridge lay rather in his innovations in logic and the philosophy of mathematics.

Perhaps the book in which Frege's specifically *philosophical* genius is most evident is the *Grundlagen der Arithmetik* (*Foundations of Arithmetic*) of 1884. The ambition of this work is to show that arithmetic is analytic. Kant had argued that it was synthetic a priori, along with geometry. Frege always accepted the latter doctrine, but for long he believed that arithmetic could be reduced to logic and that he had provided the tools for doing so. This thesis is known as *logicism*; and the fortunes of logicism are an important part of the evolution of analytic philosophy. But before we consider logicism further we must discuss the epistemological framework in which Frege worked.

Frege considers Kant's notion of analyticity too narrow, though he thinks Kant had 'some inkling' (Ff 99) of the broader notion which he himself prefers. Analyticity he thinks should be defined as derivability from pure logic with the help of definitions alone.

This is the broad notion of analyticity which we noticed in Chapter 2. The narrow notion of analyticity, on the other hand, is the one that corresponds to Mill's notion of a 'verbal' proposition or inference. As we have seen (p. 39 above), there is an important rationale for the narrow notion of analyticity, a rationale which Frege ignores. Statements which are 'analytic' in the narrow sense are indisputably unproblematic epistemologically. The broader notion—definitional reducibility to logic—does not preserve this rationale, unless one takes it that our knowledge of logic is unproblematic. It may be, as Frege suggests, that Kant was not clearly conscious of the difference between the two; but there is nevertheless clear philosophical point in his preoccupation with the narrow notion.

There is nothing to stop us using a broad notion of analyticity. But this will not prevent the problem which Kant and Mill saw about the synthetic a priori from arising just as surely for those truths which are broadly but not narrowly analytic. It is a problem which Frege evidently does not feel. He recognizes three sources of knowledge. There is sense perception, which yields a posteriori knowledge. And there are the logical and the geometrical (he sometimes calls the latter the 'geometrical and temporal') sources of knowledge. Both yield a priori knowledge, but the latter involves intuition. Thus when he eventually abandoned logicism he sought to give arithmetic an equally firm and a priori foundation by deriving it from the geometrical source of knowledge.

Frege seems to have felt no need to *explain* how an a priori logical or geometrical source of knowledge is possible; he was content with what he took to be the obvious fact that it must and does exist. He was not open, as both Kant and Mill in their very different ways were, to the thought that no a priori proposition can say anything about a mind-independent world.

His position is a Platonic version of conceptual realism, in that he does not merely hold that there are abstract existents which are neither physical nor mental, but also insists that they are known independently of sense-experience. He protests against 'Kant's dictum: without sensibility no object would be given to us' (Ff 101). Unlike Peirce's realism, therefore (p. 105 above), Frege's is of the kind Mill had thought dead: it is a doctrine which cannot be squared with concept-empiricism or with the phenomenalism which underlies it. Another Platonist of this kind, as we shall see, was Moore—Platonic forms of realism were decidedly in the air after the holistic-phenomenalist excesses of the *fin de siècle*. The realism of Frege's thought, and the rationale it provided for the technical programme of logicism, gave it a strong affinity with Cambridge.

It had to be a Platonic form of realism, if it was to underpin the a priori certainty of mathematics. For if one defended conceptual realism on pragmatist lines, in the manner of Peirce, one might well conclude that our knowledge of abstract entities was a posteriori. But Frege's lack of interest in the Critical question, how knowledge of abstract entities is possible, makes it difficult to know just how he conceived the ontological status of the non-actual real. When he touches on the question he resorts to metaphor, as in *Grundlagen* when he says that in arithmetic 'we are not concerned with objects which we come to know as something alien from without through the medium of our senses, but with objects given directly to our reason and, as its nearest kin, utterly transparent to it' (Ff 115). (He is here talking about 'objects' in the narrow Fregean sense.) He immediately adds that for that very reason these objects are not 'subjective fantasies. There is nothing more objective than the laws of arithmetic.' Elsewhere he says that how thought grasps a proposition, which is not mental but abstract, 'is perhaps the most mysterious of all' (Fp 145).

Connected with Platonic realism is the revolt against 'psychologism'. This may be the view that the laws of logic are simply the psychological laws which govern our mental processes, or again it may be the view that 'meanings' are mental entities. Frege strenuously opposes both these views in the *Grundlagen* and thinks of them as bound up with idealism; just as Mill does in the *System of Logic*. However, there is an important difference. Mill's opposition to psychologism in the above two senses is clear enough, but his case for what he takes to be ultimate principles of reasoning (induction) or ultimate ends (happiness) nevertheless rests on a naturalistic appeal to what we agree on 'in theory and practice'. The appeal, as we saw, is not a deduction of logic or ethics from psychology; but neither is it an appeal to a priori knowledge of necessary relationships between Platonic entities. What is new about analytic modernism's hostility to psychology is that it rejects the naturalistic attitude as such. Or rather, as in both Frege and Moore, it is the *combination* of that with an equally sharp opposition to any kind of idealism that is new. But neither Frege nor Moore does much to explain how it is that these opposed positions—naturalism and post-Kantian idealism—are not exhaustive.

Whatever one's verdict on the epistemological impulse of logicism, its detailed working-out was immensely influential. *Grundlagen* only sketches this programme. But it does give a sparklingly clear account of what numbers are, which has ever since won the applause of lovers of genuinely illuminating, exact thought—whether or not they agree with it. This account, which has been tremendously influential in analytic philosophy as a paradigm of conceptual analysis, will now be outlined. The reader who prefers to omit the details can skip to p. 148.

A concept can be said to have a number of instances. For example, the concept 'cup on my table' has seven instances if there are seven cups on my table, zero instances if there are no cups on my table, and so on. Having seven instances is a higher-order concept—itself instantiated by any seven-instanced concept, such as 'day of the week'. All such concepts are like-numbered: Frege says they are 'equal', using that word as an arbitrary label. This notion can be defined, without invoking the concept of number, by the idea of a one-to-one relation, such as that which holds between matched knives and forks in the place-settings on a dinner table.

A one-to-one relation can itself be defined, apparently without invoking the concept 'one', in Frege's logic. 'Matched' is a one–one relation since (i) to each knife $x$ there is matched a fork, $y$, and any fork matched with $x$ is identical with $y$, and (ii) to each fork $x$ there is matched a knife, $y$, and any knife matched with $x$ is identical with $y$. (But some protest that this does invoke the concept 'one' after all, for it invokes the concept 'identical', and 'identical' means 'is one and the same as'.) To say that two concepts are equal is now to say that their respective instances can be correlated by *some* one–one relation.

Frege now defines 'the Number which belongs to the concept $F$' as 'the extension of the concept "equal to the concept $F$"' (Ff 79–80). The *extension* of a concept is the class of entities falling under or instantiating that concept—so a number is identified with an abstract entity: a class of equal concepts. And he stipulates that '*n* is a Number' means the same as 'there exists a concept such that *n* is the Number which belongs to it' (Ff 85).

It is interesting to compare this with Mill's definition of number as an attribute of aggregates (which of course Frege knew and had considered with some care, despite the scorn he pours on it.) Mill never treats of numbers as genuine singular names. What he considers are general names, of the form '*n* in number' (as in 'The cows in the field are 7 in number'). He thinks these general names connote an attribute of aggregates, and denote the aggregates which have that attribute. From this we get to Frege in two steps: (i) by replacing the idea of 7-numbered aggregates by that of 7-numbered concepts; (ii) by introducing a singular name, '7' which denotes the *class* of aggregates (now, concepts) which are 7-numbered. Neither of these steps would have been acceptable to Mill, since in each case we introduce an abstract entity. But by showing in detail how his own proposal works, Frege has provided a quite specific and unevadable challenge to the nominalist.

Frege now defines each natural number by the following scheme:

0 is the Number which belongs to the concept 'not identical with itself'

1 is the Number which belongs to the concept 'identical with 0'

2 is the Number which belongs to the concept 'identical with 0 or with 1' (Ff 87, 90)

and so on.

This guarantees the existence of 0 from purely logical knowledge. Frege also has a definition of '*n* follows in the series of natural numbers directly after *m*'—in other words, '*n* is a direct successor of *m*'. He defines it thus: for some concept *F* and some object *x*, *x* is an *F*, *n* is the number of *F*s, and the number of objects falling under *F* but not identical with *x* is *m* (Ff 89). He is now able to show that every number has a direct successor, that is, that there is an infinity of natural numbers. He defines succession as the ancestral of the relation of direct succession, in accordance with the definition of the ancestral of a relation given in the *Begriffsschrift*. (*n* is a successor of *m* just if *n* falls under every concept *F* such that *m* is an *F* and such that for every *x* and *y*, if *y* is a direct successor of *x*, and *x* is an *F*, then *y* is an *F*.) The concept '*n* is a natural number' is then defined as '*n* is a successor of 0'. The effect is that the validity of mathematical induction for natural numbers follows from the definition of 'natural number'.

These definitions, together with definitions of arithmetical operations, show how to translate the language of arithmetic into Frege's language of logic—a rich language, which allows quantification not only over objects, including classes, but also over functions. (In other words one can speak generally about functions, as well as about objects—as the definitions do.)

The definitions do not yet show that arithmetical truths are logical truths, which is the essential logicist claim. ('There are seven objects' is stateable in Frege's language of pure thought, but it is not a logical truth.) One way of showing that would be to set out axioms which are indubitably logical truths and principles of inference which are indubitably logically sound, and to show or at least make plausible that all arithmetical truths can on translation be derived from them. This is what Frege hoped to achieve in the *Grundgesetze der Arithmetik*, the *Basic Laws of Arithmetic*, the first volume of which was published in 1893. The basic laws are indeed six propositions which Frege regarded as purely logical truths; and the rules which he states he regards as logically sound.

But as he prepared the second volume for publication in 1902 disaster struck. He received a letter from Bertrand Russell pointing out that a contradiction was derivable from one of his basic laws. This was Russell's famous paradox, which he had found in 1901 while studying Cantor's new theory of sets.

Is there a class of classes which are not members of themselves? Let us suppose there is. We now ask whether *that class itself* is a member of itself. If it is a member of itself, then it is not a member of itself. If it is not a member of itself then it is a member of itself. But—if we accept the law of excluded middle—we must agree that either it is a member of itself or it is not. It follows that it both is and is not a member of itself. Contradiction.

This looks like a *reductio ad absurdum* of our supposition, that there exists a class of classes which are not members of themselves. So 'class which is not a member of itself' does not have a well-defined extension. Sadly, Frege's basic laws entailed the existence of that class. The question now was how to repair the damage without defeating logicism. What was needed was a reformulation which must (i) itself be recognizable as logical truth, and (ii) still allow the reduction of arithmetic to logic.

We shall take up Russell's response when we come to his own logicist programme. But the effect on Frege of Russell's discovery was traumatic. He attempted a solution in an appendix, but soon abandoned it. His later view of arithmetic was no longer logicist; he rejected the notion of class as irredeemably paradoxical, and sought to define real numbers in geometrical terms. Arithmetic thus becomes, like geometry, and as Kant had claimed, synthetic a priori.

But we must now turn our attention to Cambridge in the 1890s, where George Edward Moore (1873–1958) and Bertrand Arthur William Russell (1872–1970) had arrived as undergraduates, Moore in 1892 and Russell two years earlier.

Both came from families with affiliations in that nineteenth-century English 'intellectual aristocracy' which has been remarked on by some historians. Russell was of the aristocracy proper; he was third Earl Russell—the first, Lord John Russell, had proposed the 1832 reform bill. His parents were intellectuals and reformers, friends of Mill, who became Russell's godfather. They died when Russell was very young and he was looked after by his grandmother, Lord John Russell's wife. Moore was from the professional middle class with intellectual connections. His parents had moved to Dulwich to be able to send their sons to Dulwich College.

Both had an intense teenage encounter with religion, both had lost interest in religion by the time they went to university. 'Throughout the long period of religious doubt, I had been rendered very unhappy by the gradual loss of belief, but when the process was completed, I found to my surprise that I was quite glad to be done with the whole subject' (Ra 36). Russell speaks here for the collective *geist* of English-language philosophy in the new century: after 1900 religion ceases to be a central preoccupation for innovative philosophers. This was a liberation from the slippery and dizzying manœuvres that the *fin de siècle* had found necessary to give religion intellectual house-room. The world could at last be recognized in its objectivity; it could be approached with a new incisiveness which did not constantly have to find ways of dissolving it into something else.

Moore's background was in classics, which he had studied to an extreme degree of specialization at Dulwich, Russell's was in mathematics. His brother had introduced him to Euclid when he was 11: 'This was one of the great events of my life, as dazzling as first love' (Ra 30). He started to philosophize at 15, though when he went to Cambridge the only professional work of philosophy he had read was Mill's *System*.

Both turned to philosophy as the second part of their degree. They met in Moore's first year at Cambridge; it was Russell who persuaded Moore to take up philosophy. At first they were idealists; converted by J. E. M. McTaggart, one of Cambridge's best philosophers and an admirer of Bradley. (Moore recalled McTaggart saying that when he met Bradley he felt 'as if a Platonic idea had walked into the room' (Sm 22).) Both of them became Fellows of Trinity, Russell with a dissertation on the foundations of geometry in which Kant's views were discussed, Moore with one on Kant's ethics.

Their personalities were strongly contrasted. Russell was ardent, aristocratically confident, versatile, technically effortless, Moore diffident, narrow, dogged in his effort to understand. But these Moorean qualities went with a purity and honesty of purpose and an artlessness which were evidently extraordinarily impressive to his contemporaries.

At any rate it was Moore who led the revolt against idealism. 'Moore led the way,' according to Russell, 'but I followed closely in his footsteps' (Rm 54)—though Moore later said, with equal generosity, that he knew of nothing Russell owed him other than mistakes, whereas what he owed Russell were important 'ideas which were certainly not mistakes' (Sm 15). Still, it was Moore's mistakes which liberated them.

His fellowship thesis, 'The Metaphysical Basis of Ethics', dealt with Kant's notion of freedom. It was unsuccessful when first submitted, but this gave Moore another year (1897–8) to work on it and in that year he was led, through an investigation of what Kant meant by Reason, to questions about meaning and truth. The answers he gave in a new chapter of the work were, in Britain, wholly novel in the sharpness and extremity of their conceptual realism. Moore did not at this stage know Frege's writings; his own brand of conceptual realism was in any case very different. It was closer to that of Brentano's pupil Meinong; though here too there seems to have been no influence. Like Mill and Frege, Moore stresses the distinction between what is judged and the act of judging. But unlike Mill he does not think of propositions as sentences. (This would still be too mind-dependent.) He treats them as composed of concepts: these being not mental but abstract entities, existing independently of consciousness and time.

The new chapter of Moore's dissertation was the basis of his paper, 'The Nature of Judgement', published in *Mind* in 1899. Propositions are 'composed' of concepts—being indeed themselves complex concepts. It is in virtue of this complexity that they, unlike simple concepts, can be true or false. A 'specific relation' holds between the concepts which constitute the proposition, and 'according to the nature of this relation the proposition may be either true or false. What kind of relation makes a proposition true, what false, cannot be further defined, but must be immediately recognised' (Mn 180).

There is here nothing like Frege's doctrine of incompleteness, in fact no sign that Moore considers the unity of the proposition to be a serious problem. The indefinability of truth, of which logic gives the laws, is reminiscent of Frege, but there is a further doctrine, to which nothing in Frege corresponds. Concepts are *all* there is. A true proposition does not correspond to a fact, it *is* a fact. Moore develops this out of the primitiveness of truth: 'existence is logically subordinate to truth . . . truth cannot be defined by a reference to existence, but existence only by a reference to truth' (Mn 180). The fact that this rose is red is just the fact that the truth-constituting relation holds between the concepts 'this', 'rose', and 'red'. Similarly, the fact that this rose exists consists in the holding of that same relation between the concepts 'this', 'rose', and 'exists'.

To know is to be aware of a relation between concepts—so concepts are the only objects of knowledge. They

> cannot be regarded fundamentally as abstractions either from things or from ideas; since both alike can, if anything is to be true of them, be composed of nothing but concepts. (Mn 182)

> The opposition of concepts to existents disappears, since an existent is seen to be nothing but a concept or complex of concepts standing in a unique relation to the concept of existence . . . perception is to be regarded philosophically as the cognition of an existential proposition; and it is thus apparent how it can furnish a basis for inference, which uniformly exhibits the connexion between propositions. (Mn 183)

Here is a doctrine even more extraordinary than neutral monism—conceptual monism! Concepts, not sensations, are the given. They compose the world.

Moore rejects Kant's 'attempt to explain "the possibility of knowledge," accepting [instead] the cognitive relation as an ultimate *datum* or presupposition' (Mn 183). So his position is non-Critical in the way that Frege's is. But he explains why there can be no such explanation. All explanation must either be causal or it must appeal to logical relations between concepts, but neither kind of explanation could do the transcendental work Kant requires. His appeal to this dichotomy is significant and we shall return to it.

The central point, then, is that truth is a primitive relation holding between the concepts that constitute a true proposition. In its rejection of the notion of truth as correspondence, this marks an interesting continuity with the ideas of the *fin de siècle*—which Moore would not maintain for long.

One question about it concerns the unity of the proposition—which seems to be achieved, on this conception, by the truth or the falsehood relation. But these relations are themselves presumably concepts. How then can they combine concepts into propositions? Given the idealists' preoccupation with the unity of judgement, this would have been an obvious challenge. At any rate it seems that we must also postulate a primitive falsehood relation, obtaining between all concepts between which the truth-relation does not hold. But how then is false belief possible, given that belief is immediate knowledge of a complex concept? How can we know such a concept, combined by the falsehood relation, without knowing it to be false?

In another influential paper, 'The Refutation of Idealism', published in 1903, Moore again affirms a quite general distinction between acts of consciousness (including judgements) and the objects of these acts. Although he now grants that modern idealism has performed a service in distinguishing clearly between thought and sensation, his main purpose is to deny that whatever is, is perceived. The model of cognition remains one of utter immediacy, or transparency of the world to the intellect: Moore explicitly denies elsewhere that 'the relation of knower to known is a causal relation' (Db ii. 451).

But Moore's reputation among a wider, non-philosophical audience in the 1900s was based as much or more on his ethics as on his leading role in the rejection of idealism.

'I went up to Cambridge at Michaelmas 1902, and Moore's *Principia Ethica* came out at the end of my first year . . . it was exciting, exhilarating, the beginning of a renaissance, the opening of a new heaven on earth, we were the forerunners of a new dispensation, we were not afraid of anything.' Thus wrote Keynes. Lytton Strachey declared it to have 'shattered all writers on ethics from Aristotle and Christ to Herbert Spencer and Mr Bradley', while Leonard Woolf described it as 'substituting for the religious and philosophical nightmares, delusions, hallucinations in which Jehovah, Christ and St Paul, Plato, Kant and Hegel had entangled us, the fresh air and pure light of common sense'.

These hyperbolic reactions all came, it is true, from a small coterie, the 'Bloomsbury group', all with Cambridge connexions. But they nevertheless help to evoke the change of mood in the 1900s among some determinedly modernist intellectuals. It was not just that Moore's 'fresh air and pure light' provided an escape from *fin-de-siècle* miasma. *Principia Ethica* set forth the foundations of a new era, as its very title (like Russell and Whitehead's later *Principia Mathematica*) somewhat suggests. In this respect it resembled similar revolutionary manifestos in areas of modernist activity which were otherwise quite disparate, such as music or architecture.

But what was the doctrine that seemed so liberating?

Ethics is concerned with the predicate 'good'. The first and characteristically Moorean doctrine of *Principia* is that this predicate is indefinable. It denotes a simple property which is not further analysable. In this respect it is just like 'true'.

It is a fallacy to define it by means of any other predicate— Moore calls it the naturalistic fallacy, though it would more appropriately have been called the definist fallacy. But Moore has in mind the naturalistic ethics of Bentham, Mill, and Spencer. (He notes that Sidgwick recognized the indefinability of 'good', and convicted Bentham of the fallacy (Mp 17).)

Mill is brought into the stocks, as a leading naturalistic miscreant, on the strength of his argument to the desirability of happiness from the fact that 'people do actually desire it'—even though Moore himself cites the passages in which Mill emphasizes that he is not offering a deductive proof.

Mill has made as naive and artless a use of the naturalistic fallacy as anybody could desire . . . the fallacy in this step is so obvious, that it is quite wonderful how Mill failed to see it. (Mp 66–7)

But how could Moore think Mill had committed it? Some of Mill's rhetoric invites the indictment, but there are deeper philosophical issues at stake, which require some attention.

We have seen that Moore's realism recognizes only causal relations and logical relations among concepts; or putting it another way, inductive inferences and strictly deductive, indefeasible ones. He appeals to this fork in rejecting Critical Philosophy's attempt to explain the possibility of knowledge. But Moore's fork is not just a successor of Hume's fork, at least if one interprets Hume's fork as a version of the analytic/synthetic, verbal/real distinction. It brings into view an assumption which had not previously been clearly identified, and connects it with a particularly strong Platonic realism.

The assumption is that the only source of a priori knowledge is immediate apprehension of concepts and their relations. We may call this the *relational model* of a priori knowledge, for two reasons. First, it involves the idea that all cognition involves a 'transparent', 'immediate', or 'primitive' relation of apprehension, between a thinker and some concepts; and second, it treats concepts as real non-actual entities among which real non-actual relations hold. A corollary of this relational model of a priori knowledge is the relational model of meaning; for understanding terms and sentences must on this view consist in apprehending the concepts they signify, and the relations among them that hold when a given sentence is true. It is not an *essential* part of this view that concepts are all there is, as is held in Moore's early philosophy—but that even stronger Platonism provides a natural home for it, and perhaps always exerts a continuous gravitational attraction on it.

The relational model contrasts with a view of concepts which does not hold that concepts are non-actual reals among which primitive relations *turn out*, so to speak, to hold—but treats them instead as constituted by their role in inference and the connexions of inference with experience and practice. They are *constituted* by such normative patterns of reasoning, from experience and into practice—they are not pre-existing entities which can *explain* the correctness of those norms. We shall call this the *epistemic conception* of meaning, or of concepts.

Moore's Platonism about concepts is the purest example of the relational model, in that he sees that model as an *exhaustive* account of a priori knowledge. Frege adopts a relational model of our knowledge of senses, and he also believes, as we have seen, in other kinds of non-actual reals, to our knowledge of which the same model applies. On the other hand he thinks that there is a geometrical source of a priori knowledge, which does not involve sense-perception but does involve sensible intuition; though his comments on this epistemological framework are so rudimentary that it is impossible to know whether he would have developed it in a Kantian, a Platonic, or some other direction.

Peirce treats universals as real on the basis of an *epistemic* conception of concepts and of meaning; and he derives from that his ideal convergence notion of truth. That also means that his framework does not generate Moore's fork, for there is plenty of potential scope in it for the idea of an inference which is in a certain sense a priori and yet is not deductive, and can be defeated.

We have seen that Mill thinks fundamental norms are grounded in facts about human agreement in theory and practice. The closeness of this to an ideal convergence notion of truth, applied to the special case of *fundamental norms*, is clear. Thus in arguing for hedonism he simply points out the empirical facts which ground the hedonist norm. Now the relation here, between a fundamental norm and its ground, cannot be deductive, but it is evidently not inductive either. So it must be eliminated by Moore's fork. That is why Moore so easily convicts Mill of the 'naturalistic fallacy'.

It is certainly a good *ad hominem* argument against Mill to press the question of what kind of relation it can be. He himself seems to have no scope for allowing non-deductive a priori warranting relations. The question presses him at the limits of his empiricism, in Critical spirit. Of course we cannot attribute to him the epistemic conception of meaning; but then neither can we attribute to him the relational model. What we can say, though, is that his naturalistic appeal to agreement is doomed to collapse into *fallacy* only if the epistemic conception is bankrupt.

Moore, to be fair, would quite certainly have thought it was bankrupt. He would have stigmatized it as yet another failure to distinguish between the act and the object of thought—the 'fundamental contradiction of modern Epistemology'. 'That "to be true" *means* to be thought in a certain way is', he says, 'certainly false.'

Yet this assertion plays the most essential part in Kant's 'Copernican revolution' of Philosophy, and renders worthless the whole mass of modern literature, to which that revolution has given rise, and which is called Epistemology. (Mp 133)

He goes on to argue that being thought of in a certain way can be even a *criterion* of truth only if a correlation between the two can be established by induction.

What is undeniable in this is that 'true' does not *mean* 'is thought of in a certain way'. What is not obvious, is that 'modern Epistemology' must hold that it does, or that it must fail to distinguish, in every way that is proper, being and being thought (experienced, felt, etc.). It is enough if it can justify 'being thought of in a certain way', in at least some crucial cases, as an a priori criterion of truth. To argue that a criterion of truth must always be inductively based is to beg the question against the epistemic account of concepts. However, the question Moore in effect raises is whether that account can be defended without resorting to idealism—a fundamental question in analytic philosophy, which will remain with us in the next two chapters.

Russell's and Moore's criticisms of pragmatism, which appeared in the 1900s, are in very much the same spirit as Moore's criticism of the 'naturalistic fallacy'. They take the pragmatists to be supplying a definition of the word 'true' and argue that truth is a simple, unanalysable, intuitable property. Thus, according to Russell, the pragmatists must hold that

'It is true that other people exist' *means* 'It is useful to believe that other people exist'. But if so, then the two phrases are merely different words for the same proposition; therefore when I believe one I believe the other.

The passage is quoted by James in a reply (Jp 315) which is certainly no model of clarity. But he is right to accuse Russell of 'vicious abstractionism' (Jp 314). One must take seriously—given pragmatism's epistemic conception of meaning—the possibility that though 'true' is not strictly *definable* as 'verifiable' or 'satisfactory', or whatever, some such notion nevertheless enters into an a priori criterion of truth.

We have been carried far into questions of modern Epistemology, in Moore's phrase, by considering his claim that 'good' stands for an indefinable property, and his criticism of Mill's naturalism. These are indeed epistemological claims about ethics; but it is time to turn to his substantive ethics as such.

It turns out that Moore himself is a universalistic consequentialist. In this he agrees with the utilitarians, as he also does in holding that no statement about duty and right, as against intrinsic value, can be a self-evident 'intuition'. But he does not bring to the vital question—how to apply a criterion of the good to a live ethical tradition—the historical sense, psychological insight, or political wisdom brought to it by Mill. That is the difference between nineteenth-century humanism and Bloomsbury modernism—writ large in the persons of Mill and Moore.

The right action, for Moore, is straightforwardly the one that produces the most good. (He offers no definition of moral obligation, as Bentham and Mill do.) Not surprisingly, this makes him pessimistic about the possibility of showing any action to be a duty—in fact he concludes that 'we never have any reason to suppose that an action is our duty: we can never be sure that any action will produce the greatest value possible' (Mp 149). He does grudgingly concede that there may be 'some possibility' of indicating an action likely to do most good; but the identification of 'we can never be sure that' with 'we never have any reason to suppose that' is characteristically Moorean in its cloistered quest for certainty. It is also an early symptom of the 'abstractionism' (to borrow William James's phrase) which has infected much of this century's moral theory—or lack of it.

The end is to maximize the sum total of good; but in his treatment of 'good' Moore is more primitive than Sidgwick had been in the *Methods of Ethics* (pp. 68 ff. above). Sidgwick saw that both an agent-relative and an agent-neutral notion of good could be consistently universalized, and in that light concluded that universalized egoism and utilitarianism were both rationally evident. Moore rejects Sidgwick's treatment of egoism by simply insisting that good must be a one-place predicate, that is, assuming that goodness must be agent-neutral. He quite fails to respond to the real challenge of Sidgwick's dualism of practical reason.

By far the most impressive and attractive sections of *Principia Ethica* are those in which Moore rejects hedonism and develops a new theory of intrinsic value. These were the sections that most inspired Bloomsbury. In some ways, it is true—the expectable modernist ways—Moore's treatment of hedonism is depressingly simple-minded. The subtleties in Mill's position— his attempt to introduce a distinction between higher and lower pleasures, for example, and his terminology of an end being 'part' of happiness—are given very short shrift. On the other hand, Moore responds interestingly to Sidgwick's argument for hedonism.

This has two parts. Sidgwick first argues that nothing can be good or bad 'out of relation to human existence, or at least to some consciousness or feeling . . . no one would consider it rational to aim at the production of beauty in external nature, apart from any possible contemplation of it by human beings' (quoted, Mp 81–2). On this basis he concludes that nothing can be reasonably sought after except in so far as it conduces either to happiness, or to 'the Perfection or Excellence of human existence'. His next step is to argue that 'ideal goods' such as 'cognition of Truth, contemplation of Beauty, Free or Virtuous action' are valuable only in so far as they are conducive to happiness; perfection or excellence of human existence reduces to happiness and is not a categorially separate end.

Moore disagrees with both steps. He thinks it better that a beautiful world should exist than one which is ugly: even if neither could be contemplated by a sentient being. The value of beauty is greatly increased by the enjoyment of it, he emphasizes, but it nevertheless has value in itself, even if it cannot be enjoyed.

But he thinks this error 'utterly insignificant' (Mp 85) in comparison with that made in the second step, and here he makes suggestive and substantial arguments for holding that life has ends other than pleasure. Aesthetic enjoyment and personal affection are the most important ends of life:

personal affections and aesthetic enjoyments include *all* the greatest, and *by far* the greatest, goods we can imagine . . . (Mp 189)

They are 'the *raison d'être* of virtue . . . the rational ultimate end of human action . . . the sole criterion of social progress'. But their value does not lie exhaustively in the pleasure they afford. They are 'organic unities' of emotion and *veridical* cognition. Moore's principle of organic unities states that the 'the intrinsic value of a whole is neither identical with nor proportional to the sum of the value of its parts' (Mp 184). The enjoyment which results from what is believed to be a beautiful object or a loving friendship has intrinsic value, just as the mere existence of a beautiful object or of love between friends has value. But these are all small compared to the value of the whole which includes that enjoyment of beauty or friendship together with the reality of the beauty or friendship which is enjoyed. An essential constituent of the organic whole is a knowledge-constituting relation between the state of consciousness and something outside it. Knowledge, 'though having little or no value by itself, is an absolutely essential constituent in the highest goods, and contributes immensely to their value' (Mp 199). The value of our enjoyment of beauty and personal affection is immensely reduced if the beauty and affection are unreal and our belief in them false.

Moore's criticism of the 'naturalistic fallacy' was very influential, while on the other hand the final chapter of *Principia Ethica*, on 'The Ideal', which so influenced Bloomsbury, has often since then been derided. But it is this last chapter which best survives, by its philosophical penetration and simplicity of expression. Keynes was right to describe passages from it as 'sweet and lovely' and to speak of 'the beauty of the literalness of Moore's mind, the pure and passionate intensity of his vision, *un*fanciful and *un*dressed up'. We, however, must turn from Moore's ethics to take up again the thread we dropped with Russell's discovery of the paradox of non-self-membered classes, and its devastation of Frege's logicism.

In the late 1890s Russell and Moore affirmed the independence of fact from cognition and experience. Moore led the frontal assault, while Russell concerned himself particularly with what he thought of as a logical aspect of idealist doctrine, its monism. This was the idea that relations are not ultimate

—cannot exist between ultimately distinct things—but must resolve into qualities of a complex whole, which comprehends those apparently distinct things. Against it Russell asserted what he called the 'doctrine of external relations', a pluralism in which perfectly genuine relations can exist between quite distinct things. This line of criticism runs somewhat parallel to William James's, but Russell gives it (as Peirce had earlier done) a logical rather than a psychological or experiential basis.

In lectures he gave in 1899 on Leibniz (published in 1900 as *A Critical Exposition of the Philosophy of Leibniz*) Russell argues that Leibniz's central error is the assumption that all propositions have subject-predicate form. This forces him 'to the Kantian theory that relations, though veritable, are the work of the mind' (Rl 14) and thus to his philosophy of monads. Otherwise the lectures reiterate early modernist realism: truth is not dependent on knowledge, for unless it exists independently of knowledge, there is nothing to know.

Russell knew the logical work of Boole, Peirce, Schröder; but 'had not found that they threw any light on the grammar of arithmetic' (Rm 66). Enlightenment came only in 1900 when he met Peano at the International Congress of Philosophy in Paris in June. This was 'the most important event' in 'the most important year' of his life (Sr 12). From Peano he learnt, he said, two things. One was the importance of distinguishing between singular predications and general statements of the form 'All $\phi$s are $\psi$s.' (Syllogistic syntax treated both as having the form *S is P*.) The other was that 'a class consisting of one member is not identical with that one member' (Rm 67).

Both points had already been made by Frege, but he did not know this until later. In his autobiography he records that he had been given Frege's *Begriffsschrift* by James Ward, his philosophy tutor, after becoming a Fellow of Trinity (so probably about 1896), but possessed it some years before he 'could make out what it meant' (Ra 65). He soon began to realize Frege's importance. The *Principles of Mathematics*, published in 1903, has an appendix on him, and in the preface of *Principia Mathematica* it is stated that 'In all questions of logical analysis our chief debt is to Frege' (RW, p. viii). Russell thought he had arrived at the conception of numbers as classes of equinumerous classes independently (Ri 11), but he fully recognized Frege's priority and importance.

The first draft of *Principles of Mathematics* was finished on the last day of the 19th century (the last day of 1900), the final draft on 23 May 1902. In the meantime Russell had discovered the paradox (1901); but the book argues for logicism nonetheless, though a rigorous presentation of the programme is not made, nor is any definite solution of the paradox offered.

Philosophically, the main point of logicism as Russell then saw it was to provide a definite refutation of idealism. It was in the first place aimed at Kant's theory of mathematics. As against Kant and Frege, he considers logic itself to be synthetic a priori (Rp 457). But this does not mean that he is claiming to explain the validity of logic in transcendental idealist terms. It is rather that he disagrees with the central Critical and empiricist point— that knowledge of mind-independent fact can be obtained only by experience—while he at the same time thinks there are *no* analytic truths other than tautologies of the form '*A* is *A*', which are 'not properly propositions at all' (Rl 17). Thus although his classification of propositions superficially differs from Frege's (because he takes 'analytic' very narrowly) his position is in fact close to Frege. He takes the a priori status of logical knowledge as evident while agreeing with empiricists that we cannot have a priori knowledge of the actual (spatio-temporal) world.

The idealists had thought that Absolute Knowledge is available only to the metaphysician, or indeed, as Bradley claimed, not discursively available at all. Scientific and common-sense knowledge is at best relative, and riven with contradiction. Russell's analysis of mathematics and logic provides the counter-example. For here are truths which are universal, absolute, not dependent on spatial or temporal intuition. Moreover, Kant's antinomies of space are dissolved by the treatment of real numbers and continuity provided by Cantor, Dedekind, and Weierstrass. Thus the 'two pillars of the Kantian edifice' (Rp 457) are pulled down.

Russell's position is still close to Moore's early conceptual monism. (It is not quite easy to say how close—see Rp 44.) But he tries to cope with its difficulties and this leads him into important questions about meaning. It seems to him that the concepts which constitute propositions cannot uniformly be regarded as what propositions are *about*. This is clear, for example, in the case of general propositions, such as 'any finite number is odd or even', which is true even though 'the *concept* "any finite number" is neither odd nor even' (Rp 53). We must say that the concept *any finite number* 'denotes' something like the totality of finite numbers (it is far from clear quite what entities concepts denote) and that the proposition is true because each member of that totality is odd or even.

Another kind of denoting concept is expressed by definite descriptions, such as 'the highest Alpine mountain'. The proposition expressed by 'The highest Alpine mountain is in France' is about Mont Blanc, though it does not contain Mont Blanc. On the other hand 'Mont Blanc is in France' is both about and contains Mont Blanc—which is therefore not a denoting concept, but a thing. A denoting concept such as *the golden mountain* can fail to denote anything at all, but it still has being: it is what 'the golden mountain' means, and the expression would have no meaning if the concept had no being.

This line of thought did not satisfy Russell for long; conceptual monism could not satisfy the 'robust sense of reality' (P 226) which he thought essential for scientific philosophy. The next step was 'On Denoting' published in *Mind* in 1905.

Strictly speaking this paper abolishes Russell's original concept of denoting, understood as a relation between denoting concepts and other entities. The expressions which were previously taken to express denoting concepts, such as *everything*, *nothing*, *a man*, *any man*, *the present King of France*, and so on, are now paraphrased, in Bentham's sense. Russell says that they 'never have any meaning in themselves, but that every proposition in whose verbal expression they occur has a meaning' (Rlk 43). Elsewhere he calls them 'incomplete symbols'.

The concept he now takes as primitive is that of a *propositional function*, '$C(x)$', which is thought of as an entity essentially containing a *variable*, $x$. We can say such things as that '$C(x)$' is always true of $x$, or always false of $x$: these respectively para-phrase '$C$(everything)' and '$C$(nothing)'.

'The father of Charles II was executed' is then paraphrased as follows:

It is not always false of $x$ that $x$ begat Charles II and that $x$ was executed and that 'if $y$ begat Charles II, $y$ is identical with $x$' is always true of $y$. (Rlk 44)

This is Russell's 'theory of descriptions'. In terms of the notation introduced earlier (p. 136 above) the paraphrasis is this:

$(Ex)$ $(x$ begat Charles II & $x$ was executed & $(y)$ $(y$ begat Charles II $\rightarrow y \equiv x))$.

'On Denoting' is a classic paper, but its philosophical impor-tance derives in great part from the context in which it was produced. It is easiest to appreciate if we contrast the Cam-bridge conception of meaning (of Moore, Russell, and of Wittgenstein in the period covered in this chapter) with that of Mill or of Frege. For both Mill and Frege meaning is indirect or mediate. There is the expression, and then there is its sense, or connotation, which in turn determines its reference, or deno-tation (in Mill's sense) where it has one.

Mill of course thinks that proper names have no connotation, but he also says they have no meaning. With that exception, he applies his doctrine to all, and only to, names—other expres-sions he treats syncategorematically, so whatever has meaning has connotation. Frege and Cambridge in contrast seek a uniform treatment of *every* expression.

This is an important contrast; but it is even more important that Cambridge philosophy rejects any distinction between con-notation and denotation, or sense and reference. Meaning is held to be a direct and immediate relation between the ex-pression and the entity it means. Every expression which has independent meaning, every complete symbol, signifies an en-tity which has being: to have significance is to signify some entity. It is this direct conception of meaning, rather than conceptual monism as such (which rather flows from it) that generates problems—for example, about expressions that stand for nothing that exists, about identity and generality. Russell's original account of denoting was a response to these problems which in fact involved a falling-away from the direct conception, a falling-away which 'On Denoting' remedies.

With the direct conception of meaning goes the *principle of acquaintance*, which Russell states in many places. In 'On Denoting' he puts it thus:

in every proposition that we can apprehend (i.e. not only in those whose truth or falsehood we can judge of, but in all that we can think about), all the constituents are really entities with which we have immediate acquaintance. (Rlk 56)

Russell draws a contrast between knowledge by acquaintance and knowledge by description; but his model of acquaintance is much tighter than the common-sense contrast between, say, my knowing Smith by acquaintance, but Jones only by the description 'the Welsh full-back'. *Acquaintance* for Russell is an immediate cognitive relation, such as I may have only to a concept, a percept, or an inner feeling. It is the primitive cognitive relation between a mind and an entity.

If I understand a sentence it must be analysable into one that is composed entirely of expressions which mean entities with which I am acquainted; for those *are* the meanings of the expressions, and I cannot grasp a meaning by description. Nor can that sentence contain an empty expression, one which purports to mean, but in fact means no entity. For if an expression means nothing it is meaningless, and the sentence containing it is meaningless.

The significance of 'On Denoting' must be seen in this context. Yet in that context Russell has not fully solved the problem. For there remains the question of how the variable and the propositional function mean. Moore wrote to Russell (23 October 1905) asking the question:

You say '*all* the constituents of propositions we apprehend are entities with which we have immediate acquaintance.' Have we, then, immediate acquaintance with the variable? And what sort of entity is it?

Russell replied

The view I usually incline to is that we have immediate acquaintance with the variable, but it is not an entity. Then at other times I think it is an entity, but an indeterminate one. In the former view there is still a problem of meaning and denotation as regards the variable itself. I only profess to reduce the problem of denoting to the problem of the variable. This latter is horribly difficult, and there seem equally strong objections to all the views I have been able to think of.

The 'problem of the variable' does not, to be sure, arise if we read the theory of descriptions in the context of Frege's syntax of predicates and his conception of quantifiers as second-order predicates. Frege's predicates are not the same as Russell's propositional functions: the former take truth or falsehood as values, feature as inherently 'incomplete' components of every sentence, and have sense and reference; the latter take propositions as values and have neither sense nor reference—they are not thought of as 'incomplete' and not every proposition has a propositional function as a constituent. But if we put the theory of descriptions into Fregean syntax can we not also call upon Frege's semantics of sense and reference? There is then no need for a theory of descriptions—even though it remains an elegant, and for many purposes a clarifying, device.

The first volume of *Principia Mathematica,* the joint work of Russell and the philosopher–mathematician A. N. Whitehead, appeared in 1910. The immense and influential technical achievement of Russell and Whitehead's book, in which arithmetical concepts are reduced to set theory, and arithmetical truths to truths of set theory, is not our direct subject here. (Russell claimed that he was never able to think so abstractly again.) We must, however, pay some attention to the theory of types which Russell had meanwhile developed to deal with the paradoxes, and which is deployed therein.

Spotlighting the paradoxes is perhaps the most significant contribution of logicism to general philosophy. For the paradoxes—of which the paradox of non-self-membered classes (p. 147 above) is only one—pin-point questions about the limits of meaningfulness, and they seem to imply that we cannot talk unrestrictedly about *everything* there is. This conclusion is already foreshadowed in Frege's distinction between objects and functions. It is also at least *pleasing* to Kantian idealists. In these ways and others the paradoxes are at the heart of analytic modernism.

For Russell and Moore's early realism—which is intended as the diametric opposite of transcendental idealism—they posed particularly acute problems. For any technical escape from them seems to cloud the lucid simplicity of the realist vision. In that vision there is a plurality of entities only some of which exist, but all of which have being, can be thought of and meant. In that sense they all have the same ontological status, and there seems no reason why the *totality* of them should not have being and be capable of being thought of and meant. But among these entities, on realist principles, will be classes of entities. And now an argument from Cantor, which proves that the number of subclasses of any class is greater than the number of members of that class, immediately leads to paradox. For the totality of entities is nothing but the class of all entities. By Cantor's argument the number of subclasses of *this* class is greater than the number of its members. So there is a class greater in number than the class of *all* entities.

It does not solve the problem to dismiss classes from the realm of genuine entities—as Russell saw quite clearly. He does in fact develop a way of paraphrasing talk of classes into talk of propositional functions, so that class-words become 'incomplete symbols'. But paradoxes can still be formulated if we allow ourselves to talk unrestrictedly about all entities. Consider, for example, the propositional function '. . . is a propositional function which cannot be truly applied to itself', and ask: can it be truly applied to itself?

The resulting paradox is blocked if we cease to hold that this expression is unambiguously applicable to all entities, and this is the effect of Russell's theory of types. Its main idea is that a propositional function is of higher order than any entity which the function can take as argument, or that falls in the range of any quantifier contained in the function. One consequence of this is that a propositional function cannot take itself as argument. Another is that we cannot talk unrestrictedly about all entities, but only about entities of a given type—where the propositional function '. . . is an entity of type α' cannot itself be said to be an entity of type α—that is, cannot take itself as argument.

The paradoxes have something like the effect on Moore and Russell's early realism that perceptual illusion has on naïve realism about the perception of physical objects. They force Russell to introduce distinctions of type which cannot readily be defended as deliverances of immediate apprehension. Russell brings to their defence the famous 'vicious circle principle' (it derives originally from Poincaré), according to which 'Whatever involves *all* of a collection must not be one of the collection' (Rlk 63), or again, 'no totality can contain members defined in terms of itself' (Rlk 75). He gives various other formulations of the principle, and the task of finding a precise interpretation of it is not a trivial one. But the point for our purposes is that the metaphysics of early Russell/Moore realism can provide no *justification* for the vicious circle principle. For the principle really belongs to a 'constructive' view of logical entities, in which one such entity cannot be 'constructed' by using another entity whose construction requires the previous construction of the first. (This would be the vicious circle.) Not only does such a view, with its Kantian flavour, sin against the early Cambridge doctrine that entities pre-exist the subject which thinks about them, it sins also against the view that they bear only external relations to each other. For now one entity may presuppose the construction of another, and hence could not exist if the other did not exist. (Classes could not exist without their members. But Russell treated them as paraphrasable fictions—not as genuine, but 'constructed', entities.)

The introduction of type-theory marked a retreat from pure logicism, as well as from pure realism, for it necessitated the introduction of postulates which could hardly be regarded as logical, even when set theory is counted as part of logic. These (the 'axioms' of infinity and reducibility) need not concern us here. We have already seen that the complete success of pure logicism would still have left undecided the epistemological status of logic. That issue, between Millian radical empiricism and transcendental idealism, can be formulated irrespectively of the truth of logicism, and in the next chapter we shall see how the Vienna Circle handled it.

After his intense concentration on questions in logic and the philosophy of mathematics in the 1900s, Russell's interests widened to include epistemology, and particularly the problem of our knowledge of the physical world. His views in this field and also in general metaphysics—though Cambridge called this, too, logic—went through a rapid and interesting succession of changes.

In general metaphysics the end of the 1900s saw the end of conceptual monism. Russell and Moore ceased to believe in the identity of propositions and facts, both philosophers being moved in particular by the problem of what it is to have a false belief. Russell developed a view according to which truth ceases to be indefinable and becomes a relation of correspondence between beliefs and facts, beliefs being treated as relations between the thinker and the various objects, particular and universal, of the belief.

In the philosophy of perception, the two philosophers became preoccupied by the notion of 'sense-data', understood not as states of individual minds but as direct objects of perception, which yet are not physical objects either. The problem this curious notion raises as to the relation of sense-data to physical objects, and the nature of our knowledge of the latter, is obvious. Russell first postulated physical objects, on grounds of simplicity and natural instinct, as the causes of sense-data (Rpp 24–5), but a few years later, in *Our Knowledge of the External World as a Field for Scientific Method in Philosophy*—the Lowell lectures delivered in Harvard in 1914—he concluded that they are constructs: complicated classes whose first-order constituents are sense-data.

The influence of this book will be touched on again in the next chapter. But it was not the end of Russell's evolution. By about 1919 he had come to accept neutral monism and this, together with philosophical behaviourism, is defended in *The Analysis of Mind* of 1921 (eventually it was itself abandoned).

The general direction of the evolution is evident—in a very broad sense it is a movement away from the pattern of realism. Not that Russell ever relaxed his anti-Kantian vigilance. His empiricism always tended to the realist rather than the Critical. Thus his attitude towards the principle of induction moved from the view propounded in the *Problems of Philosophy*, that it is intrinsically evident, to a more agnostic view which does not claim that it is known, but yet emphasizes in common-sense fashion that it is required for all empirical reasoning. He certainly does not defend it as a transcendental presupposition of knowledge.

In these ways Russell's philosophy partook in the general movement away from realism which followed the First World War, without ever moving away from it to the extent others did. But this movement away from realism belongs to the next chapter. In the meantime we must turn to the third and the most broadly influential of the great Cambridge trio, Ludwig Wittgenstein (1889–1951).

Wittgenstein is one of the great masters of twentieth-century modernism. Like some others, he is simultaneously a maker of modernism and a hostile critic. He is a pivot between Cambridge and Vienna, and between the two phases of analytic modernism. However, he is a good deal more even than that. His later philosophy criticizes its way out of the assumptions of analytical modernism which he himself did so much to shape. Wittgenstein is just as important in breaking the mould of the analytic tradition as in shaping it. But that comes after our period. In this book we shall encounter him only in the latter role.

Wittgenstein came from a Viennese milieu of the greatest bourgeois affluence, achievement, and culture. Karl Wittgenstein, his father, was a powerful character and an important man in Vienna. Of Christianized German Jewish stock (the Wittgensteins had come to Vienna in the 1850s), he built up the family's already considerable fortunes, becoming a major iron and steel master of the Austrian Empire. The family was large, close, and intensely musical—intense in fact in every way.

In his musicality and his general culture Wittgenstein was strongly oriented to the earlier 19th century. One of his sayings was that culture comes to an end with Schumann; Alban Berg's music seemed to him a scandal. Yet his distaste for both liberal and *fin-de-siècle* Vienna was just as great as that of other Viennese modernists. In Karl Kraus he found a fellow-spirit, especially in Kraus's concern with purifying language. It is right to relate his own concern with the distinction between saying and showing, and with crystalline purity of statement, to this Viennese matrix.

Wittgenstein received his training as a mechanical engineer in the *Technische Hochschule* in Charlottenburg. He came to Britain in 1908 to continue engineering studies at Manchester. But in the autumn of 1911 he went to Cambridge. It seems that quite early in his engineering days at Charlottenburg he had become interested in the philosophy of mathematics; he had read Frege and Russell's work, and thought hard about the paradox. In Manchester he finally decided to study the philosophy of mathematics, went to Jena to consult with Frege, probably in the summer of 1911, and was advised to study with Russell.

The encounter with Russell was momentous for both sides, deeply productive and deeply strained, an exhausting, tense wrestling-match between the aristocratic Edwardian and the tortured, uncertain, but intransigent Viennese. Russell, after being unsure for some time what to make of 'my German engineer', came to see Wittgenstein as his true heir in logic—just when his own logical flame was dying down. But despite Wittgenstein's lifelong engagement with the philosophy of mathematics (more than half his writings concern it), that was not the final centre of his thought. Technical paradoxes or challenges were for him a starting-point of comtemplation, an indication of something not utterly clear.

Eventually their paths diverged, personally and then intellectually. Russell thought Wittgenstein's later philosophy was intellectual suicide. But it was he who found a means of publishing Wittgenstein's first great contribution, which Wittgenstein had completed while a combatant in the war—the

*Logische-Philosophische Abhandlung* (1921)—it was in fact published only because Russell supplied an introduction for it. And it was Moore who suggested the title for its English translation: *Tractatus Logico-Philosophicus*.

The expository structure of the *Tractatus* is an integral part of its content and force. It consists of seven theses, numbered consecutively. The text consists of comments on them, comments on comments, and so on. Thus '4.31' is the first comment on the third comment on the fourth thesis. (But the system is not quite perspicuous—for example, '6' is followed by '6.001'.)

The first thesis is 'The world is all that is the case', the final thesis 'What we cannot speak about we must pass over in silence.' In a sense, these suffice for Wittgenstein, and are indeed already too much.

But before we sniff the work's heady mystical vapours too deeply, it is better to begin in the middle, with the second, third, fourth, and fifth theses. 'What is the case—a fact—is the existence of a state of affairs'; 'A logical picture of facts is a thought'; 'A thought is a proposition with a sense'; and 'A proposition is a truth-function of elementary propositions.' They all express aspects of the Tractarian 'picture theory of meaning'.

The central point is that *only a fact can represent a fact*. It is a point about the essence of representation, which comes from reflection on what unifies the proposition—the question we have encountered repeatedly in this chapter and the last.

'Only facts can express a sense, a set of names cannot' (3.142). Propositions—whatever represents a 'state of affairs'—are themselves facts. (In the terminology of the *Tractatus* a 'state of affairs' is a possible—actual or non-actual—fact.)

Wittgenstein had been working out the implications of this in Cambridge and Norway before the war. The problem-context would have been familiar to Moore and Russell from their early period of conceptual monism. Moore too had then identified propositions with facts—but Wittgenstein's point was now quite different. A proposition is a fact which pictures *another*, actual or possible, fact. From this basic insight about the nature of signification, or symbolization, many consequences flow.

Propositions—facts which represent—are combinations of

names. The names directly stand for, go proxy for objects; the possible combinations of names represent possible configurations of objects (thus, states of affairs).

One name stands for one thing, another for another thing, and they are combined with one another. In this way the whole group—like a tableau vivant—presents a state of affairs. (4.0311)

It is the fact of their being combined in a particular way that represents—as the fact that the light is moving in this direction across the screen, represents that the aeroplane is flying in that direction over that bit of country. It is not the sentence considered as an inscription or utterance—an object—which means, but the *fact* that the names in it are configured in a particular way:

Instead of, 'The complex sign '*aRb*' says that *a* stands to *b* in the relation *R*', we ought to put, '*That* '*a*' stands to '*b*' in a certain relation says *that aRb*'. (3.1432)

Frege had sought to account for the unity of the proposition by means of the doctrine of incompleteness. The proposition for him is a sense, a complete entity which can be referred to, but it has an identifiable ingredient which is incomplete. It results that none of the following—a function, a predicate, the sense of a predicate—can be the referent of a singular term. And hence we get the paradox of the concept *horse*.

For Wittgenstein a proposition contains no ingredient which is 'incomplete'—the Fregean doctrine of incompleteness is rejected along with the Fregean distinction of sense and reference. A proposition is a fact, a configuration of names which cannot itself be named. Tractarian objects—the simples which are named—already determine their own possibilities of configuration. His doctrine of propositions as facts nonetheless produces closely related paradoxes of unsayability. Since facts cannot be named, the picture theory itself must be unsayable. But Wittgenstein enormously widens the realm of unsayability. We are eventually led by Wittgenstein's principles to the conclusion that not only semantics and metaphysics, but also ethics and mathematics are strictly unsayable.

While a proposition, as we have seen, can picture a non-actual state of affairs, a name cannot fail to name. If it did it would lack meaning and could not enter into a proposition. Thus any object, in the Tractarian sense, must subsist as a condition of the existence of any state of affairs: the set of possible states of affairs is the set of possible configurations of objects. 'Objects make up the substance of the world' (2.021). 'If all objects are given, then at the same time all *possible* states of affairs are also given' (2.0124).

Obviously, then, these propositions and names are not what we ordinarily think of as propositions and names. Nor are the objects ordinary objects. How then do they enter the ordinary world? The answer is to be found in the fifth thesis, 'A proposition is a truth-function of elementary propositions.' It might have been better to say: what is normally called a proposition, what is expressed by an ordinary sentence, is a truth-function of propositions.

Facts cannot have properties or relations, for they are not objects. It follows that any proposition which seems to predicate a property of a fact cannot really do so. But propositions are themselves facts. So there cannot be propositions about propositions. In particular, connectives do not stand for objects and truth-functions are not configurations of objects:

there are no 'logical objects' or 'logical constants' (in Frege's and Russell's sense). (5.4)

Wittgenstein calls this his 'fundamental idea' (see e.g. 4.0312), and it is indeed equivalent to the factuality of propositions. Truth-functions, he says, are operations on propositions. Thus negation reverses the sense of a proposition (which Wittgenstein thinks of like a vector, or an arrow); double negation reverses it twice, leaving us with the original proposition. Or we can think of a proposition as dividing logical space cleanly in two; its sense determines which portion is affirmed. Negation, like a toggle-switch, alternates the affirmed portion. The toggle switch does not itself represent anything *in* logical space. Thus $\sim\sim P$ says the same thing as $P$. To take the equivalence as an axiom of logic, as Frege does, is wrong.

All of this can be made clearer by the use of a truth-table notation. Wittgenstein did not claim to have invented truth-tables—we saw that Frege in effect used them in explaining the connectives in the *Begriffsschrift*. What Wittgenstein did was to use them as a way of representing truth-functions of propositions (by the truth-table which determines them). All our ordinary propositions are such truth-functions, 'results of truth-operations on elementary propositions' (5.3).

To get to this beautiful result Wittgenstein treats generality as conjunction across all objects $((x) \, \phi x = \phi a \, \& \, \phi b \, \& \, \ldots)$. And he also draws on Russell's theory of descriptions, using it to paraphrase out all ordinary singular terms. That requires him to give an account of identity, which, as we have seen, is used in Russell's theory. For let '*a*' and '*b*' be Tractarian names. Then '*a=b*', if a genuine proposition, would have to be necessarily true. But it could not picture a state of affairs, so it cannot be a genuine proposition. Wittgenstein simply eliminates the identity sign, showing how to formulate the theory of descriptions without it (5.53 ff.).

The picture theory of propositions and the doctrine that there are no logical constants are unified in Wittgenstein's thinking with the other cardinal thesis of the *Tractatus*; that logic is formal. 'There are no pictures that are true a priori', (2.225). There are no *facts* of logic; 'there can be no representatives of the *logic* of facts' (4.0312). Logic is a priori just because it says nothing about the world; it is *expressed* by a perfect symbolism. For to symbolize is to picture a state of affairs, or to play a role in the picturing of states of affairs. Since any proposition shares its formal structure with the state of affairs (the possible fact) which it pictures, it *can* only picture a possible fact.

It is a beautiful idea that logic expresses the essential structure of fact—the logical structure of the world—that is, of everything that is the case. It also follows that there can be no logical relations between distinct facts. For the existence of such a relation would itself be a fact, so that logic would after all be factual.

Russell's theory of types is now seen to be superfluous,

because no symbol can be used illogically. What it attempts to say can only be shown. The propositions of logic are contentless tautologies; truth-functions which come out true whatever truth-value is assigned to the elementary propositions from which they are built. Thus Wittgenstein honours the thesis of epistemological empiricism, that no a priori proposition can have real content. Its underlying idea is captured with Wittgenstein's crystalline purity:

A priori knowledge that a thought was true would be possible only if its truth were recognizable from the thought itself (without anything to compare it with). (3.05)

If the truth of a proposition does not *follow* from the fact that it is self-evident to us, then its self-evidence in no way justifies our belief in its truth. (5.1363)

Wittgenstein takes with unprecedented strictness the idea that logic is purely formal—and with equal strictness the idea that what is not formal is empirical:

The so-called law of induction cannot possibly be a law of logic, since it is obviously a proposition with sense.—Nor, therefore, can it be an a priori law. (6.31)

[It] has no logical justification but only a psychological one. (6.3631)

What then of the apparent non-truth-functionality of those contexts which Frege had handled by his theory of indirect reference? Wittgenstein cannot allow that 'propositions in psychology, such as "*A* believes that *p* is the case" and "*A* has the thought *p*", etc.' (5.541) express a relation between a subject and a proposition. For by his general principles, a proposition is not an object and cannot be denoted by a name. The solution, apparently, is to do away with the empirical subject:

'*A* believes that *p*', '*A* has the thought *p*', and '*A* says *p*' are of the form ' "*p*" says *p*'; and this does not involve a correlation of a fact with an object, but rather the correlation of facts by means of the correlation of their objects. (5.542)

This hardly shows how propositions of the form ' "*p*" says *p*' avoid naming facts—Wittgenstein's hand-waving, and his tendency to pull metaphysical rabbits out of a hat which is supposed to be rigorously formal, are particularly flagrant here. The only available conclusion on his principles is that psychological propositions are unsayable, along with everything syntactic or semantic, everything a priori and everything ethical.

All too much becomes unsayable in the *Tractatus*. On the other hand, if we allow ourselves to *say* the unsayable we find that it contains some good old-fashioned transcendental theses. The disconcerting point is that these are, somehow, supposed to emerge from Wittgenstein's demonstrations that only what can be pictured can be said, and that the propositions of logic are contentless. Not that he succeeds in this—the Millian insight that logic contains real propositions remains intact. It is not true that all logic can be reduced to tautologies; but in any case the propositions which are 'tautologies' in Wittgenstein's sense cannot all be empty or analytic in the strict or narrow sense which is required in the debate between radical empiricism and transcendental idealism.

But we cannot stop to demonstrate this in detail. We must consider further the transcendental, that is, 'unsayable', and the modernist strands in the *Tractatus*.

The fundamental transcendental presupposition is that there are objects—the world has substance (Cp. 5.552, 5.5521). But also 'something about the world must be indicated by the fact that certain combinations of symbols . . . are tautologies' (6.124).

What? Wittgenstein does not say. If what does the indicating is that tautologies are contentless, then what it must indicate is that the classical laws of truth—bivalence and exclusion—are not themselves either empty or real but somehow transcendental presuppositions of any proposition's being empty or real. It is hard indeed to know what to make of this. And then there is the question of Wittgenstein's apparent transcendental solipsism, which seems to be also connected.

*The limits of my language* mean the limits of my world. (5.6)

This is a leading comment on thesis 5, which says that propositions are truth-functions of elementary propositions. So the limits Wittgenstein has in mind seem to be those set by the names of my language and their possibility of configuration.

We cannot say the world might have consisted in other objects—that would be to think beyond the limits. Wittgenstein says that this provides the key to how much truth there is in solipsism:

what the solipsist *means* is quite correct; only it cannot be *said*, but makes itself manifest. (5.62)

He has already inferred the non-existence of the empirical subject from his treatment of 'propositions in psychology'. But now he talks of 'the metaphysical subject', which he says is the 'limit of the world' (5.632). What brings it 'into philosophy is the fact that "the world is my world" ' (5.641).

Perhaps the connexion is with the transcendental question of how it is possible for names to signify objects. Obviously it cannot be by any empirical process which is *in* the world. For then the objects would *already* have had to have been represented for names to be attached to them. And any such naming process, being an empirical state of affairs, might not have occurred. It would only be a contingent fact that all objects had been named. But if they had not been, language would not be isomorphic with the world, which is impossible. So to think of the naming process as empirical leads to a *reductio ad absurdum*. To be, we are forced to conclude, is to be named. But naming and language cannot exist without a namer and language-user. So perhaps we can detect here the underlying notion that the metaphysical subject, the transcendental language-user, constitutes objects in naming them. But this can only be conjecture—the text we are given does not provide enough secure guidance to follow Wittgenstein's thought through.

Woven into these themes in the *Tractatus* there is another, which figures greatly in the modernist spirit. It is the bifurcation between what can be said and has no value (the propositions of natural science) and what has value but cannot be said.

All propositions are of equal value. (6.4) [namely, none]

The sense of the world must lie outside the world . . . *in* it no value exists. (6.41)

Ethics (and, which is the same thing, aesthetics) is transcendental (6.421). So is the will—'in so far as it is the subject of ethical attributes' (6.423). ('And the will as a phenomenon is of interest only to psychology.')

If nothing in the world, no contingent project in itself, has value, what does? The good will, which is associated with the impersonal—the mystical—sense of the world.

It is not *how* things are in the world that is mystical, but *that* it exists. (6.44)

Feeling the world as a limited whole—it is this that is mystical. (6.45)

But we cannot ask *why* the world exists.

When the answer cannot be put into words, neither can the question be put into words. (6.5)

There are indeed things that cannot be put into words. They *make themselves manifest*. They are what is mystical. (6.522)

Immediately on these words there follows a description of 'the correct method in philosophy':

The correct method in philosophy would really be the following: to say nothing except what can be said, i.e. propositions of natural science—i.e. something that has nothing to do with philosophy—and then, whenever someone else wanted to say something metaphysical, to demonstrate to him that he had failed to give a meaning to certain signs in his propositions. Although it would not be satisfying to the other person—he would not have the feeling that we were teaching him philosophy—*this* method would be the only strictly correct one. (6.53)

This conception of the traceless, self-cancelling, work of philosophy is of the utmost importance to analytic modernism. It is stated in the *Tractatus* with wonderful elegance and simplicity; we shall see another attempt to ground it in the next chapter. It remained with Wittgenstein throughout his life—when he had long given up the doctrines of the *Tractatus*. But it is no easy solution. It must somehow come from a conception of meaning which is powerful enough to dissolve the metaphysical questions which press on us—while yet itself not being metaphysical.

Does analytic modernism find a way of dissolving metaphysics—without somehow reintroducing transcendental idealism in the very dissolving agents it uses? We shall come back to the question for a last time in Chapter 6. Certainly Wittgenstein did not find the way in the *Tractatus*. There, the metaphysical subject still haunts the scene.

The self-dissolving conception of philosophy was always liberating, rather than stultifying, for Wittgenstein. It can seem to be stultifying—to send one back, chastened, to the tedium of the natural attitude. But at the time of the *Tractatus* particularly, when the war had quickened his mystical and quietist impulse, it had a powerful spiritual value for him. 'The solution of the problem of life is seen in the vanishing of the problem' (6.521). He did not mean that it could be solved by being ignored. On the contrary, its solution is its dissolution, and only the most intense and pure meditation provides an adequate solvent. It leaves everything in the world as it is—but it does not leave the will as it is.

Wittgenstein's mysticism is already present in the picture theory, with its emphasis on 'representing', 'going proxy for'—on the homology between picture and pictured, the picturing fact *re-presenting* the fact. He senses it himself when he speaks of the 'internal relation of depicting that holds between language and the world' and draws this comparison: '(Like the two youths in the fairy-tale, their two horses, and their lilies. They are all in a certain sense one)' (4.014). The Eleatic impulse is very close to the surface here, and it is present in the idea, which I have suggested underlies Wittgenstein's notion of the truth in solipsism, that to be is to be named.

Later, when mysticism and logic were no longer fused in his thought (at least by explicit doctrine), Wittgenstein still found spiritual sustenance in the very peculiar clarity the philosopher is left with, when philosophy has done its self-dissolving work. Evidently it does not dissolve only itself. It must also dissolve pressures or distortions of which it is only one possible effect—but a very special one, because for him at least, it is the only effect which contains the promise of cure. But this is to go beyond our limits into the later Wittgenstein.

# Modernism II: Vienna

The important phases in the development of the analytic tradition fall rather neatly into two periods. The first phase develops mainly before the First World War; it includes the Cambridge revolt against idealism, Moore and Russell's early assertion and abandonment of conceptual monism, the first response to the work of Frege, the discovery of the paradoxes and the arrival of Wittgenstein in Cambridge. It culminates with the publication of the *Tractatus* in 1921. The second phase is mainly in Vienna in the 1920s and 1930s, and is the subject of this chapter, which will outline the work of the Vienna Circle—the movement know as 'logical positivism'.

If the mood of the first phase can be said to be primarily logical and ethical, that of the second is scientific and political. The change is part of a broader change in the spirit of modernism, before and after the Great War. Certainly the new logic, and its continuing development, is just as important to the Vienna Circle as it was in Cambridge. But increasingly it is put to work as a tool of epistemological analysis, rather than being itself made an object of metaphysical reflection.

Russell, it is true, was throughout his life a political activist. His first book (1896) was on *German Social Democracy*, and a stream of social and political writings followed. But there was a divide between these writings and his 'professional' (as it could by now be called) philosophy, a divide which did not exist in the philosophy of Mill and Green. Moreover Russell stood out by his political activity; it was one part of that whole side of his character which put his relations with both Moore and Wittgenstein under strain. Overall the influence of early Cambridge philosophy was toward a quietist Platonic ethic of the soul and its personal relations.

Russell's political writings have not entered the canon of political philosophy, and the Vienna Circle produced no classic text of political philosophy either. In fact the absence of really serious political *philosophy* in analytic modernism is its most telling limitation (a limitation of modernism as such). The closest this period came to making a permanent contribution to political philosophy was at its very end, in Karl Popper's companion volumes, *The Poverty of Historicism* and *The Open Society and its Enemies* (1944, 1945). These look likely to join the canon, though that is not yet quite clear. But though Popper was an Austrian scientist–philosopher, and had associations with the Vienna circle, he was decidedly not a member of it; nor does he belong to analytic modernism. Though not free of modernist influences he was in important ways a critic of its Viennese phase—its epistemology, its theory of meaning, and its politics.

The Vienna Circle produced no great work of political philosophy, but it would be a mistake to see it as engaging simply in the technical science of science. It differed in its intellectual foci from the philosophic radicalism of Bentham and his circle, yet in its way it was just as much a *movement* for intellectual and social reconstruction, with a strongly secular-socialist-planning tinge. This has the same flavour as the older nineteenth-century Positivism; it was not to the taste of Moritz Schlick, its founder, or of Wittgenstein, its greatest outside mentor—they both belonged to the earlier, élitist–quietist phase of modernism. But it was very much the mood of its most important younger members, Rudolf Carnap and—especially—Otto Neurath.

The *Tractatus* is a pivot between the two phases of analytic modernism. After its publication Wittgenstein retired from philosophy. He thought he had solved the problems. But he had also been deeply changed by the war, in which he had fought (with truly desperate bravery) on the Eastern front. He now gave up his fortune and tried to make a career as an elementary schoolteacher in the Austrian countryside. The Tolstoyan endeavour ended in failure and humiliation. To fend off accusations that he gave excessively severe corporal punishment to some of the children, Wittgenstein found himself telling lies.

This haunted him for long after. (It was part of the same intensity that he took immense pains with his better pupils.) The real trouble was that Wittgenstein, however he sought it, could not endure the company of the *NormalMensch*. In the latter half of 1926 he was back in Vienna, engaged with Paul Engelmann, a close friend who was an architect, on the design of a house for his sister Margaret Stonborough. A comment he made on it much later, in his personal notes, is interesting:

the house I built for Gretl is the product of a decidedly sensitive ear and *good* manners, an expression of great *understanding* (of a culture, etc.). But *primordial* life, wild life striving to erupt into the open—that is lacking. And so you could say it isn't *healthy* (Kierkegaard). (Hothouse plant.) (Wc 38)

(This is from a selection of the notes which contains many interesting and moving things.)

Meanwhile the *Tractatus* was finding in Vienna a small but distinguished group of readers. Hans Hahn, a mathematician who was also one of the original members of the discussion group which became the Vienna Circle, gave seminars on it in 1922. But the most influential Viennese philosopher to take up its cause was the founder of that group, Moritz Schlick (1882–1936).

Schlick was a German, not an Austrian, from a well-to-do family. He was a physicist by training, completing a doctorate (on an aspect of the physics of light) at the University of Berlin under Max Planck. After philosophical posts at Rostock and Kiel he came to Austria in 1922 to take the Chair of the History and Philosophy of the Inductive Sciences at the University of Vienna. (It had been founded in 1895 to attract Ernst Mach from Prague. He had to resign it in 1901 because of a stroke and was succeeded by Ludwig Boltzmann, who changed its title to Theoretical Physics and Natural Philosophy, from dislike of Mach's philosophical activity; Schlick restored the original title.)

Schlick was a philosopher of general culture and wide interests. But it was as a philosopher of science and an epistemologist that he first made a mark. In 1915 he published a paper on 'The Philosophical Significance of the Principle of

Relativity' and in 1917 a book on *Space and Time in Contemporary Physics*. Through his own work and through his encouragement of younger philosophers of science, he helped to put modern physics, particularly the analysis of Einsteinian space–time, on the philosophical agenda. (Philosophers in Cambridge had also taken an early interest.) He was not so interested in modern logic—it was pre-eminently Carnap who added that to the Vienna Circle's curriculum, producing the distinctive fusion of modern physics and modern logic which stamps their epistemology. But that is to anticipate.

Einstein was sufficiently impressed to champion Schlick's cause, observing in a letter to Born: 'Schlick has a good head on him; we must try to get him a professorship.' But he thought it would be difficult, 'as he does not belong to the philosophical established church of the Kantians' (Sg, p. xv). Certainly Schlick's *General Theory of Knowledge* (published in 1918 under the German title *Allgemeine Erkenntnislehre*, and in a considerably revised edition in 1925) is outside that church. It belongs to the tradition of epistemology as naturalistic 'science of science' which we saw developing in the 19th century. Epistemology interprets, clarifies, and codifies scientific knowledge. Schlick rejects Kant's view that there are synthetic a priori truths and he also rejects the claim that any truths are self-evident. In all this he is on the side of Mill and Mach.

The book is also, however, a late manifestation of the realist turn in philosophy around the turn of the century. But in this case the realism is not Platonic but scientific. Schlick criticizes both Kantians and Millian or Machian empiricists in this spirit—arguing against them that science can legitimately transcend experience and give us knowledge of entities which we do not directly experience.

That is one broad difference between him and the older empiricism. Another, more clear-cut, is that Schlick sharply distinguishes between the logical and the empirical. Mill and Mach held—in Mill's case, as we saw, very carefully and explicitly—that logic and mathematics are empirical. In contrast, Schlick holds that they are a priori because empty of content. 'Every judgement we make is either definitional or cognitive' (Sg 69).

His main impulse is to account for the unchallengeable exact-
ness and certainty of logic and mathematics:

the radical empiricism of John Stuart Mill [like 'the doctrine of the
sophist Gorgias']—if carried out with thoroughgoing consistency—
results in the [view that] absolute certainty cannot be claimed for any
knowledge, not even for so-called pure conceptual truths, such as the
propositions of arithmetic. [It has no way of] saving the certainty and
rigor of knowledge in the face of the fact that cognition comes about
through fleeting, blurred experiences . . . (Sg 30)

To remedy this defect epistemology must investigate whether the content of all concepts is to be found ultimately only in intuition [i.e.
'immediate experience'], or whether under some circumstances it may
make sense to speak of the meaning of a concept without reducing it
to intuitive ideas. The determinateness of such concepts could thus be
guaranteed independently of the degree of sharpness that character-
izes our intuitions. We would no longer have to be dismayed by the
fact that our experiences are in eternal flux; rigorously exact thought
could still exist. (Sg 31)

Schlick shares this urge to reassert the dichotomy between
the exact and certain—the rigorous—on the one hand, and the
blurred and defeasible—the empirical—on the other, with all
analytic modernists. (And he, too, strictly separates the logical
and the psychological.) But Schlick and Wittgenstein are the
first among them to base it on the thesis that all rigorous sciences are formal: contentless. This goes with another point of
agreement between them—both of them deny logical as against
psychological standing to the principle of induction. On this
point Schlick, like Mach whom he otherwise criticizes, finds
cause to go back to Hume.

But where Wittgenstein defends the dichotomy by the
argument that logic consists of tautologies and mathematics
of identities, Schlick comes at it differently. He argues for it on
the basis of the mathematician David Hilbert's notion of *implicit
definition*. Here is one important source of a theme which will
occupy us—the Vienna Circle's conventionalism.

The work to which Schlick refers is David Hilbert's
*Grundlagen der Geometrie* of 1899 (Foundations of Geometry).
In this, Hilbert provides the first fully satisfactory set of axioms

for Euclidean geometry, and he suggests that the primitive terms used therein (such as 'point', 'straight line', 'plane', 'between', 'outside of', etc.) can be thought of as implicitly defined by the axioms. In other words, it is to be simply *stipulated* that they denote any entities which as a class satisfy the axioms.

An implicit definition contrasts with an explicit definition, such as ' "square" means "plane figure bounded by four equal rectilinear sides" ', which allows substitution of the defined term by its definiens. Schlick also recognizes what he calls 'concrete definitions', as against 'logical definition proper' (Sg 30). In these the meaning of a simple concept is ostensively exhibited in experience—for example the note 'A' is concretely defined by sounding a tuning-fork. It is only through such definitions that we set up a connexion between concepts and reality.

Pure geometry is thus a formal science which studies logical consequences in an axiom system. The axioms themselves, since they have the status of definitions, are not genuine cognitive judgements at all. The formal system turns into a component of physical geometry when its primitive concepts are 'co-ordinated' with physical facts. Schlick holds that such co-ordinations essentially involve *conventions*—he points out that he is using the term in a narrow sense (which he ascribes to Poincaré), since 'in the broader sense, of course, all definitions are agreements' (Sg 71).

The co-ordination is between two definitions: an implicit definition with a concrete definition, for example of 'point' by ostending a grain of sand, or 'straight line' by ostending a taut string. There is an empirical element here—it is a *hypothesis* that the principles of the formal system, thus interpreted, will turn out to yield correct predictions. But if predictions are to be possible at all we must also define units of measurement as part of our co-ordination, and it is here that a convention in Poincaré's sense comes in. Thus a unit length could be defined by a particular taut string, or a rigid rod, which is then laid off against other straight lines to measure their length. Schlick's example is the unit of time-measurement. We can define a day as the period the earth takes to rotate about its axis (the side-real day). We could equally have chosen 'the pulse beats of the Dalai Lama' as units. But the rate at which the processes of nature run their course would then depend on the health of the Dalai Lama; for example, if he had a fever and a faster pulse beat, we would have to ascribe a slower pace to natural processes, and the laws of nature would take an extremely complicated form.

We choose the metric which yields the simplest laws. So, for example, the sidereal day may come to be abandoned as a unit of measurement—it may be more 'practical'

to assert that, as a consequence of friction due to the ebb and flow of the tides, the rotation of the earth gradually slows down and hence sidereal days grow longer. Were we not to accept this, we would have to ascribe a gradual acceleration to all other natural processes and the laws of nature would no longer assume the simplest form. (Sg 72)

In general, the simplicity of the total system of laws of nature taken as a whole is the criterion for choosing units of measurement. It is only 'as that stage', Schlick rather curiously says, 'that the unit of time acquires the character of a convention in our sense'. We shall come back to this point.

But has Schlick's appeal to the notion of implicit definition successfully demonstrated his claim—which was that logic and mathematics are a priori, exact and certain because they consist of definitions? The following passage is representative:

In the class of definitions in the wider sense, we include also those propositions that can be derived by pure logic from definitions. Epistemologically, such derived propositions are the same as definitions, since ... they are interchangeable with them. From this standpoint purely conceptual sciences, such as arithmetic, actually consist exclusively of definitions; they tell us nothing that is in principle new, nothing that goes beyond the axioms. (Sg 73)

Here Schlick allows that definitions can be deduced from definitions. This may already be questioned, if we insist that definitions are rules, rather than propositions apt to play the role of premise or conclusion. But let us waive that point and ask instead the crucial question—what is the status of the 'pure logic' by which the theorems of the axiom-system are derived?

Pure geometry, on Schlick's reading, is a set of logical truths about the relations of derivability between certain 'definitions'. But if those truths are not contentless—because they are a posteriori or synthetic a priori—then Schlick's goal has not been achieved.

Can we apply the same treatment to logic itself—treating its axiomatized principles as implicit definitions of the primitive logical constants? It seems that Schlick has something like this in mind when he says that the principles of contradiction and excluded middle 'merely determine the nature of negation' and 'may be looked upon as its definition' (Sg 64, cp. 337). But this does not explain how truths about derivability within a formal logical system are contentless. For the same question now arises about the meta-logical principles by which the theorems of the axiomatized logical system are derived.

Schlick does not push the question so far. But it was to become important in the later development of logical positivism, and we shall return to it.

The other important theme in the *General Theory of Knowledge* is Schlick's treatment of consciousness and his criticism of what he calls the 'immanence standpoint'. This holds that all realities are immanent in experience—nothing transcends it. It is in other words the thesis we have called 'strong phenomenalism' (p. 56 above). Against this Schlick argues that objects inferred by scientific methods are just as legitimately held to exist as those given in experience. Rather misleadingly he calls such objects, 'whose reality is asserted without their being directly *given*' (Sg 195), *things-in-themselves*. They are indeed by definition not things-as-they-appear. But Schlick warns that his use of the term is special—he does not have in mind the notion Mach derided, of a bare particular stripped of all properties, nor the notion of Kant, of an object which transcends all empirical scientific enquiry as such. Moreover, things-in-themselves need not be things but may be events and processes. His criterion is that 'everything is real that must be thought of as being at a specific time' (GTK 194) and his point is that science and common sense itself necessarily postulate experience-transcendent entities which are by this criterion real. The laws of science themselves imply that not everything real can be humanly perceivable:

Science goes beyond [unperceived but perceivable objects] to things that, in virtue of its very own principles, cannot be given to man. It makes judgements about the interior of the sun, about electrons, about organic field strengths (for which we do not possess any sense organs) and so forth. (Sg 203)

He thinks that what forces people to abandon common sense and seek refuge in the standpoint of immanence comes down to just one 'dreaded' problem, that of mind–body dualism, which has haunted philosophers since Descartes. This is the problem conjured up by Mach, and Schlick makes the empirio-critics, Avenarius and Mach, together with Bertrand Russell as represented by his position in *Our Knowledge of the External World*, the main objects of his criticism.

Russell's basic principle is that anything real must be a possible object of acquaintance. But this is to confuse acquaintance (*Kennen*) with knowledge (*Erkennen*). Moreover, in postulating sense-data or sensibilia which exist unsensed, Russell violates Occam's razor, and in any case already infringes the standpoint of immanence as clearly as postulating Schlickian things-in-themselves does. For it is futile to pretend that unsensed sensibilia can have the same epistemological and metaphysical status as actual sense-contents. But Schlick's entities are simply the physical objects postulated by science, while Russell's are philosophical excrescences from which physical objects still have to be constructed.

While Russell offers a genuine, though untenable alternative to Mill, the empirio-critics cannot distinguish their position from his. The immanence-standpoint 'if developed with consistency, leads inevitably to Mill' (Sg 213), and is thus open to the same objections.

The basic objection is that Mill makes subjunctive conditionals baldly true. 'Reducing the real to the possible must always be counted a *hysteron-proteron*' (Sg 184). Mach claims to substitute for Mill's possibilities 'something much sounder', the idea of functional relations between sensations, in the mathematical sense of 'function'. But this, Schlick rightly observes, is an alternative only if we treat functions as real things, that is, if we reify concepts.

There is in short no consistent way of expanding from the bankrupt view that *only* what is given is real, without wholeheartedly giving up the immanence-standpoint:

we deny any difference in reality between objects perceived and objects inferred by rigorous methods. We attribute reality to both kinds equally. (Sg 218)

Causal laws can then be formulated between things-in-themselves—the more fundamental the laws, the more remote those things are from the given. Contrary to neutral monism, objects perceived by several individuals are not a numerically identical series of sensations, occurring in two different minds. That problem, insoluble from the standpoint of immanence, disappears.

It turns out that the founder of the Vienna Circle had already provided devastating objections to positivism! At least it was to positivism understood in one standard sense, as strong phenomenalism. Schlick's own view (like Poincaré's) is a form of structural realism. He agrees with Kant on the 'ideality' (he prefers to call it the subjectivity) of intuitive space. 'Representable or imaginable *extension*', along with representable duration, is a property of subjective sensible qualities, not of things-in-themselves; the 'popular concept of the bodily' therefore joins together features that, *realiter*, are incompatible: a body is supposed to be a thing-in-itself . . . yet at the same time it is burdened with the intuitive, perceivable property of extension' (Sg 291). Physical, as against intuitable, space is the objective pure-geometric ordering of things-in-themselves:

reality is called 'physical' *in so far as it is designated by means of the spatio-temporal quantitative conceptual system of natural science* . . . the space of physics, as we have seen, is not in any way (intuitively) representable; it is a wholly abstract structure, a mere scheme of ordering. (Sg 294)

This structural realism in Schlick's view solves the mind–body problem. He agrees with Avenarius's criticism of what the latter termed 'introjection', the error of locating the sensible qualities in the head (Schlick's phrase). For Schlick it is the error of *locating* them at all. They are not in space. Schlick's argument partly overlaps with Reid's criticism of the Ideal System—he criticizes Kant for treating sensible qualities as 'appearances'—but only partly. For Schlick *also* rejects, with Kant, the common-sense notion of a perceived body with sensible qualities existing *outside* the mind.

Thus it appears that we have on the one hand the theoretical terms of science, implicitly defined by their place in its 'wholly abstract structure', and on the other the states of consciousness of subjects. (It is not quite as clearcut as that, because Schlick retains—for non-trivial reasons—a Kantian tendency to talk of intuitive space as ideal but nevertheless empirically real.) As to subjects, Schlick aspires to an anti-Cartesian stance, which eliminates the metaphysical subject without denying the Kantian 'unity of consciousness'. The contents of consciousness, from which neutral monism sought to build the world, have no existence independent of consciousness (or at least they become, in the just-noted Kantian sense, ideal).

'Kant brings space into consciousness, Avenarius extends consciousness over space' (Sg 307). But Schlick insists, neither is in the other. This is the key to the mind–body problem. What is describable by psychological concepts may also be described by physical ones:

in place of the dualistic assumption we introduce the much simpler hypothesis that the concepts of the natural sciences are suited for designating every reality including that which is immediately experienced. The resulting relation between immediately experienced reality and the physical brain processes is then no longer one of causal dependency but of simple *identity*. What we have is one and the same reality, not 'viewed from two different sides' or 'manifesting itself in two different forms', but designated by two different conceptual systems, the psychological and the physical. (Sg 299)

Schlick here introduces a position on the mind–body question which has become celebrated in contemporary philosophy as the 'identity-theory'. With it, naturalism has finally found its fully worked-out ontological expression:

according to our hypothesis the *entire world* is in principle open to designation by that conceptual system. Nature is all; all that is real is natural. Mind, the life of consciousness, is not the opposite of nature, but a sector of the totality of the natural. (Sg 296)

Notice that the conceptual system of natural science is not an uninterpreted formal system, but a system of empirical hypotheses. Therefore, just as pure geometry becomes empirical—physical—geometry only when it is 'co-ordinated' with physical facts, so must the system of the physical sciences as a whole be somehow co-ordinated with 'immediately experienced reality'—which Schlick, in the last but one quotation, takes to consist in processes of consciousness. But these *are* physical brain processes. Now co-ordination must be with the given, that is, something ostensible in a concrete definition. If states of consciousness are given, brain-processes are given—but not as brain-processes. There may or may not be a problem lurking there. (Schlick needs not just the notion of two conceptual systems but the obscurer notion of two modes of presentation of the same fact.) Another point is that to take the given as states of consciousness is to subjectivize it, in a way in which identifying it with the inter-subjective world of intuitive space does not. Does not communication require that the 'given', that which supplied the ostensions required by concrete definition, be inter-subjective? Here is one good reason for retaining intuitive space as at least 'empirically' real. But how to understand this, without some sort of Kantian framework, remains a long-term problem for the analytic tradition.

Another leading figure in the Vienna Circle, and eventually a more influential one, was Rudolf Carnap (1891–1970). Carnap, like Schlick, was a German. He studied at the Universities of Jena and Freiburg im Breisgau, specializing in mathematics and philosophy and then physics and philosophy. At Jena he attended a number of Frege's courses, on the *Begriffsschrift* and its applications in the construction of mathematics. Like Schlick, he too began work on a doctorate in physics—in his case on an aspect of the theory of electrons. But this was interrupted by the outbreak of war, in which Carnap served as an officer in the German army, and it was never finished; when he came back after the war he sought a new topic which would allow him to combine his interests in philosophy and theoretical physics.

In 1917 on the Western front he had read Einstein, delighting in the new theory's elegance; in 1919–21 he read *Principia Mathematica*, with its development of the theory of relations, Frege's *Grundgesetze*, and Russell's *Our Knowledge of the External World*. In his intellectual autobiography he quotes the following passages from the closing pages of the last:

The study of logic becomes the central study in philosophy: it gives the method of research in philosophy, just as mathematics gives the method in physics . . .

All this supposed knowledge in the traditional systems must be swept away, and a new beginning must be made . . . The one and only condition, I believe, which is necessary in order to secure for philosophy in the near future an achievement surpassing all that has hitherto been accomplished by philosophers, is the creation of a school of men with scientific training and philosophical interests, unhampered by the tradition of the past, and not misled by the literary methods of those who copy the ancients in all except their merits. (quoted, Sc 13)

He felt as though this appeal had been directed to him personally: 'To work in this spirit would be my task from now on!' (Sc 13). It was indeed his life's work, and his migration to the United States in 1935 produced a further round of Anglo-German inter-influence; the Russellian ideal of scientific philosophy, reinterpreted in Vienna-Circle terms, becoming a crucial presence in American philosophical debate. (The continuing development of American pragmatism was another—and after the post-war dissolution of logical positivism it came into the ascendant. But it would require another chapter to trace its fortunes between the wars.)

Carnap now saw, as he had not before, the general philosophical significance of the new logic. His new thesis (awarded 1921) was on space; it bore the subtitle, 'A Contribution to the

Philosophy of Science' (*Der Raum: Ein Beitrag zur Wissenschaftslehre*). In 1923 he met Hans Reichenbach at a conference in Erlangen—they had corresponded before. Reichenbach too was to become an important figure in the logical positivist movement, and like Carnap ended his career in America. (He taught in Berlin and was an associate but not a member of the Vienna Circle). Reichenbach's early work, a little later than Schlick's, was on relativity and the philosophy of space and time; the German first editions of his *The Theory of Relativity and A Priori Knowledge* and *The Philosophy of Space and Time* appeared in 1924 and 1928 respectively. Through Reichenbach Carnap met Schlick, in the summer of 1924.

He must have made a strong impression, for in the following year, 1925, we find him giving lectures to Schlick's Philosophical Circle on his own work (the *Aufbau*—see below), and in 1926, at the invitation of Schlick, he becomes a *privatdozent* (instructor) at the University of Vienna, and begins regular attendance at meetings of the Circle.

In his thesis Carnap had distinguished three notions of space —formal, intuitive, and physical. This was similar to Schlick's analysis, but less radical in its departure from Kant. Formal space was, as in Schlick, an uninterpreted 'abstract system, constructed in ... the logic of relations' (Sc 12), our knowledge of it was logical. Intuitive and physical space corresponded to Schlick's division, but Carnap still thought, under neo-Kantian influence, that 'pure intuition', independent of 'contingent experience', could provide synthetic a priori knowledge of properties of intuitive space, to which physical space must conform. However, he limited these to certain topological properties; like Schlick he considered that the metric of physical space was determined conventionally, and otherwise took its properties to be empirical. It is an important corollary of this metric conventionalism, endorsed also by Reichenbach, that the choice of geometry is conventional. (The thesis attempts to work out a predictively accurate description of the earth, based on the assumption that it is a flat surface in a Riemannian finite space.) Carnap, as we shall see, was to remain very consistent in holding that neither observation nor philosophical theory forces us to choose one particular theoretical framework or 'language-form' over another.

The work which first gives Carnap a distinctive place in the development of the analytic tradition is *Der Logische Aufbau der Welt*, translated into English as *The Logical Structure of the World*. It was drafted in 1922–5 and published in 1928. This is as much a monument of analytic modernism as the *Tractatus* or *Principia Ethica*—though all three works are utterly different. Carnap's aim is to construct all the concepts we use in describing reality (or, as he also says, to construct the objects corresponding to those concepts) from a small number of fundamental concepts; and his method is 'the analysis of reality with the aid of the theory of relations' (Ca 7).

He outlines a way of constructing the world from 'auto-psychological' elementary experiences. These are the experiences of a single self. (The experiences of other selves he calls 'heteropsychological'—they must themselves be constructed from physical objects which are in turn constructed from elementary experiences.) Elementary experiences are not Machian elements, the simple sensations of empiricist tradition—they are total unanalysable states of consciousness or *gestalts*. Carnap rather prides himself on this anti-atomistic point, and it gives him an opportunity for some constructional pyrotechnics, when he shows how to construct analogues of the traditional atomic sensations as complicated classes of elementary experiences.

The 'methodological solipsism' of the autopsychological construction is, Carnap stresses, optional—methodological not metaphysical. The world, including experiences, can equally be constructed by taking physical objects as primitive. The choice of construction is nothing more than the choice of language. So it seems that the question whether there are really only elementary experiences or really only physical things, at least taken in the philosophical spirit in which it is asked, is quite simply out of order. For the statement 'Only elementary experiences exist' will be false in both the autopsychological construction and in the physical construction; since objects in the empirical sense include those which are constructed—Carnap calls these 'quasi-objects'. We can of course say, if we adopt the autopsychological construction, 'Only elementary experiences are objects—all other empirical objects are quasi-objects.' But this is a sentence about the syntax of the autopsychological language. Carnap would insist that it had no ontological significance.

This is a startling position, which makes the *point* of Carnap's constructional project extremely elusive. Getting hold of it is made no easier by the technical deficiencies in his reduction, and, especially, by the eccentricity in his account of what constructing a concept is. His general claim is that it consists in showing how to 'transform' all sentences which contain it into sentences which do not. This sounds like paraphrasis in the style of Bentham and Russell; but it is not, because Carnap does not require that transformation should preserve synonymy or even logical equivalence. More must be required than that transformed and transforming sentences should have the same truth-value—in the preface to the second edition he says it should have been law-like coextensiveness of the concepts themselves, but this raises many questions. Altogether, the rationale of Carnap's construction is thoroughly unclear compared, for example, to the logical-reductionist programme of the *Tractatus*, which has a clear semantic framework.

Perhaps for expository as against critical purposes we can get along by saying, loosely, that Carnap thinks both the autopsychological and the physical construction would in their different ways 'capture everything genuinely objective that science has to say'. This connects with the structuralism that is such a strong theme in Carnap, Schlick, and before them, Poincaré (it is a neo-Kantian theme, echoed also, for example, in Green): what is objective is the relations between objects. Only structures, not phenomenal contents on the one side or 'things-in-themselves' on the other can be communicated and intersubjectively verified. But do we not have to require that the structures be co-ordinated to reality through the ostension of something which is given? Is it Carnap's doctrine that physical objects and elementary experiences may each indifferently be regarded as given? And are the physical objects denizens of intuitive space, or Schlickian things-in-themselves? Carnap was always maddeningly taciturn about such crucial philosophical questions which are raised by his technical projects.

Is the point the ontological unity of science? Consider the following passage.

The constructional system shows that all objects can be constructed from 'my elementary experiences' as basic elements. In other words (and this is what is meant by the expression 'to construct'), all (scientific) statements can be transformed into statements about my experiences (more precisely, into statements about relations between my experiences) where the logical value is retained. Thus, each object which is not itself one of my experiences, is a quasi object; I use its name as a convenient abbreviation in order to speak about my experiences. In fact, within construction theory, and thus within rational science, its name is *nothing but* an abbreviation. Whether, in addition, it also designates something which 'exists by itself' is a question of metaphysics which has no place in science. (Ca 255)

Here Carnap does say that the construction shows that all statements can be interpreted as speaking about (relations between) my experiences and that names of quasi-objects are used just as 'a convenient abbreviation to speak about my experiences'. Does that not show that only 'my' experiences exist? (Carnap reduces the self to them too.) Yet there is supposedly the equal possibility of a physicalist construction. So all statements can equally be interpreted as speaking about (relations between) physical objects. Should we then say: relative to the physical construction only physical objects exist; relative to the autopsychological construction, only experiences exist? The question then is what these two statements mean. We have already noticed that they are not true *within* the construction.

In fact Carnap explicitly gives an internal, intra-linguistic, account of 'real' (the 'empirical concept of reality'—sections 170–4); he has previously explained that the question 'What is the nominatum [the referent] of this object sign?' should strictly be phrased as 'Which sentences in which this object sign can occur are true?', adding

*We can make an unambiguous assessment only of the truth or falsity of a sentence, not of the nominatum of a sign, not even of an object sign. Thus . . . the indication of the nominatum of the sign of an object, consists in an indication of the truth criteria for those sentences in which the sign of this object can occur. (Ca 256–7)*

This can be read as stripping paraphrasis of its ontological significance—'construction' as against *reduction*. It seems to follow that the choice of the *framework of construction*, of the objects from which quasi-objects are constructed, itself carries no ontological significance, just as it carries no epistemological significance. Carnap's position, one might say, is *ontological neutralism*—for the same things are real on either construction. He is *neither* a strong-phenomenalist *nor* a physicalist, so he is not claiming that science is entirely about experiences, or entirely about physical objects. The point is rather that science can be ontologically unified in either way. But on Carnap's official account of the 'empirical concept of reality', this point cannot be made! On his own showing, it can only be a non-internal, metaphysical thesis.

It is illuminating to see how Carnap applies this neutralism to the mind–body problem. He imagines a 'brain mirror' which allows the processes of a living brain to be observed. From the point of view of physical construction we then have, constructionally speaking, a correlation between two physical sequences, one of brain events and the other of behaviour. No philosophical problem here. From the point of view of 'autopsychological' construction, on the other hand, we have two sequences of (complicated sets of) elementary experiences, between which, again, a straightforwardly empirical correlation is discovered. On the constructional approach, the metaphysical (as against the empirical) problem of psychophysical interaction cannot be formulated.

Schlick's naturalistic realism and his identity-theory are both more contemporary and less modernist than this neutralist 'solution' of the problem. On Carnap's view there is an internal scientific question and also a metaphysical problem, which he has somehow peeled off from it. The metaphysical problem, therefore, is not answered by any particular scientific discoveries about the relation between physics and psychology. An elegant response—the only trouble is that the problem has in fact been pushed under the carpet by the unclarities in Carnap's notion of 'construction'. Nevertheless, ontological neutralism remains Carnap's distinctive contribution to the analytic tradition. It developed in his thinking, and we shall be touching on it again.

The most famous Vienna-Circle doctrine, *verificationism*, is not found in the *Aufbau*. One might expect Carnap to say that metaphysical questions about whether an object-sign designates something which 'exists by itself' are meaningless; questions of existence can be raised only internally, within the framework of a constructional language. But he does not do so. The result is a little lame: metaphysical problems are dismissed as metaphysical, as out of order from the scientific or constructional viewpoint—but what is the significance of calling them metaphysical? And why should this lead to their dismissal?

What is needed to round off Carnap's position is a conception of meaning which would transform metaphysical issues into senseless pseudo-questions. Among these pseudo-questions would be questions about what ultimately exists—experiences or physical objects. The *only* trace then left by the pseudo-theses of idealism, solipsism, and realism, would be a conventional choice between language frameworks; ontological neutralism would then be the view, not that idealism and realism are equally 'correct', but that they are senseless and that there is only a choice of convention involved. The conception of meaning that is required is clearly the epistemic conception (p. 154 above), on which sentences have a meaning only by having an epistemic role—assertoric and inferential—*within* a language-framework.

The necessary step is very soon taken, but when the epistemic conception does appear, in Carnap's *Pseudo-Problems in Philosophy* (1928, written at the end of 1927), it appears in the interestingly extreme form of strict verificationism; and here it seems, by Carnap's own account, that the influence of Wittgenstein was at work.

Schlick had written to Wittgenstein in 1924 describing himself as an 'admirer of your *Tractatus Logico-Philosophicus*' and suggesting that they might meet. Nothing came of this till Wittgenstein was back in Vienna in 1926, engaged on the house for Gretl. The following February she invited Schlick to lunch, to meet her brother. He went (according to his wife) with 'the reverential attitude of the pilgrim. He returned in an ecstatic state, saying little' (Wv 14).

On his side, Wittgenstein quickly came to like and respect Schlick. Eventually, he was persuaded to meet other members of the Circle and regular discussions took place. Carnap was one of these, but only for a short while, for Wittgenstein found him hard to bear.

The tension between these two masters of analytic modernism epitomizes the conflict in its innermost spirit, a conflict which has been with us throughout this study, between enlightenment and the mystical impulse. Carnap later said that he had 'sometimes had the impression that . . . any ideas which had the flavour of "enlightenment" were repugnant to Wittgenstein' (Sc 26). If we judge by his recollections of the period, his attitude to Wittgenstein was modest but strong-minded and perceptive, somewhat as Moore's was:

His intellect, working with great intensity and penetrating power, had recognised that many statements in the field of religion and metaphysics did not, strictly speaking, say anything. In his characteristic absolute honesty with himself, he did not try to shut his eyes to this insight. But this result was extremely painful for him emotionally, as if he were compelled to admit a weakness in a beloved person. Schlick, and I, by contrast, had no love for metaphysics or metaphysical theology, and therefore could abandon them without inner conflict or regret . . . I had the impression that his ambivalence with respect to metaphysics was only a special aspect of a more basic internal conflict in his personality from which he suffered deeply and painfully. (Sc 27)

A small incident is revealing about both of them. Schlick 'unfortunately mentioned that I was interested in the problem of an international language like Esperanto'. Wittgenstein did not like this at all:

I was surprised by the vehemence of his emotions. A language which had not 'grown organically' seemed to him not only useless but despicable. (Sc 26)

It was not just a question of the need for a religious attitude. It was the old contrast again, say between Bentham and Coleridge —with Schlick, who needed religion no more than Mill, but like Mill had a great capacity of reverence (not the same as Carnap's modesty), playing something like the role of Mill between the two, in this case, younger men.

In January of 1929 Wittgenstein went back to Cambridge and, as it soon turned out, to active philosophy. He did not see Schlick again until he returned for a visit to Vienna the following Christmas.

Meanwhile the Vienna Circle had issued a manifesto, the inspiration of its younger members. It was mainly drafted by Neurath, though Carnap and Hans Hahn also signed the preface as editors, and it was entitled *Die Wissenschaftliche Weltauffassung: Der Wiener Kreis* (The Scientific Conception of the World: The Vienna Circle). The dedication was to Schlick, in gratitude for his decision to stay in Vienna with his friends when he had been offered a chair in Bonn.

The manifesto famously rejects metaphysics as nonsensical, because 'there is no such thing as philosophy as a basis or universal science alongside or above the various fields of the one empirical science' (N 316), and it affirms the tautological character of logical and mathematical truths. It appends a list of members of the circle, of sympathizers elsewhere (including Hans Reichenbach in Berlin and Frank Ramsey in Cambridge) together with three 'leading representatives of the scientific world conception'—Albert Einstein, Bertrand Russell, and Ludwig Wittgenstein. Wittgenstein's reaction was predictable:

Just because Schlick is no ordinary man, people owe it to him to take care not to let their 'good intentions' make him and the Vienna school which he leads ridiculous by boastfulness. When I say 'boastfulness' I mean any kind of self-satisfied posturing. 'Renunciation of metaphysics!' As if *that* were something new! What the Vienna school has achieved it ought to *show* not *say* . . . The master should be known by his *work*. (Letter to Waismann, Wv 18)

Of course Wittgenstein does not here demur at the renunciation of metaphysics as such. It was he above all others who asserted the strict *senselessness* of metaphysics, and the self-dissolving character of philosophy. This was true in both the *Tractatus* and in his later philosophy—if anyone spent a lifetime trying to achieve a totally perspicuous *übersicht* on the pseudo-problematic nature of philosophical questions, it was Wittgenstein.

In the *Tractatus* the meaninglessness of philosophy had been proclaimed on the basis of the picture theory of meaning, a conception strictly non-epistemic, which grows out of the realism of that earlier period. The *Tractatus* combines the doctrine that the sense of a proposition is determined by its truth conditions with an absolutely pure adherence to the correspondence conception of truth. Wittgenstein would at this stage have relegated all questions about what it is to *understand* a proposition, how one *grasps* its sense, to psychology.

But by the time he had his conversations with Schlick and others from the Vienna Circle, his views were rapidly changing. The question of what it is to understand an expression or a sentence now began to assume a central role, and his first line of thought took a very strict verificationist form. The record made by Friedrich Waismann of these conversations contains many formulations of it.

'The sense of a proposition is the method of its verification' (Wv 79, cp. e.g. Wv 227). We can take it that a proposition is a declarative sentence with a sense, and that to verify a proposition is to establish that it is true. Wittgenstein takes this quite strictly to mean '*indefeasibly* establish'. He describes (in Waismann's record) two conceptions of verification. According to one I cannot verify a proposition—for example, 'Up there on the cupboard there is a book'—completely.

A proposition always keeps a back-door open, as it were. Whatever we do, we are never sure that we were not mistaken.

The other conception, the one I want to hold, says, 'No, if I can never verify the sense of a proposition completely, then I cannot have meant anything by the proposition either. Then the proposition signifies nothing whatsoever.'

In order to determine the sense of a proposition, I should have to know a very specific procedure for when to count the proposition as verified. (Wv 47)

Applying the procedure must yield a definite and indefeasible result. But if understanding a sentence *is* knowing an effective way of determining its truth-value—and is nothing else—then it will also follow that a proposition cannot be true when there is not a method of verifying it. So the proposition is true if and only if there is a procedure which, if applied, would indefeasibly warrant us in holding it to be true—and this biconditional must itself be an analytic truth—a 'grammatical' truth, as Wittgenstein would now say. It also follows that if there is more than one verification procedure for a sentence (as with most sentences in 'everyday language') then that sentence has more than one sense. It expresses more than one proposition. And, of course, where there is no such procedure the sentence lacks sense.

Schlick was the closest of the Vienna Circle to Wittgenstein, yet it is nevertheless somewhat unexpected that he should have been the one who took strict verificationism most to heart. In the *General Theory of Knowledge* he refers to pragmatism, 'which some time ago caused a not inconsiderable stir in philosophical circles', says it maintains that 'the very essence of truth is to be found in' the process of verification, and bluntly concludes that 'this thesis is totally incorrect' (Sg 165).

Nevertheless it is Schlick who develops an argument for strict verificationism most explicitly. In his paper 'Positivism and Realism' (1932) he starts from the Tractarian point, that a proposition *means* by expressing the state-of-affairs which renders it true—its truth-condition. This doctrine was often treated by verificationists in the 1930s as already an expression of their view. Schlick fills in the line of thought by asking what it is to understand a sentence, and thus grasp its truth condition.

One understands the sentence by understanding the words which compose it, but this cannot proceed wholly by explicit definition:

the meaning of a word must ultimately be *shown*, it has to be *given*. This takes place through an act of pointing or showing, and what is shown must be given, since otherwise it cannot be pointed out to me.

In order, therefore, to find the meaning of a proposition, we have to transform it by introduction of successive definitions until finally only such words appear in it as can no longer be defined, but whose meanings can only be indicated directly. (Sp ii. 264)

Schlick deduces from this principle, namely that the meaning of all elementary signs must be ostensively given, the conclusion that grasp of a truth-condition is always grasp of an *observable* state of affairs, one which can be 'found in the given'. The deduction is erroneous—and it is at variance with his earlier, pre-positivist position. For there he had accepted the premise but in effect rejected the conclusion, that truth-conditions are always observable states of affairs, Wittgenstein's impact must indeed have been a powerful one!

Schlick does not however restrict the observable, and thus verifiable, to what we in practice can observe:

The statement that 'there are 10,000 ft mountains on the far side of the moon' is beyond doubt absolutely meaningful . . . it would remain just as meaningful even if we knew for certain, on scientific grounds of some kind, that no man would ever reach the far side of the moon. Verification always remains *thinkable*, we are able to say what sort of data we should have to encounter, in order to effect the decision; it is *logically* possible, whatever the situation may be as regards the actual possibility of doing it. And that is all that is at issue here. (Sp ii. 265)

The essence of the view is that to understand a sentence is to picture the encounterable data which make it true; to verify it is to 'encounter' those data.

This now leads him to conclude that 'propositions about bodies can be transformed into propositions of like meaning about the regularity of occurrence of sensations' (Sp ii. 283). He also argues that general propositions are rules.

This position has come to be thought of as canonical of 'logical positivism'. It is verificationist, it reduces physics to incorrigible statements about data, and it dichotomizes cognitively significant propositions strictly into those which are true or false by virtue of the meanings of their constituent words alone, and those whose truth or falsity can be decided by possible observation.

In fact it captures one position in a debate among philosophers in Vienna (inclucing Wittgenstein) which was full of cross-currents and sea-changes.

The verificationist idea itself was subject to them. It helps to distinguish two guiding ideas about what it is to understand a sentence: (1) picturing to oneself on encounterable state of affairs, (2) knowing how to follow a procedure of verification. Each of them can lead to strict verificationism, each of them can be used to elucidate the slogan 'To understand a sentence is to grasp its truth-condition', but they belong to quite different seas.

(1) results from combining a leading theme of traditional positivism, that the real is observable, with the strictly non-epistemic conception of meaning advanced in the *Tractatus*. It is true that Schlick is not quite happy with the term 'positivism' and that he rejects the statement that 'only the given is real' as meaningless (Sp 283)—but he does so on grounds which would have been understandable to Berkeley or Mill. It is also true that if Schlick's argument were valid we would not need to bring in the traditional positivist thesis as a separate premise; we would be able to argue directly to (1) from Tractarian principles about the meaning of sentences and names. Either way, verificationism, when reached in this way, does not flow from the epistemic conception of meaning.

(2) on the other hand is a version of the general conception of meaning which we have called 'epistemic'—though it is a particularly narrow one. On this general conception, understanding a word or a sentence is knowing what can be done with it in communication and action—knowing the rules which govern its role in our practices of assertion and inference. One may get from this to verificationism by highlighting *assertion*, and the conditions which warrant an assertion. Or one may stress *inference*—and thus the expectations licensed by an assertion. Pragmatism, taken as a theory of meaning, is a version of the epistemic conception, just as verificationism is. So is the conception

of meaning as 'use' which Wittgenstein gradually developed (and, needless to say, liked to be coy about). The appeal to 'use' is helpful, if it liberalizes the epistemic conception—allowing all the norms which govern what we assert and infer to be taken into account.

It is curious that Schlick abandoned his earlier scientific realism through being converted to a form of *metaphysical* realism. For that is what the Tractarian doctrine was, despite Wittgenstein's proscription of metaphysics. It adhered to an untenably metaphysical version of the idea that truth is correspondence, a version which radically divorces our grasp of what it is for a proposition to be true, from our grasp of rules which determine what would justify us in holding it true. That was in effect Neurath's criticism, as we shall in a moment see.

Notice also that in his argument Schlick makes no mention of the idea of implicit definition, which had been so important in his earlier work. He assumes that when a term is not explicitly defined it must be ostensively defined. This reflects a crucial point: on the non-epistemic form of verificationism (comparing the picture with reality) only one interpretation can be made of the idea that aprioricity is truth in virtue of meaning. It is the verbal one endorsed by Mill and by Kant (on the strict or narrow reading of 'analytic').

The same cross-currents were affecting Wittgenstein, and it is probably impossible to know just what his thinking at this time was. He could certainly have been getting to verificationism from the *Tractatus*, in something like the manner of Schlick. He too emphasized at this time that generalizations are not propositions but rules. That would be expectable—given that he had abandoned the idea that universal generalizations are reducible to a conjunction of their instances—if he still nevertheless retained the idea that propositions are pictures. For on the properly epistemic conception, attention ought rather to focus on the way in which we *actually* justify the assertion of universal generalizations. On that approach, the 'problem' of their significance ought to seem like a pseudo-problem.

On the other hand pragmatism may have had some influence on Wittgenstein's thinking, through his friend Frank Ramsey, a brilliant young Cambridge mathematician and philosopher who was greatly interested in it. Ramsey visited Wittgenstein in Austria and talked philosophy with him in 1923 and 1924. After Wittgenstein's return to Cambridge, they frequently discussed philosophy until Ramsey's tragically early death in 1930 at the age of 26. Wittgenstein was also greatly stimulated by a lecture L. E. J. Brouwer gave in Vienna in 1928—though his own strict verificationism did not cast doubt on the law of excluded middle as Brouwer's mathematical intuitionism did. He was also experimenting at this time with rather Kantian themes, about phenomenal or intuitive space, which gave him some sympathy with the synthetic a priori—though he always insisted on treating it in terms of his mysterious notion of grammar (one of his least helpful legacies). One thing that was clear to him was that there were 'grammatical statements' which were not Tractarian tautologies. And this, like the notion of implicit definition, is not stably reconcilable with a non-epistemic form of verificationism.

Another stream of cross-currents came from the redoubtable Otto Neurath (1882–1945), who has already figured several times. He was an Austrian who had been educated at the universities of Vienna and Berlin, studying mathematics and then linguistics, law, economics, and sociology. He was an active social democrat with strong Marxist sympathies (to which his holism and materialism in philosophy bear witness); after the First World War he directed central planning under the short-lived social-democratic and revolutionary governments in Bavaria. When the revolutionary government fell, he was sentenced to imprisonment and released only on the intervention of the Austrian Government.

Metaphysics was Neurath's *bête noire*, physicalism (rather than empiricism—in accord with fine old-fashioned anti-bourgeois tradition) his pride and joy. When the Circle discussed the *Tractatus*, Neurath kept interjecting 'Metaphysics!',

to the irritation of Moritz Schlick who finally told him he was interrupting the proceedings too much. Hans Hahn, as conciliator, suggested to Neurath just to say 'M' instead. After much humming . . . Neurath made another suggestion to Schlick: 'I think it will save time and trouble if I say "non-M" every time the group is *not* talking metaphysics'. (N 82–3)

Under Neurath's influence the Circle's 1929 manifesto greatly stressed the project of a unified science, which would be public, achieved by collective effort, and would exhibit the unity of social and natural science. Neurath and Carnap influenced each other a good deal. Carnap went over to a preference for physicalistic language, while Neurath was persuaded that physicalism was a metaphysical pseudo-thesis. But he still insisted that the choice of language was a practical and political choice, and that an intersubjective physicalistic language would better serve the needs of the community.

Of this language Neurath takes a radically coherentist view. *All* its empirical propositions, Neurath holds, are corrigible by further enquiry. Theory can override observation sentences— there are no incorrigible sentences expressing immediate experience. 'It is therefore meaningless to talk ... of a private language';

It is always science as a system of statements which is at issue. *Statements are compared with statements*, not with 'experiences', 'the world', or anything else. All these meaningless *duplications* belong to a more or less refined metaphysics and are, for that reason, to be rejected. Each new statement is compared with the totality of existing statements previously coordinated. To say that a statement is correct, therefore, means that it can be incorporated in this totality. What cannot be incorporated is rejected as incorrect ... The definition of 'correct' and 'incorrect' proposed here departs from that customary among the 'Vienna Circle', which appeals to 'meaning' and 'verification'. In our presentation we confine ourselves always to the sphere of linguistic thought. (Ns 291)

This was the point of his famous comparison of science to a ship afloat on the ocean, which cannot berth in a dry dock but can only be mended plank by plank, from within. In Neurath's coherence theory *nothing* outside the system of scientific sentences rationally constrained the system. (He abolished the ocean as well as the dry dock.)

In response to the objection advanced by Schlick that many incompatible systems of sentences could be internally coherent, Neurath and Carnap replied that the correct one was the one accepted by scientists of one's 'culture circle'. 'I do have trust in those good fellows,' Schlick replied 'but that is because I always found them to be trustworthy wherever I was able to test their enunciations' (Sp ii. 404). A. J. Ayer, taking the position somewhat more seriously, gave a neat refutation. He pointed out that each competing system could contain a sentence asserting that it alone was accepted by scientists in one's culture circle. If to this it was replied that only one of them was accepted in fact, an appeal was made to a fact outside the system of sentences—thus abandoning the theory.

But why were they led into this 'astonishing error', as Schlick called it (Sp ii. 376)? There were good reasons and bad. The good reason was that they appreciated the holism of scientific theory: the total fabric of science and observation hangs together and no empirical sentence is unrevisable. The bad reason is the curious idea that 'statements are compared with statements'— and cannot be 'compared' with experiences.

'It is my humble opinion', Schlick replied, 'that we can compare anything to anything if we choose' (Sp ii. 401). Unfortunately he does not drive this home. The point that is really at issue is whether something that is not a sentence can warrant the assertion of a sentence. Specifically, can an experience, such as I could describe by saying 'I seem to see something blue over there'—call this *S*—warrant a sentence? The question is *not* whether *S* warrants a sentence, but whether the experience it describes does. If it does, the relation between the percept and the warranted sentence is the dreaded comparison of statements with experience, which breaks out of the circle of sentences. It puts rational constraints on that circle other than internal ones.

Of course such a rule can only be stated in a sentence. Thus perhaps:

> (*R*) If one seems to see something blue one is warranted (in the absence of counter-evidence) in saying, 'There's something blue.'

On the epistemic conception this rule may be seen as a linguistic rule, partially determining the use, and thus the meaning, of the word 'blue' in the 'object language', i.e. the language which is the object of discussion. It is itself, however, stated in the 'meta-language' (these terms are Carnap's). It concerns a relation between a state of affairs and a sentence in the object language, not a relation between two sentences in it. In other words it is a semantic, not a syntactic rule—syntactic rules determine which sentences are well formed and how sentences can be transformed into other sentences by rules of inference (this is Carnap's 'logical syntax').

The point was one about which Carnap was later quite clear—instead of seeing philosophy as being concerned exclusively with logical syntax he came to see it as the meta-theoretical study of possible languages, including their semantic (and 'pragmatic') aspects as well. But once the point is clear it undermines the bad argument for Neurath's coherentism.

Schlick however does not seize on the key point, that a relation of rational warrant can exist between an experience and a sentence. He focuses rather on what he calls *Konstatierungen*—'affirmations', which are incorrigible propositions about immediate experience. These are not observation sentences belonging to the public—and, as Schlick agrees, always corrigible—corpus of science. But at this point he is snookered by his own structuralism: insofar as they are not public and communicable, they are not objective at all. They cannot therefore provide an objective foundation for science—

In no sense do they lie at the basis of science, but knowledge, as it were, flickers out to them, reaching each one for a moment only, and at once consuming it. And newly fed and strengthened, it then flares on toward the next. (Sp ii. 387)

This was the kind of thing that made Neurath call Schlick a 'metaphysician and a poet' (Sp ii. 400, see also 407 ff.). It is certainly not easy to see what epistemic role Schlick's private 'affirmations' are supposed to play; the relevant anti-Neurathian point could have been made without bringing them in at all. Yet there remains something curiously glamorous and perplexing about these incorrigible *Konstatierungen* in their private language. Can experiences play an epistemic role in my thought without being thought? And if they are thought, must not the language in which they are thought be private? 'Affirmations' continued to feed Wittgenstein's thinking—one might expect him to be fascinated by them. Eventually they produced his celebrated argument against the possibility of a private language, in the *Philosophical Investigations*. Neurath would have been delighted. 'Non-M!', he might at last have said.

If the notion of incorrigible propositions is dropped, so must strict verificationism be. For now we see that however strong the justification for any statement, further evidence or theory may yet emerge to defeat it. These insights were promoted in the Circle by Neurath's bluff emphasis on the public and holistic character of knowledge, and they helped to blow away the non-epistemic (for him 'metaphysical') form of verificationism coming from Schlick and Wittgenstein. Of course Wittgenstein was already moving in this direction himself. But it is important to be aware that the demythologizing of analytic modernism's earlier conceptions of language and thought was in no way Wittgenstein's single-handed contribution. It was part of a general Viennese drift which developed strongly in the 1930s and which opened the way for further exploration of the epistemic conception of meaning. The meaning of a sentence— its epistemic role—could now be approached more liberally in terms of its place with other sentences in inference and the degrees of confirmation it received from observations. It was no longer necessary to hold that theoretical sentences were *translatable* in any sense into observational ones.

This was the direction in which Carnap's thinking developed. It partly came from greater emphasis on the corrigibility of *all* scientific, and thus all objective, discourse. (Karl Popper's *Logic of Scientific Discovery (Logik der Forschung)* 1935, which Carnap read in manuscript, also contributed to this.) And it also came from the shift to a 'meta-theoretical' conception of philosophy which was semantic and pragmatic as well as syntactic.

An important catalyst of this shift was the semantic concept of truth developed by the Polish logician Alfred Tarski ('The Concept of Truth in Formalized Languages'; Polish publication, 1933, German publication, 1935). Tarski considered instances of the schema '$S$ is true in language $L$ if and only if $p$' (restricting them to avoid the famous truth-paradoxes, such as the

Cretan). The syntax of the object-language $L$ is formally specified, as are the semantics of its primitive terms. Tarski stipulates that instances of the schema are so selected that '$p$' is always a translation into the meta-language of $S$, and he shows how to derive them formally from the semantic axioms for the primitive terms of $L$.

For some of the Vienna Circle, and for Popper, this rescued truth from the limbo of metaphysics—though Otto Neurath remained stoutly unconvinced. It is indeed far from clear why it should do so. Philosophers who need a complex technical development in formal logic to achieve a glimpse of the philosophically obvious may be thought to demonstrate their scientistic limitations. The philosophical irrelevance of such technical logical results was a point Wittgenstein liked to dwell on. Yet he himself had earlier anathematized all semantic and syntactic discourse as meaningless. It was no mean effort on Carnap's part to break out of this dogma, by producing detailed and patently meaningful specimens of such discourse. (The problem of the unity of the proposition had meanwhile somehow simply vanished away.)

On the other hand, to see it from Neurath's point of view, if the essential target is the correspondence notion of truth—understood not as a platitude but as a metaphysical thesis—Tarski's demonstration of how to determine 'true-in-$L$' extensionally becomes irrelevant. Since the coherence theorist can agree without trembling to the platitude (that 'Snow is white' is true if and only if snow is white, etc.), he can applaud and accept Tarski's technical achievement—as a technical achievement. So here Neurath and Wittgenstein could have agreed. But of course Wittgenstein would hold that *both* the correspondence *and* the coherence theories of truth are senseless metaphysical theses.

As for Carnap, his new position was explained in two important papers, 'Testability and Meaning' (1936–7) and 'Truth and Confirmation' (1936). With a new clarity he makes the point that 'true' does not mean 'verified', 'confirmed', etc.—appealing to Tarski's semantic account of truth and pointing out that if truth is equated with confirmation it becomes necessary to abandon the law of excluded middle.

To distinguish 'true' from such concepts is to accept that it is not itself an epistemic notion. It does not help to strengthen them by appeal to what would be *ideally* verified or confirmed. One cannot identify truth even with idealized convergence. (Though the weaker pragmatic thesis, that assertion as such commits one to expecting that ideal enquirers would converge on what one has asserted, can still stand.) Can one then continue to defend an epistemic conception of meaning? If the meaning of a sentence is determined, on the model Tarski provides, by the way in which its truth-condition is derived from the semantic values of its terms, what scope is left for the notion that meaning is epistemic role?

These are questions frequently raised in current philosophy. The answer must lie in distinguishing between a 'theory of meaning'—a formal expansion, for a particular language, of the truism that meaning is determined by truth-conditions; and, on the other hand, the continued philosophical enquiry into what it is to understand a language or possess a system of concepts. In that latter enquiry Carnap and Wittgenstein always continued to think in terms of an epistemic conception—they broke definitively with the Platonic realism, and the relational model of meaning, characteristic of earlier analytic modernism (p. 154 above). They would have disagreed sharply on how far the enquiry could issue in a *theory* of concepts and language-understanding, but on that question we do not yet know, I think, who was right.

We have seen that the earlier phase of analytic modernism broke off abruptly from the great debate between naturalism and the post-Kantian tradition of idealism, without providing an answer to it. The period we have surveyed in this chapter effectively resumes that debate. It resumes it—and it also purports to dissolve it.

By the 1930s all the philosophers we have been considering in this chapter would have agreed that 'naturalism', 'idealism'—'realism', 'physicalism', 'materialism', 'solipsism'—are all pseudo-theses lacking cognitive significance. But had they succeeded in showing that? It can be argued that they had only found a new formulation for idealism.

The nub of Kant's critique, as we have repeatedly seen, lay in the question, how is knowledge possible? Naturalism led to the epistemological-empiricist conclusion that no real proposition or inference is a priori—and that in turn to a collapse into complete scepticism.

All the analytic modernists, early and late, are agreed in rejecting Millian empiricism about logic; on the other hand, the Vienna Circle and Wittgenstein appear to agree with him that no real proposition or inference is a priori. Thus it seems that they check the Kantian argument at the point where it seeks to collapse epistemological empiricism into scepticism—and hence they escape having to give a transcendental rationale for the 'synthetic a priori'. But these appearances are misleading.

To avoid being misled, we must consider more carefully the Vienna Circle's conventionalist reading of the a priori. One source of this, as we have seen, is the development of geometry and physics which produced relativity theory. In the logical positivists' treatment of this there is in fact considerable continuity with the Kantian tradition, which is brought out clearly, for example, in Reichenbach's *The Theory of Relativity and A Priori Knowledge* (1920). They agree with Kant that the objectivity of scientific discourse presupposes certain a priori rules—in their case these are the 'co-ordinative' conventions that determine the metric of space–time. Where they disagree is in regarding these conventionally determined a priori rules as unrevisable. They are *chosen* and the choice can be varied if doing so provides a convenient simplification of the discourse as a whole.

Further inputs into their thinking were provided by logicism and the *Tractatus*. Now we have already seen that the *Tractatus*, which did not endorse logicism, did make a serious effort to explain the emptiness of pure logic by means of the doctrine of tautology; and of mathematics by the treatment of it as consisting in identities. But we have also seen that these lines of defence could not be held.

In the case of logicism, on the other hand, our question has been whether the reduction of arithmetic succeeds in showing it to be analytic or verbal in the important *narrow* sense that is required to eliminate the debate between Kant and Mill. This is not essentially a matter of whether set theory can be counted as logic, or whether some of the axioms of *Principia Mathematica* are genuinely logical; it is a question of whether logic itself is analytic in the required sense.

Carnap continued to endorse logicism, and to apply the *term* 'analytic' to logic and mathematics, but in *The Logical Syntax of Language* (*Logische Syntax der Sprache*, 1934) his conception of it moved towards the treatment of the a priori which the positivists had already given in the case of geometry.

The neutralism of the *Aufbau* is now enunciated as the 'principle of tolerance': '*It is not our business to set up prohibitions, but to arrive at conventions*' (Cl 51). The point is that languages and logics are chosen, as geometries are.

In other words, there is no attempt to show that certain privileged principles of logic are analytic in the *narrow* sense, and thus unchallengeable, or known by a priori cognition of an objective world to be laws of truth—and thus again unchallengeable. Any system of logic is adopted by convention. Different choices of logic lead to different languages with different syntaxes, which may be more or less expedient. To be analytic in *L* is to be a syntactic truth of *L*. We shall call this *Carnap's neutralism*.

It confronts us with the same question which we earlier raised in discussing Schlick's analysis of implicit definition (p. 187 above): what is the status of the *meta-logic*, by means of which syntactic truths in the object-language *L* are established? The only possible answer now is that it is itself conventional.

If this is coherent, it is significant that it raises the same questions of coherence as radical Millian empiricism does. If everything is empirical how do we tell what follows from an empirical datum? If everything is conventional, how do we tell what follows from a convention? The answer in both cases is that the rules which determine what follows are themselves empirical, or conventional—but that *what the rule requires* involves a notion of consistency which is not empirical or conventional, yet still does not reinstate the notion of an unrevisable truth. It is the notion of *consistency in carrying out one's intention*, and it is one of the routes which lead to Wittgenstein's later preoccupation with the question of what is involved in interpreting a rule.

But of course there is an important difference between Millian empiricism and Carnap's neutralism, which is that logic and mathematics for Carnap is 'analytic': it expresses conventions of syntax. Those conventions can indeed be changed, but to change them is to opt for a new language.

From one point of view this carries on Mach's thought-economical conception of science. From another point of view it stands in the Kantian tradition, which stresses the constitution of objectivity by postulates which are presupposed by objectivity. Carnap had indeed originally wanted to give the *Aufbau* the Kantian title, 'Prolegomena to a Theory of the Constitution of Reality' (*Eines Konstitutionstheorie der Wirklichkeit*).

Does conventionalism really escape idealism? This is a highly elusive question, as we have seen in our earlier discussion of the *Aufbau*. At least this much is unchallengeable: conventionalism is supposed to *elucidate* how it is that certain principles are a priori. One seeks to do that by saying 'This principle, $P$, is a priori because it is true by convention.' What then is the force of this elucidation, of the word 'because'? Does it mean, 'Given another convention, it would not have been true that $P$'? At this point Carnap might accuse us of falling into what he called the 'material mode of speech', with all its obfuscation.

But without it, it is impossible to state the *distinctive* thesis of conventionalism. For anyone at all can agree with the meta-linguistic formulation: 'Given another convention, "$P$" would not (or at least might not) have been true.' For this allows any conventional change in the meanings of words, and it is trivial that '$P$' might not have been true if it had meant something different. Allowing the material mode, on the other hand, we find that what is true depends on our choices—a relativized and de-subjectivized version of idealism. In that case, Carnap's neutralism does not supersede the Mill–Kant debate, but falls on the idealist side of it.

Alternatively, if we do not allow the material mode of speech, we can ask what is the *point* of calling the transformation rules of logical syntax 'conventions'?

Calling them that presupposes a distinction between conventions and facts. We do not make a sentence conventional rather than factual by calling it a 'principle of logical syntax'. (Carnap was aware of these criticisms, which came from Quine and Tarski, but he was never persuaded by them.) In particular, to see a choice motivated by simplicity as a conventional one, it is necessary to see the requirement of simplicity as purely practical or 'psychological', rather than as itself having an epistemological claim. But what is the status of that distinction itself? It seems inevitable that this question, together with the holistic arguments which rightly drove the Circle to acknowledge that all propositions in the public language of 'science' are corrigible, will force the conclusion that the alleged distinction between 'fact' and 'convention' is untenable.

If, finally, we have not said much about the ethics of this period it is because there is not much to say. Ethics in the second phase of analytic modernism is a bit like the incident in the Sherlock Holmes story, of the dog that did not bark (let alone bite) in the night. At least three factors lay behind this barrenness. First, the preoccupations of this period are social and political rather than ethical. On the other hand, second, the modernist obsession with being scientific about man and society undermined confidence in common-sense moral psychology and in historical sense—the intellectualized practical wisdom which is essential in any serious normative thought about political, as well as moral, issues. And lastly, positivism's official philosophy of value, 'emotivism', which held that value judgements are not genuine *assertions*, but expressions of emotional attitude, was not conducive to the attempt, in the manner of Mill, Sidgwick, or Green, to reason normatively about social issues. All these are aspects of the revolt against the liberal apogee of the mid-nineteenth century, even though in other aspects the Vienna Circle marks a return to the tradition of enlightenment. It is an instance of the general principle that the rise and fall of modernism is the fall and rise of liberalism. For the central philosophical idea which causes trouble to the logical positivist is that key liberal notion, rational autonomy—which seems to require categorical principles of practical reason, and thus an unreconstructed synthetic a priori.

Emotivism stands to Moore's earlier ethical intuitionism (that is, the view that fundamental ethical propositions are known solely by self-evident intuition) exactly as conventionalism stands to the earlier logical intuitionism. And emotivism continues to influence our culture as profoundly as conventionalism does. (Trenchant critics of 'logical positivism' who have fully swallowed and digested these, its most characteristic doctrines, are legion.) But it also raises the same problems as to its own intelligibility.

Conventionalism holds that certain statements are true because of our conventions. Emotivism may hold that others—evaluative statements—are true because of our emotional reactions. If it is formulated in this way, we can again ask what the force of 'because' is. Consider, for example, ' "Causing pain is wrong" is true because of our emotional reactions against the causing of pain.' Obviously, the emotivist does not mean this to be equivalent to an eccentric object-language moral judgement: 'What makes causing pain wrong is the fact that we are against it.' *That* is not what makes causing pain wrong.

An emotivist philosopher is more likely to say that value judgements are not genuine statements at all, but express emotional attitudes. One may similarly hold that a priori judgements are not genuine statements, but express conventions. (So the only genuine statements are factual ones, which are true or false according to the facts.) Much philosophical analysis in this century starts from these positivist *idées maîtresses*, and then tries to reconcile them in ever more subtle ways with common sense and common usage. The difficulty, as we have seen with conventionalism, is to find a way of doing so which does not make them trivially false on the one hand—or contentless on the other.

It is a revealing difficulty, and quite possibly a fatal one. Modernism sought to assert absolute distinctions between the domain of fact and the domain of logic and value. In the analytic tradition this was attempted, first, by a Platonic realism about concepts and values, and second, by the denial that logic and ethics literally *say* anything. If these attempts fail, are we returned to the questions as they stood in the 19th century? The next chapter says a few final words about this.

# 6

# Epilogue: After Modernism

This has been a thematic history in which three themes have played a role. The first and most important has been the conflict between naturalism and idealism. The second (an offshoot of the first) has been the problem of subjectivity and consciousness. And the third (a much remoter offshoot) has been the fortunes of utilitarian and liberal philosophy.

In the last two areas developments from around 1960 suggest a new phase, which follows after analytic modernism but no longer shares its spirit. Today the 'identity-theory', the view that mental processes *are* bodily physical processes, has become a very influential thesis in the English-language world. (Which is not to say that it is unproblematic, or that it is generally thought to be so.) We have seen it make a brief and rather obscure appearance in Schlick's early work; but it was overshadowed by the continuing preoccupation with strong phenomenalism, or, for a period after the war, with a somewhat shadowy 'philosophical behaviourism'. Its clearcut emergence is one symptom of a new shift to the reassertion of naturalism in philosophy. The word 'naturalism' itself is now fashionable as it would not have been in the two modernist periods.

Ethics, and from around the 1960s again, political philosophy, have staged a remarkable revival. Although doughty descendants of emotivism remain, fighting ever more ingenious campaigns, the broad impulse of the last thirty years has been towards the reassertion of the objectivity of ethics, though in a broadly naturalistic rather than a Platonic mode. With it has come a new interest in moral theory. The revival of political philosophy has been pre-eminently a revival of the liberal tradition. The debate there, which is again about freedom, justice, and community, is between liberalism and its critics, while the debate in ethics is in good part at least between utilitarianism, or descendants of it, and critics.

Altogether the student of Mill and the 19th century can hardly help noticing parallels. But just as Mill rightly recognized 'the whole difference of level which has been gained in philosophy through the powerful negative criticism of Kant' (M ix. 1), so, to philosophize seriously today, one must recognize a similar 'whole difference of level' gained by analytic modernism.

In part this new level is owed to the great development of logic, and associated methods of analyis, described in Chapter 4. But like Kant, analytic modernism also produced a 'powerful negative criticism', and I would like to end by considering that criticism a little further. It is a criticism of philosophy itself, for it asserts that philosophical questions are pseudo-questions. This is the most intriguing legacy of modernism, which still I think remains puzzling.

I have suggested that the self-dissolving view of philosophy must be founded in a conception of meaning. This cannot be strict verificationism, which is itself a metaphysical thesis. But what *is* essential is the epistemic conception of meaning itself, in which meanings are constituted by rules, rules which determine concepts' and expressions' *roles* in reasoning, acting, and communicating.

Kantians criticized naturalistic philosophers as being 'pre-Critical'. Can we say that modernism has found a way of being post-Critical? And if so, does our current preoccupation with naturalism mark a lapse from that?

The self-dissolving conception would deserve to be called post-Critical, if it found a way of dispelling such philosophical theses as idealism, realism, and scepticism—without itself propounding philosophical theses. This was Wittgenstein's Holy Grail, and not many people can be confident whether he found it, or just thought he did. At any rate, it is his late work that provides the best evidence that he found it. In that respect it takes forward a central theme of analytic modernism, even though it discards some of its most characteristic preoccupations.

If I am right in thinking that the self-dissolving view of philosophy requires the epistemic conception of meaning, then that conception had better not be itself a *philosophical thesis*. It is still more obvious that it had better not *itself* be a form of idealism. Otherwise it will not be post-Critical, but simply a continuation of the Critical philosophy, with the word 'epistemic' replacing the word 'transcendental'.

We have seen that Carnap's neutralism, which was a way of implementing the self-dissolving view, either slides, when pushed, to a form of idealism, or retreats from any genuine use of the distinction between fact and convention. Still, while conventionalism requires the epistemic conception of meaning, the reverse does not hold. Perhaps the epistemic conception of meaning gives us the wherewithal to defend the notion of a defeasible a priori warrant—a default rule of reasoning—*without* grounding that notion on a convention, a choice. This could give Thomas Reid epistemological grounds for his notion of a system of common-sense principles, grounds which he needed but could not himself provide.

One example of such a principle might be (R) on p. 208 above. To hold that (R) is partially constitutive of the concept *blue*, or the meaning of the word 'blue', is to adopt the epistemic conception of meaning. It is to say something more than '*x* satisfies the predicate 'blue' just if *x* is blue', which is the axiom needed for an empirical theory of meaning for English. Note also that an assertion licensed by (R) is defeasible—I may seem to see something blue, but have evidence that I am under blue light or whatever, and thus not be justified in asserting 'There's something blue.'

What then is the status of (R)? It is a rule which partly constitutes the concept *blue*. The *statement* in the object-language that corresponds to it is, 'If one seems to see something blue then there is there something blue.' That statement can be empirically false even if (R) is a priori.

In similar spirit, the warrant for fundamental logical or ethical principles—as against basic perceptual statements—could reside in an agreement, reached through reflective scrutiny, that the principle in question is indeed obvious. Once again the warrant could be defeated; by further reflection (as with the discovery of the paradoxes), or, in the case of logic, by a development of scientific theory, which led us to discard the principle. So the position is reconcilable with Mill's epistemological empiricism, inasmuch as it can concede that even principles of logic are revisable in the light of experience. (It is sometimes said that accepting such principles is part and parcel of understanding the logical concepts which they contain. But my understanding of a logical concept is not constituted by *accepting* the relevant principles; it is constituted by finding these principles primitively obvious, and counting that as a *warrant* for accepting them. The warrant can still be defeated.)

What I have outlined is a version of the epistemic conception which promises to dissolve metaphysical theses, and does not involve conventionalism. Is it itself a piece of metaphysics, a new form of idealism? It does not *seem* to be—it seems simply to make a point about what is involved in possessing a concept, or grasping a meaning. But a very little further probing soon shows that the question is more difficult than that suggests. Perhaps the difficulty lies in finding a clearcut contrast between naturalism and idealism. That is very much the post-Critical philosopher's point—when the debate gets to this stage, he would say, there is no longer any substantive question at stake. This line of thought has been continued and developed by philosophers influenced by pragmatism, or by the Viennese trends we have studied. But that, as they say, is another story.

# Notes

## Chapter 1

4    *every immediate object of the mind in thinking*: this is from Locke's Second Letter to the Bishop of Worcester.

7    *non-Euclidean geometry of visibles*: for more on this see Norman Daniels, *Thomas Reid's Inquiry: The Geometry of Visibles and the Case for Realism* (New York, 1974).

13    *a great commentator*: Norman Kemp-Smith, *The Philosophy of David Hume* (London, 1964), 564.

17    *'that capacity of "patient thought"'*: The comment is Dugald Stewart's (R 4).

18    *I ever knew ... heaven*: Hazlitt, *Selected Essays*, ed. Geoffrey Keynes (London, 1942), 724–5.

18    *To Coleridge I owe education*: *Essays and Tales*, ed. J. C. Hare, 2 vols. (London, 1848), vol. i, p. xv.

25    *the philosophic radicals*: for John Stuart Mill's distinction between three kinds of radical see p. 30 below. He makes it in 'Fonblanque's England under Seven Administrations' M VI 353.

## Chapter 2

37    *'the logic of the moral sciences'*: this is the title of the sixth book of his *System of Logic*, which discusses psychology and the social sciences.

39    *Kant ... have all along been thought in it*: this is from Kant's *Critique of Pure Reason*, trans. N. Kemp Smith (London, 1968), 48.

46    *Kant ... 'Copernican Revolution'*: he describes it thus in *Critique of Pure Reason*, 22.

51    *Sidney Smith said*: quoted in Sir Leslie Stephen's entry on Whewell in the *Dictionary of National Biography*, lx (London, 1899), 460.

54    *'the Ideas of the Divine Mind'*: the phrase is from Whewell's article 'On the Fundamental Antithesis of Philosophy' (see his *On the Philosophy of Discovery* (London, 1860), appendix E).

73   *'permanent interests of a man as a progressive being'*: cp. Cole-
     ridge: 'The imagination is the distinguishing characteristic of
     man as a progressive being;... it ought to be carefully guided
     and strengthened as the indispensable means and instrument of
     continued amelioration and refinement' (*The Complete Works of
     Samuel Taylor Coleridge*, ed. W. G. T. Shedd, 7 vols. (1884), iv.
     317–18).

## Chapter 3

75   *Mill's public influence*: A. J. Balfour, *Theism and Humanism*
     (London, 1915), 138; A. V. Dicey, 'Lecture on the Relation be-
     tween Law and Public Opinion in England during the Nineteenth
     Century' (London, 1914), 306.

75   *Mill will have to be destroyed*: Henry Sidgwick: A Memoir by
     A. S. and E. M. S. (London, 1906), 133–4.

77   *certain solid wilfulness*: quoted by M. Richter, *The Politics of
     Conscience* (London, 1964), 46, from a letter from Sidgwick to
     Mrs Green.

79   *The forties ... was the time of doubts*: Owen Chadwick, *The
     Secularization of the European Mind in the Nineteenth Century*
     (Cambridge, 1975), 184.

79   *My father was brought up scientifically*: quoted in Israel Scheffler,
     *Four Pragmatists: A Critical Introduction to Peirce, James, Mead,
     and Dewey* (London, 1974), 5.

79   *the mistake of subjecting to human judgement*: J. H. Newman,
     *Apologia Pro Vita Sua* (London, 1913), 493.

79   *the doubts and difficulties*: The Complete Prose Works of Matthew
     Arnold: Philistinism in England and America, ed. R. H. Super
     (Ann Arbor, 1974), 165.

80   *No longer is it possible*: Edward Caird, *Hegel* (Edinburgh, 1883),
     55.

89   *'the crude and raw and provincial' utilitarians*: quoted in Alan
     Donagan, 'Victorian Philosophical Prose: J. S. Mill and F. H.
     Bradley' in S. P. Rosenbaum (ed.), *English Literature and British
     Philosophy* (London, 1971), 208–28, 222.

93   *The completeness and self-consistency*: J. H. Muirhead, 'Hegel',
     *Encyclopaedia Britannica*, 11th edn. (Cambridge, 1911), xiii. 207.

95 *gave ... letters of credit*: H. J. Laski, *The Decline of Liberalism* (London, 1940), 11.

109 *Peirce was above all a logician*: John Dewey, 'Le Développement du pragmatisme américain', *Revue de Métaphysique et de Morale*, xxix, 411–30.

112 *neutral monism*: the term itself is Bertrand Russell's.

115 *and surely such a trifle*: quoted in G. Bird, William James (London, 1986), 199; cp. Jp 210.

120 *weekend huntsman*: quoted in A. Hamilton, 'Ernst Mach and the Elimination of Subjectivity', *Ratio*, NS 3 (1990), 119.

## Chapter 4

129 *of all silly superficialities*: quoted in John Passmore, *A Hundred Years of Philosophy* (Harmondsworth, 1968), 86–7.

132 *the most important date*: William and Martha Kneale, *The Development of Logic* (Oxford, 1971), 511.

148 *intellectual aristocracy*: see Paul Levy, *Moore: G. E. Moore and the Cambridge Apostles* (Oxford, 1982), ch. 1, 'The Intellectual Aristocracy', which describes Moore's family background.

152 *'I went up to Cambridge ...'*: J. M. Keynes, *Two Memoirs* (London, 1949), 81–2.

152 *shattered all writers*: quoted in David Gadd, *The Loving Friends* (London, 1974), 23; the passage from Leonard Woolf is also quoted there (p. 24).

152 *Bloomsbury Group*: the group and Moore's relations with it are described in Levy, *Moore*.

159 *the beauty of the literalness of Moore's mind*: Keynes, *Two Memoirs*, 92, 94. (The whole of Keynes's second memoir, 'My Early Beliefs', is worth reading.)

164 *Moore wrote to Russell*: the exchange of letters between Moore and Russell is quoted in Peter Hylton, *Russell, Idealism, and the Emergence of Analytic Philosophy* (Oxford, 1990), 255–6.

# Further Reading

The literature on most of the philosophers discussed in this book is vast. The following is only a small selection of starting points for further reading.

## Chapter 1

The most recent general study of Reid is Keith Lehrer, *Thomas Reid*, (London, 1989). For the intellectual and cultural tradition of generalist Scottish common sense, see George Davie, *The Democratic Intellect* (Edinburgh, 1961). A general study of Bentham's philosophy is Ross Harrison, *Bentham* (London, 1983). For Coleridge's Philosophy J. H. Muirhead, *Coleridge as Philosopher* (London, 1930) may still be consulted. The plagiarism issue is fully covered in the introduction and notes of C vii.

## Chapter 2

A general study of Mill's philosophy is John Skorupski, *John Stuart Mill* (London, 1989). Alan Ryan, *John Stuart Mill* (London, 1974) is briefer but also broader in its coverage of Mill's writings and activities. The fullest account of Mill's moral and political philosophy is Fred R. Berger, *Happiness, Justice and Freedom: The Moral and Political Philosophy of John Stuart Mill* (London, 1984).

   J. B. Schneewind, *Sidgwick's Ethics and Victorian Moral Philosophy* (Oxford, 1977) provides everything promised by its title and a great deal of cultural context as well. On Whewell see Menachem Fisch and Simon Schaffer (eds.), *William Whewell, A Composite Portrait* (Oxford, 1991).

## Chapter 3

John Passmore, *A Hundred Years of Philosophy* (Harmondsworth, 1957, and more recent editions), provides a much wider survey of philosophers and movements in the period covered in this and the next two chapters than is offered here (though it does not deal with moral and political philosophy).

   There are useful sketches of Green's and Bradley's metaphysics in Peter Hylton, *Russell, Idealism and the Emergence of Analytic Philosophy* (Oxford, 1990). Peter P. Nicholson, *The Political Philosophy of the British Idealists* (Cambridge, 1990) is a comprehensive account of that side of Green, Bradley, and Bosanquet. Melvin Richter, *The Politics of Conscience: T. H. Green and His Age* (London, 1964) is a study not only of Green but also of Oxford culture in Green's time. See also Richard Wollheim, *F. H. Bradley* (Harmondsworth, 1969). On pragmatism, Israel Scheffler, *Four Pragmatists: A Critical Introduction to Peirce, James, Mead, and Dewey* (London, 1974) is an excellent starting-point. See also A. J. Ayer, *The Origins of Pragmatism* (London, 1968), Christopher Hookway, *Peirce* (London, 1985) and Gerald E. Myers, *William James* (New Haven and London, 1986). For Mach's 'neutral monism' see Andy Hamilton 'Ernst Mach and the Elimination of Subjectivity', *Ratio*, NS 3 (1990); on Mach and on nineteenth-century positivism in general see also M. Mandelbaum, *History, Man, and Reason* (Baltimore and London, 1971), chapters 1 and 14.

## Chapter 4

It is difficult to find a clearer exposition of Frege than Frege's. Michael Dummett, 'Frege's Philosophy', in his *Truth and Other Enigmas* (London, 1978), makes a good starting-point.

On Moore and Russell, see Peter Hylton, *op. cit.* See also Thomas Baldwin, *G. E. Moore* (London, 1990), Mark Sainsbury, *Russell* (London, 1979). Nicholas Griffin, *Russell's Idealist Apprenticeship* (Oxford, 1991) is an account of Russell 'pre-Russell'. On Wittgenstein see Robert J. Fogelin, *Wittgenstein* (London, 2nd edn. 1987). Allan Janik and Stephen Toulmin, *Wittgenstein's Vienna* (New York, 1974), is inaccurate on philosophical detail, but penetrating on psychological and historical context.

## Chapter 5

A. J. Ayer, *Language, Truth and Logic* (1936; 2nd edn. with additional introduction, Victor Gollancz, 1946) is a fine work of philosophy which brought the Vienna Circle to Britain. J. Alberto Coffa, *The Semantic Tradition from Kant to Carnap: To the Vienna Station* (Cambridge, 1991) is a study of the Vienna Circle and its antecedents which came too late for me to take it fully into account in this book. However I have benefited from the writings of Coffa's colleague, Michael Friedman— see as a starting point Michael Friedman, 'The Re-evaluation of Logical Positivism', *Journal of Philosophy*, 10 (1991). See also Andy Hamilton, 'Carnap's *Aufbau* and the Legacy of Neutral Monism', *Ratio*, NS 3 (1990), and Pierre Jacob, 'The Neurath–Schlick Controversy', *Fundamenta Scientiae*, 5 (1984).

# Index

**OXFORD**

# MORE OXFORD PAPERBACKS

This book is just one of nearly 1000 Oxford Paperbacks currently in print. If you would like details of other Oxford Paperbacks, including titles in the World's Classics, Oxford Reference, Oxford Books, OPUS, Past Masters, Oxford Authors, and Oxford Shakespeare series, please write to:

**UK and Europe:** Oxford Paperbacks Publicity Manager, Arts and Reference Publicity Department, Oxford University Press, Walton Street, Oxford OX2 6DP.

Customers in UK and Europe will find Oxford Paperbacks available in all good bookshops. But in case of difficulty please send orders to the Cash-with-Order Department, Oxford University Press Distribution Services, Saxon Way West, Corby, Northants NN18 9ES. Tel: 0536 741519; Fax: 0536 746337. Please send a cheque for the total cost of the books, plus £1.75 postage and packing for orders under £20; £2.75 for orders over £20. Customers outside the UK should add 10% of the cost of the books for postage and packing.

**USA:** Oxford Paperbacks Marketing Manager, Oxford University Press, Inc., 200 Madison Avenue, New York, N.Y. 10016.

**Canada:** Trade Department, Oxford University Press, 70 Wynford Drive, Don Mills, Ontario M3C 1J9.

**Australia:** Trade Marketing Manager, Oxford University Press, G.P.O. Box 2784Y, Melbourne 3001, Victoria.

**South Africa:** Oxford University Press, P.O. Box 1141, Cape Town 8000.

## THE GREAT PHILOSOPHERS

*Bryan Magee*

Beginning with the death of Socrates in 399, and following the story through the centuries to recent figures such as Bertrand Russell and Wittgenstein, Bryan Magee and fifteen contemporary writers and philosophers provide an accessible and exciting introduction to Western philosophy and its greatest thinkers.

Bryan Magee in conversation with:

| | |
|---|---|
| A. J. Ayer | John Passmore |
| Michael Ayers | Anthony Quinton |
| Miles Burnyeat | John Searle |
| Frederick Copleston | Peter Singer |
| Hubert Dreyfus | J. P. Stern |
| Anthony Kenny | Geoffrey Warnock |
| Sidney Morgenbesser | Bernard Williams |
| Martha Nussbaum | |

'Magee is to be congratulated . . . anyone who sees the programmes or reads the book will be left in no danger of believing philosophical thinking is unpractical and uninteresting.' Ronald Hayman, *Times Educational Supplement*

'one of the liveliest, fast-paced introductions to philosophy, ancient and modern that one could wish for' *Universe*

Also by Bryan Magee in Oxford Paperbacks:

*Men of Ideas*
*Aspects of Wagner* 2/e

# OPUS

*General Editors: Walter Bodmer, Christopher Butler,
Robert Evans, John Skorupski*

## A HISTORY OF WESTERN PHILOSOPHY

This series of OPUS books offers a comprehensive and
up-to-date survey of the history of philosophical ideas
from earliest times. Its aim is not only to set those ideas in
their immediate cultural context, but also to focus on
their value and relevance to twentieth-century thinking.

## CLASSICAL THOUGHT

### *Terence Irwin*

Spanning over a thousand years from Homer to Saint Augustine, *Classical Thought* encompasses a vast range of material, in
succinct style, while remaining clear and lucid even to those with
no philosophical or Classical background.

The major philosophers and philosophical schools are examined—the Presocratics, Socrates, Plato, Aristotle, Stoicism,
Epicureanism, Neoplatonism; but other important thinkers,
such as Greek tragedians, historians, medical writers, and early
Christian writers, are also discussed. The emphasis is naturally
on questions of philosophical interest (although the literary and
historical background to Classical philosophy is not ignored),
and again the scope is broad—ethics, the theory of knowledge,
philosophy of mind, philosophical theology. All this is presented
in a fully integrated, highly readable text which covers many of
the most important areas of ancient thought and in which stress
is laid on the variety and continuity of philosophical thinking
after Aristotle.

Also available in the History of Western Philosophy series:

*The Rationalists*   John Cottingham
*Continental Philosophy since 1750*   Robert C. Solomon
*The Empiricists*   R. S. Woolhouse

# PAST MASTERS

## General Editor: Keith Thomas

The *Past Masters* series offers students and general readers alike concise introductions to the lives and works of the world's greatest literary figures, composers, philosophers, religious leaders, scientists, and social and political thinkers.

'Put end to end, this series will constitute a noble encyclopaedia of the history of ideas.' Mary Warnock

# HOBBES

## Richard Tuck

Thomas Hobbes (1588–1679) was the first great English political philosopher, and his book *Leviathan* was one of the first truly modern works of philosophy. He has long had the reputation of being a pessimistic atheist, who saw human nature as inevitably evil, and who proposed a totalitarian state to subdue human failings. In this new study, Richard Tuck shows that while Hobbes may indeed have been an atheist, he was far from pessimistic about human nature, nor did he advocate totalitarianism. By locating him against the context of his age, Dr Tuck reveals Hobbs to have been passionately concerned with the refutation of scepticism in both science and ethics, and to have developed a theory of knowledge which rivalled that of Descartes in its importance for the formation of modern philosophy.

Also available in Past Masters:

*Spinoza*   Roger Scruton
*Bach*   Denis Arnold
*Machiavelli*   Quentin Skinner
*Darwin*   Jonathan Howard

# PAST MASTERS

## General Editor: Keith Thomas

*Past Masters* is a series of authoritative studies that introduce students and general readers alike to the thought of leading intellectual figures of the past whose ideas still influence many aspects of modern life.

'This Oxford University Press series continues on its encyclopaedic way ... One begins to wonder whether any intelligent person can afford not to possess the whole series.' *Expository Times*

# KIERKEGAARD

## Patrick Gardiner

Søren Kierkegaard (1813–55), one of the most original thinkers of the nineteenth century, wrote widely on religious, philosophical, and literary themes. But his idiosyncratic manner of presenting some of his leading ideas initially obscured their fundamental import.

This book shows how Kierkegaard developed his views in emphatic opposition to prevailing opinions, including certain metaphysical claims about the relation of thought to existence. It describes his reaction to the ethical and religious theories of Kant and Hegel, and it also contrasts his position with doctrines currently being advanced by men like Feuerbach and Marx. Kierkegaard's seminal diagnosis of the human condition, which emphasizes the significance of individual choice, has arguably been his most striking philosophical legacy, particularly for the growth of existentialism. Both that and his arresting but paradoxical conception of religious belief are critically discussed, Patrick Gardiner concluding this lucid introduction by indicating salient ways in which they have impinged on contemporary thought.

Also available in Past Masters:

*Disraeli*   John Vincent
*Freud*   Anthony Storr
*Hume*   A. J. Ayer
*Augustine*   Henry Chadwick

# ANTHONY TROLLOPE IN THE WORLD'S CLASSICS

Anthony Trollope (1815–1882), one of the most popular English novelists of the nineteenth century, produced forty-seven novels and several biographies, travel books, and collections of short stories. The World's Classics series offers the best critical editions of his work available.

## THE THREE CLERKS

### Anthony Trollope
### Edited with an Introduction by Graham Handley

*The Three Clerks* is Trollope's first important and incisive commentary on the contemporary scene. Set in the 1850s, it satirizes the recently instituted Civil Service examinations and financial corruption in dealings on the stock market.

The story of the three clerks and the three sisters who become their wives shows Trollope probing and exposing relationships with natural sympathy and insight before the fuller triumphs of Barchester, the political novels, and *The Way We Live* Now. The novel is imbued with autobiographical warmth and immediacy, the ironic appraisal of politics and society deftly balanced by romantic and domestic pathos and tribulation. The unscrupulous wheeling and dealing of Undy Scott is colourfully offset by the first appearance in Trollope's fiction of the bullying, eccentric, and compelling lawyer Mr Chaffanbrass.

The text is that of the single-volume edition of 1859, and an appendix gives the most important cuts that Trollope made for that edition.

Also in the World's Classics:

*The Chronicles of Barsetshire*
*The Palliser Novels*
*Ralph the Heir*
*The Macdermots of Ballycloran*

# LITERARY BIOGRAPHY AND CRITICISM IN OXFORD PAPERBACKS

Oxford Paperbacks's impressive list of literary biography and criticism includes works ranging from specialist studies of the prominent figures of the world literature to D. J. Enright on television soap opera.

## BRITISH WRITERS OF THE THIRTIES
### *Valentine Cunningham*

'He has steeped himself in the period . . . *British Writers of the Thirties* is by far the best history of its kind published in recent years . . . and it will become required reading for those who wish to look back at a society and a culture in which writers, for all their faults, were taken seriously.' Peter Ackroyd, *The Times*

'a serious and often brilliant book, provoking one to argument, forcing one back to known texts and forward to unread ones . . . it is simply so packed with information that it will speak as much to readers with an interest in social history as to the students of literature for whom it was first intended.' Claire Tomalin, *Independent*

'this should henceforth be the standard treatment . . . a minor classic of literary history' Frank Kermode, *Guardian*

'brilliant survey and analysis . . . Mr Cunningham's narrative is cleverly constructed, wonderfully detailed, and he deploys his findings to great effect.' Charles Causley, *Times Educational Supplement*

Also in Oxford Paperbacks:

*Fields of Vision*   D. J. Enright
*Modern English Literature*   W. W. Robson
*The Oxford Illustrated History of English Literature* edited by Pat Rogers
*The Pursuit of Happiness*   Peter Quennell